THE POLITICS OF THE
(IM)POSSIBLE

Thank you for choosing a SAGE product! If you have any comment, observation or feedback, I would like to personally hear from you. Please write to me at contactceo@sagepub.in

—Vivek Mehra, Managing Director and CEO,
SAGE Publications India Pvt Ltd, New Delhi

Bulk Sales

SAGE India offers special discounts for purchase of books in bulk. We also make available special imprints and excerpts from our books on demand.

For orders and enquiries, write to us at

Marketing Department
SAGE Publications India Pvt Ltd
B1/I-1, Mohan Cooperative Industrial Area
Mathura Road, Post Bag 7
New Delhi 110044, India
E-mail us at marketing@sagepub.in

Get to know more about SAGE, be invited to SAGE events, get on our mailing list. Write today to marketing@sagepub.in

This book is also available as an e-book.

THE POLITICS OF THE (IM)POSSIBLE

Utopia and Dystopia Reconsidered

Edited by

BARNITA BAGCHI

$SAGE www.sagepublications.com
Los Angeles • London • New Delhi • Singapore • Washington DC

First published in 2012 by

 SAGE Publications India Pvt Ltd
B1/I-1 Mohan Cooperative Industrial Area
Mathura Road, New Delhi 110 044, India
www.sagepub.in

SAGE Publications Inc
2455 Teller Road
Thousand Oaks, California 91320, USA

SAGE Publications Ltd
1 Oliver's Yard, 55 City Road
London EC1Y 1SP, United Kingdom

SAGE Publications Asia-Pacific Pte Ltd
33 Pekin Street
#02-01 Far East Square
Singapore 048763

Published by Vivek Mehra for SAGE Publications India Pvt Ltd, Phototypeset in 10/12pt Times New Roman by Star Compugraphics Private Limited, Delhi and printed at Rajkamal Electric Press, Kundli, Haryana.

Library of Congress Cataloging-in-Publication Data Available

ISBN: 978-81-321-0734-7 (HB)

The SAGE Team: Neelakshi Chakraborty, Arpita Dasgupta, Nand Kumar Jha

Contents

PART III   Coda: Resistance

Acknowledgements

The conference from which this book originates was held in February 2008 in Paris, under the auspices of the Indo-French Cultural Exchange Programme. All the articles are revised, modified versions of the conference presentations. We thank the Fondation Maison des Sciences de l'Homme (FMSH), Paris, France; the Indian Council for Social Science Research (ICSSR), New Delhi, India; and Institute of Development Studies Kolkata (IDSK), India, for their unstinting support. We are particularly grateful to France Bhattacharya in Paris and Amiya Bagchi and Ramkrishna Chatterjee in Kolkata for all levels of support, from the intellectual to the administrative. Martine Spensky co-organised and contributed to the conference and was a delight to work with. Unfortunately, heavy academic commitments prevented her from co-editing this volume. Subhoranjan Dasgupta provided critical logistic support and was a solidly supportive presence. We thank Hind Benfares in Paris, and Sanchari Guha, Madhusri Ghosh, Bijoy, Ashok, and Goutam in Kolkata for logistical support. In the final stages of planning the conference, I was on a fellowship at the South Asia Institute in the University of Heidelberg, Germany; I thank Subrata Mitra and the Rosa Luxemburg Foundation for supporting that visit. I thank, from the bottom of my heart, each of the contributors to this volume. In particular, I thank Sonia Dayan-Herzbrun, Rachel Foxley, and Marie-Claire Caloz-Tschopp for their camaraderie and support in this endeavour. France Bhattacharya, Waddick Doyle, Claude Safir, and Gilles Tarabout enriched the original conference as discussants. This book was completed at Utrecht University, the Netherlands; I acknowledge the nurturing presence of senior colleagues, Ann Rigney in particular. Our gratitude to Elina Majumdar, formerly at SAGE, who had commissioned this volume. We thank Neelakshi Chakraborty, Arpita Dasgupta, Rekha Natarajan, all at SAGE, for their continued interest in the volume in its gestation. Finally, I thank my parents, my sister, and friends (notably Ayu Yusoff, Somdatta Ghosh and Kasturi Banerjee) for their love and common sense, without which this volume could not have been completed.

1

Introduction

Barnita Bagchi

It is the dream of a just society which seems to haunt the human imagination ineradicably and in all ages, whether it is called the Kingdom of Heaven or the classless society, or whether it is thought of as a Golden Age which once existed in the past and from which we have degenerated.

George Orwell, 'Arthur Koestler'[1] (1944)

This volume brings together chapters on utopia and dystopia, from a rich breadth of disciplines: history, literature, gender studies, political science, sociology, anthropology, and Native American Studies. It is also a truly international volume, with contributors from India, France, the United Kingdom, Ireland, Canada, Switzerland, and the United States. The origins of the volume lie in an international symposium on 'Utopia, Dystopia, and Concepts of Development' co-organized by Indian and French scholars in Paris in 2008.

Utopia is a resonance, a mode, a perspective. Utopia, with its Greek pun on a 'good place' (*eu-topos*) and 'no place' (*ou-topos*), offers simultaneously a locus of possibilities for human development, as well as a sense that this conceptualization, being speculative, idealized or fictive, might be difficult or impossible to actualize in reality. Utopia is at one level a topos in writing and in literature. Topos (Greek 'place'), in Latin locus, refers in classical Greek rhetoric to a standardized method of constructing or developing an argument. Ernst Curtius studied topoi as commonplaces, or reworkings of established, standardized subjects, particularly the descriptions of standardized settings.[2] Such rhetorical

---

[1] George Orwell, Review of 'The Complete Works of Arthur Koestler'. http://www.george-orwell.org/Arthur_Koestler/index.html (accessed 17 June 2010).

[2] Ernst Robert Curtius, *European Literature and the Latin Middle Ages* (Princeton: Princeton University Press, 1953), passim.

settings offer an important clue that 'topos' is also a space and a place. The utopian mode works with both of these meanings of topos: a way of writing or constructing an argument, and an account of a space or a place.

Utopia has become one of the most resonant political, philosophical, and literary concepts of our times. Utopia is at once a place of dreams, a place of the good, and a place which is nowhere to be found. First coined by Sir Thomas More in his book in Latin, *Utopia* (1516), 'utopia' has become more than a word or a culture-specific term; it is not limited to Europe or Eurocentric writing and thought. If More had not invented the word utopia, we would still have had the notion with us. There are numerous utopias and dystopias, occupying and spanning numerous disciplines and domains, from different kinds of creative writing to history, politics, philosophy, and sociology. Utopian narrative writing allows the unfolding and description of a concrete place, whether idealized or demonized, and a detailed description of its topographical as much as moral–political contours. Such writing also moves fluidly between fiction and non-fiction. Equally, the double burden of awareness entailed in the term 'utopia' leads to every successful conceptualization of utopia having as its Janus face a dystopia: one (wo)man's utopia is often another's dystopia, and vice versa.

There has been a distinguished tradition of self-conscious theorization and practice of utopianism in Europe and North America, from More in the sixteenth century to Owen, Fourier, and the Saint-Simonians in the nineteenth century, and down to numerous utopian communities set up in the United States from the eighteenth century onwards. Such work and writing have been analysed by scholars in some detail,[3] though until recently with a masculinist bias. The work of feminist activists and scholars has now opened up the recovery of a rich body of female-centred and feminist utopian projects, from the medieval writer Christine de Pizan's imagined community of the City of Ladies populated by female worthies in *Le Livre de la Cite des Dames* (1405), down to feminist science

---

[3] It is not the intention of this brief introduction to analyse the corpus of utopian studies. Apart from critics such as Ernst Bloch, Ruth Levitas, Krishan Kumar, Fredric Jameson, Karl Mannheim, discussed later, see, for example, F.E. and E.P. Manuel, *Utopian Thought in the Western World* (Oxford: Oxford University Press, 1979); Tom Moylan, *Demand the Impossible: Science Fiction and the Utopian Imagination* (London: Methuen, 1986); Kenneth Roemer, *The Obsolete Necessity: America in Utopian Writings, 1888–1900* (Kent, Ohio: Kent State University Press, 1976); Lyman Tower Sargent, *British and American Utopian Literature, 1516–1985: An Annotated, Chronological Bibliography* (New York: Garland, 1988); Roland Schaer, Gregory Claeys, and Lyman Tower Sargent, eds., *Utopia: The Search for the Ideal Society in the Western World* (Oxford: Oxford University Press, 2000).

fiction and radical feminist periodicals and communes of the 1970s, 1980s, and beyond.[4] The history of socialism is another area that has brought to scholarly notice numerous political utopian experiments. Even the distinction made by Engels between 'utopian socialism' and 'scientific socialism'[5] (that is, Marxism) has proved to be the product of a particular historical moment. Later Marxist scholars such as Ernst Bloch, writing in the wake of the real-life dystopia of Nazi Germany, resurrected and reinvested in utopia as a realm of hopeful possibility. Bloch's *The Principle of Hope* (1952–59),[6] written in German in the United States, sees emancipatory potential in a huge array of phenomena. Even though Bloch is a Marxist thinker, the text is remarkably open-ended and indeterminist in seeing the principle of hope, operating through a vast number of phenomena, as the utopian impulse. Originally intended by Bloch to be titled *Dreams of a Better Life*, the book analyses daydreams; fashion; advertising; display; fairy tales; travel; film; theatre; jokes; social and political utopias; technological, architectural, and geographical utopias; quests for world peace and a life of leisure; and 'Wishful Images of the Fulfilled Moment', including morality, music, images of death, religion, and the highest good.

Krishan Kumar's *Utopia and Anti-utopia in Modern Times*,[7] an engaging, rigorous analysis of Western utopian writing, takes the strong position that utopia is not universal, that it is not a natural propensity of the human mind (contra Bloch), and that it is not a resonance or mode. Although I disagree with this position, and though this collection shows how sweeping, global, and trans-historical utopia is as a mode and a resonance, Kumar's work remains one of the best in laying out the argument that the Classical and Christian heritage together give birth to a particular kind of European utopian thought and writing. He also makes a strong and early case, which we agree with, that in twentieth-century writing, utopia and anti-utopia/dystopia are mutually dependent, complementary forms.

---

[4] For fiction, see, for example, Joanna Russ, *The Female Man* (London: Women's Press, 1975); Suzy Mckee Charnas, *Motherlines* (first published in 1978) (London: Women's Press, 1981); Marge Piercy, *Woman on the Edge of Time* (New York: Alfred Knopf, 1976).

[5] Frederick Engels, 'Socialism: Utopian and Scientific' (1880), The Marx Engels Library, http://www.marxists.org/archive/marx/works/1880/soc-utop/index.htm (accessed 18 June 2010).

[6] Ernst Bloch, *The Principle of Hope*, 3 vols, trans. Neville Plaice, Stephen Plaice, and Paul Knight (Cambridge: MIT Press, 1995).

[7] Krishan Kumar, *Utopia and Anti-Utopia in Modern Times* (Oxford: Basil Blackwell, 1987).

The work of Ruth Levitas[8] sees utopia as grounded in desire, and as a flexible form. She argues that we need to recognize that some utopias are set in the future, others are not. Some may hark back to the past; some may simply be set somewhere else in our world. She, importantly, sees utopia as socially, materially grounded articulations of desire. Whether and to what extent utopias are realizable within the realms of possibility, including political possibility, depends on the specific context, she argues.

The real-life context is extremely important, indeed, for utopian and dystopian thought, writing, and practice. There has always been a transaction and exchange between utopia as an imaginative possibility and as a real-life actualization. Eighteenth-century British, Bluestocking, real-life female philanthropic communities were founded by Elizabeth Montagu and Sarah Scott. Scott delineates a fictional community of this nature in *Millennium Hall* (1762);[9] Romantic-era experiments such as Pantisocracies[10] (involving the poets Samuel Taylor Coleridge and Robert Southey), or Owenite and Saint-Simonian communities disseminated their ideas through an explosion of writing.[11] Later Emersonian and Thoreauvian real-life utopic communities were imaginatively represented by these writers and their followers in essays and memoirs.[12] Indian feminist women in the colonial era, such as Ramabai Saraswati, founded real-life female communities and wrote fiction and non-fiction delineating such imagined places.[13] Utopian writing and practice abound in such examples, in which literature and life have come close, have on many occasions coalesced, have seen the shattering of utopian dreams, or viewed utopia turning into grim dystopia.

---

[8] Ruth Levitas, 'The Elusive Idea of Utopia', *History of the Human Sciences* 2003 (16, no. 1), 1–10; Ruth Levitas, *The Concept of Utopia* (Syracuse: Syracuse University Press, 1990).

[9] On Bluestocking utopia, see, for example, Nicole Pohl, *Women, Space and Utopia 1600–1800* (Aldershot: Ashgate, 2006); Sylvia H. Myers, *The Bluestocking Circle: Women, Friendship, and the Life of the Mind in Eighteenth-century England* (Oxford: Clarendon Press, 1990).

[10] See Tim Fulford, *Romantic Indians: Native Americans, British Literature, and Transatlantic Culture, 1756–1830* (Oxford: Oxford University Press, 2006), 120–21.

[11] John Harrison, *Robert Owen and the Owenites in Britain and America: The Quest for the New Moral World* (Re-issue) (London: Routledge, 2009).

[12] Richard Francis, *Transcendental Utopias: Individual and Community at Brook Farm, Fruitlands, and Walden* (Ithaca: Cornell University Press, 2007).

[13] Ramabai Saraswati, *Pandita Ramabai in Her Own Words*, introduced and part-translated by Meera Kosambi (Delhi: Oxford University Press, 2000).

Utopian and dystopian writing and practice thus offer a complex interplay between the actual and the possible, dream and reality, spaces and temporalities, and competing versions of the ideal or the monstrous communities. Some of the most pressing intellectual, social, political, and cultural topics of our time, such as colonialism, imperialism, movements for women's liberation, masculinity, the culture, politics, and economies of indigenous and pre-modern peoples and tribes, nation states as imagined communities, and globalization, are illuminated when approached through rich concrete universals embedded in utopian/dystopian texts. This volume, focusing on the period after the seventeenth century, moves us through transformative epochs (economically, socially, and culturally) of human history, in which industrial and political revolutions, colonization and decolonization, and movements for the emancipation of marginalized groups, such as women, and indigenous peoples, have all occupied the centre stage.

The utopian and dystopian mode is a site of paradoxes. Such paradoxes are never to be divorced from material conditions of life, whether historical, economic, political or the literary context. Such awareness of paradoxes, contradictions, and heterogeneities pervades and lights up this volume. Utopia and dystopia, it cannot be over-emphasized, are modes and resonances present in all parts of the world, not just Europe and white North America. Equally, utopian and dystopian thought and practice is and has always been gendered. Utopia, memory, and temporality intersect in often strange and surprising ways. These three dimensions: the relationship between utopia/dystopia, time, and memory; the focus on Europe and areas outside Europe at the same time; and the gendered analysis of utopia/dystopia are also central to the enterprise undertaken in this volume. These dimensions are not discrete or sutured, clearly; they mutually interweave and inflect each other.

Utopia is frequently inflected by a sense of time, sometimes describing places which are in the future or futuristic. However, utopian and dystopian writing can also limn places which are in the past, or preservations of the past in the present. The work of remembrance, seen in a social and transnational context, draws together the past, the present, and the future in often surprising and unexpected ways. Utopia, equally, is on many occasions as much about going back to a (reinvented) past, as it is about conceiving possibilities, which may or may not align with the future. Utopia moves restlessly between the past, present, and future, much as the work of memory does.¹⁴ Indeed, to see memory as aligned with the past and utopia with the future, now seems hopelessly naive.

The vast majority of utopian writing and thinking has thought beyond national boundaries. One of the most generative present-day fields for the study of memory and utopia, in this connection, is the utopian thought and practice of indigenous peoples/communities/nations/tribes in countries such as Australia, New Zealand, Canada, and India; here, a very strong explicit relationship is posited between the past and what is desired: the pre-colonial or pre-nation state past is re-viewed, re-invented, re-politicized, and re-grounded.¹⁵ We think of the indigenous people's Dreamtimes and Songlines in Australia, of utopia as a golden age set in the pre-colonial past, capturable in the present in indigenous communities' myths, stories, rituals, and practices, which propose an alternative to a mechanistic, late-capitalist universe.

Historically, as well as in our times, religion, memory, and utopia often go together, as in the example of the utopian practices and thought of many radical sects and movements, in a host of countries. Foxley's chapter on seventeenth-century radical utopian thinking, for example, shows how such writing and movements posited the desired future as a return to a lost, better world of liberties, often coupled with radical Christianity. The relationship between religion, memory, and utopia therefore needs also to be squarely in our field of analysis.

Ernst Bloch argued that anamnesis, or mere recollection, is not utopian, while anagnorisis or recognition, which renovates memory, is utopian.¹⁶ Recent scholars, such as Geogheghan, have been arguing that Bloch's distinction is too rigid and reductive.¹⁷ Utopian studies as a field has been highly aware, particularly since the 1990s, that it is a fallacy

---

¹⁴ Luisa Passerini, *Memory and Utopia: The Primacy of Intersubjectivity* (London: Equinox, 2007). This book analyses memory and utopia as a relationship, as experienced by subjects in Europe, with the 1968 political movements in Europe analysed as a conjunction when the past, present, and future came together in utopian ways for the participants.

¹⁵ Peter Kulchyski, *Like the Sound of a Drum: Aboriginal Cultural Politics in Nunavut and Denendeh* (Winnipeg: University of Manitoba Press, 2005).

¹⁶ Michael Landmann, 'Talking with Ernst Bloch: Korcula 1968', *Telos* 25 (Fall 1975): 165–85.

¹⁷ Vincent Geoghegan, 'Utopia, Religion, and Memory', *Journal of Political Ideologies* (12, no. 3) (October 2007): 255–67; Vincent Geoghegan, 'Remembering the Future', in *Not Yet: Reconsidering Ernst Bloch*, ed. J.O. Daniel and Tom Moylan (London: Verso, 1997), 15–32.

to think of utopia and the future as invariably or naturally or seamlessly associated. As Levitas and others have pointed out, utopia tends to have a very strong relationship with desire.[18] Utopia frequently shows desire for emplaced communities whose histories, stories, myths, and narratives have to be recovered, reinvoked, and reconfigured. Utopia always has an important element of critique of the present. Utopian practice also, far oftener than recognized, legitimizes novelties on the basis of an invented tradition.

We also argue that non-Eurocentric resonances of utopia/dystopia are rich and in urgent need of analysis. Native American studies and the utopic space of indigenous peoples of North America, nineteenth-century colonial middle-class Bengali males' dystopia in which educated women rule a world turned upside down, early-twentieth-century Muslim women activist-educators' utopic imagination of a world free of colonial rule where emancipated educated women rule a peaceful, technologically futuristic yet pastoral world: such rich concrete universals embedded in written texts are manifestations of the utopic/dystopic resonance outside Europe and white North America.

'The Peach Blossom Spring', a Chinese poem by Tao Yuanming (365–427) or Tao Quian describes a happy peasant society encountered by the narrator in the spring of 376–77.

> The peach trees stopped at the stream's source, where the fisherman came to a mountain with a small opening through which it seemed he could see light. Leaving his boat, he entered the opening. At first it was so narrow that he could barely pass, but after advancing a short distance it suddenly opened up to reveal a broad, flat area with imposing houses, good fields, beautiful ponds, mulberry trees, bamboo, and the like. The fisherman saw paths extending among the fields in all directions, and could hear the sounds of chickens and dogs. Men and women working in the fields all wore clothing that looked like that of foreign lands. The elderly and children all seemed to be happy and enjoying themselves.[19]

Many other kinds of utopia, including golden ages and happy worlds, as well as dystopia, including topsy-turvy worlds of misrule, can be found in the whole range of cultures and religions, including Daoism,

---

[18] Levitas, *The Concept of Utopia*.

[19] Translated by Rick Davis and David Steelman. http://www.xys.org/forum/db/190133.html (accessed 16 June 2010).

Confucianism, Buddhism, Hinduism, Islam, and African indigenous religions.[20] Within the present collection, northern Canadian native American
communities, contemporary African radical women writers, South Asian
feminists and anti-feminists—all make their voices heard, and speak
to European and Eurocentric utopian and dystopian projects also analysed in the volume, such as the white, imperialist, moderately feminist
women for whom emigration to colonies offered an ambiguous, exclu-
sionary utopia.

The utopia of the Hindu epic Ramayana posits as utopia 'Ramrajya'
or the 'Rule or Kingdom of Ram', presided over by the hero-king Lord
Rama. This is also an ambiguous utopia, in which women and lower-
caste individuals (Sita, Ram's wife, and Sambuka, the ambitious Shudra)
have to be disciplined and unjustly punished. Later, in the colonial period
in India, utopian thinking became rich and fertile with the pressures
and influences of historical circumstances. In late-nineteenth-century
and early-twentieth-century colonial India, women such as Pandita
Ramabai and Rokeya Hossain both narrativize and create, in real-life terms,
female communities with names such as Mukti Sadan (Freedom House)
and Tarini Bhavan (Salvation Hall), where there is innovative and wide-
ranging developmental work in areas such as education, vocational training, and gender justice. The work of M.K. Gandhi and Rabindranath
Tagore, too, is particularly resonant with utopian overtones since both
believed in renovation of society through construction and radicalization of particular communities: Tagore's real-life utopia of Shantiniketan
(Abode of Peace), a settlement in rural Bengal, featured an innovative
school, a university, a training centre for the arts, and a centre for rural
development—all built up on the model of a Vedic ashram, but one which
was also highly internationalist, paying particular attention to the cultivation of Asian languages and cultures such as the Chinese and the Japanese. Gandhi, who had been deeply influenced by Tolstoy and Ruskin,
was involved in building up Phoenix Farm in Durban and Tolstoy Farm
in Transvaal in South Africa; later, he built up the Sabarmati Ashram in
present-day Gujarat and Sevagram in Wardha in present-day Maharashtra.
His ashram communities stressed manual labour, moral purity, and indigenous handicrafts. Key texts in the utopian oeuvre of Gandhi and Tagore
include Gandhi's *Hind Swaraj* (1909) and Tagore's *Red Oleanders*
(1923–24), *Muktadhara* (The Waterfall, 1922), and *Tasher Desh* (Land

---

[20] See Lyman Tower Sargent, 'Utopia: Non-western Utopianism'; http://science.jrank.
org/pages/11553/Utopia-Non-Western-Utopianism.html#ixzz0r0mvcuH (accessed 21 June
2010).

of Cards, 1933). In these, there is an intricate interplay between the local, the national, and the international, and an attempt to synthesize Indian tradition with innovative modernity, while we can trace the various influences of European and Asian thinkers and practices on this writing and practice. For both writers, their sense of internationalism remained in creative tension with their two very different models of decolonization and national movements. Both also believed in open utopic communities welcoming colleagues and comrades from all nations, cultures, and races.

Indeed, there is much exciting work to be done on the transnational connections in the utopian writing and practice of Tagore or Gandhi. Tagore, for example, corresponded with the Dutch utopian thinker and writer Frederik van Eeden, who admired Tagore's work, translated him,[21] and gave talks about him. Van Eeden in turn had a utopian community, Walden, and attempted to spread his experiments to the United States. Van Eeden met Tagore in the Netherlands, and the fascinating cosmopolitan correspondence between them,[22] in which we find expressions of Van Eeden's yearning that Tagore take on a powerful role in bridging east and west, offers many suggestive leads for transnational and simultaneously non-Eurocentric utopian studies.

Many scholars in this book examine 'Ladylands' (the name of the utopic country in Rokeya Sakhawat Hossain's *Sultana's Dream*), whether real-life or imaginative, whether utopian or dystopian. A broad look at utopian currents globally illuminates women's agency in radical movements in arts and literature; feminist, transnational, and national movements; and the domain of human development. In India, for example, Gandhian women writers, such as Jyotirmoyee Devi in Bengal combined feminism and anticolonialism in their works, and delineated different kinds of ideal community where women could find a space for emancipation. Male-authored utopian works are also constitutively gendered, and sometimes overtly so. In eighteenth- and nineteenth-century Chinese fiction, for example, we find, in male-authored works, anatomies of powerful

---

[21] Among Van Eeden's many translations of Tagore are: Rabindranath Tagore, *Wijzangen /Gitanjali*, trans. Frederik van Eeden (Amsterdam: Versluys, 1914); *Uit het Land van Rabindranath Tagore: Brieven van 1885–1895*, trans. Frederik van Eeden (Amsterdam: Versluys, 1923); *De Vluchtelinge*, trans. Frederik van Eeden (Amsterdam: Versluys, 1923).

[22] See Rokus de Groot, 'Van Eeden en Tagore. Ethiek en muziek', *Tijdschrift van de Koninklijke Vereniging voor Nederlandse Muziekgeschiedenis* 49, no. 2 (1999): 98–147; Liesbeth Meyer, 'Tagore in the Netherlands'. http://www.parabaas.com/rabindranath/articles/pMeyer.html (accessed 30 December 2011).

female worlds and characters, in texts such as *Dream of the Red Mansion* (1749–59), or *Destiny of Flowers in the Mirror*.[23] In the latter, we find the episode of the Country of Women: a matriarchal society where relations between men and women are reversed. Samita Sen's chapter in this volume describes another such reversed-gender-roles world, in a misogynist dystopia from colonial India and Bengal. We also examine early-twentieth-century South Asian Muslim women activist-educators' utopic imagination of a world free of colonial rule where emancipated educated women rule a peaceful, technologically futuristic yet pastoral world:

> We do not covet other people's land, we do not fight for a piece of diamond though it may be a thousand-fold brighter than the Koh-i-Noor, nor do we grudge a ruler his Peacock Throne. We dive deep into the ocean of knowledge and try to find out the precious gems, which nature has kept in store for us. We enjoy nature's gifts as much as we can.[24]

Rokeya Hossain's *Sultana's Dream* was published before the American feminist Charlotte Perkins Gilman's *Herland*. Hossain was 20 years younger than Gilman. Both women led lives dedicated to writing and social activism. While *Herland* brings three male travellers into an all-female, isolated country where parthenogenetic reproduction rules, in *Sultana's Dream* a South Asian woman travels in a dream with another female friend and guide, Sister Sara, to Ladyland, where the men are banished to the inner quarters, in the *mardana* (inversion of the *zenana*). Fascinatingly different, both the white North American woman's utopian land and the South Asian Muslim woman's imagined female utopias nonetheless share a common concern with the furtherance of women's education and socialization, and a desire to reformulate humanity's relationship with the environment, by creating a greener, ecologically sustainable world. Yet we find surprising features, as for example in the colonial subject Rokeya Hossain's far greater desire for scientific and technological prowess wielded by women, with schemes for cultivation of land through electricity, the harnessing of solar power, the control of weather, and aerial transportation.

The dual application of gender and colonial and postcolonial studies, indeed, yields rich dividends in this volume. Female agency, whether

---

[23] Qian Ma, *Feminist Utopian Discourse in Eighteenth-century Chinese and British Fiction: A Cross-cultural Comparison* (Aldershot: Ashgate Publishing, 2004).

[24] Rokeya Sakhawat Hossain, *Sultana's Dream* (1905); http://digital.library.upenn.edu/women/sultana/dream/dream.html (accessed 17 June 2010).

valorized or demonized, emerges, very clearly, as a powerful theme in the texts and contexts we analyse. If from a white imperial feminist perspective it seems heroic as well as competent to exercise female agency in the white settler colonies, equally, some colonial Bengali men frequently view female professionalism and competence as demonic and sexually licentious. We stated earlier that one (wo)man's utopia is very often another man's dystopia: this is also one of the conclusions thrown up by this collection.

The chapters in this book are divided into three parts. The first part, 'Utopia and Dystopia: Debates and Resonances', has chapters on the history, political theory, and cultural politics of utopia–dystopia. The second part, 'Engendering Utopia and Dystopia', is on the gender politics of utopia and dystopia. The third part consists of an extended chapter by Caloz-Tschopp which acts as a finale to the volume. We are making a point in devoting half the volume to a gendered study of utopia, and in co-locating these with chapters which do not focus on gender. However, we are fully aware that gender is not a discrete category. What we wanted to do, in the conference as well as in the book, was to get scholars working on gendered utopia/dystopia to engage in discussion and dialogue with those whose work on utopia is not overtly focused on gender; equally, as we reiterate, we engaged consciously in a dialogue between those who work on utopia/dystopia in contexts such as Asia and Africa and those who work on European or the European-inflected utopian/dystopian currents.

Chapters in this volume, among other topics, discuss the vision of a dystopia described in a Bengali (vernacular) popular tract named *Meye Parliament ba Dwitya Bhag Bharat Uddhar* (Women's Parliament or Second Part of Rescue of India); analyse narratives of gendered utopia and dystopia in the essays, polemical writing, and fiction of the South Asian Bengali Muslim feminist Rokeya Hossain; critique Fredric Jameson's important reflections on utopian thought, in light of the grounded utopian politics of indigenous communities in Northern Canada; consider the nature of early modern, seventeenth-century English radicalism, using the concept of utopianism to interrogate the ways in which it was possible to frame demands for fundamental change within early modern English society; analyse early twentieth-century plans, disseminated through periodical literature, for emigration of white women to colonies such as Australia; analyse the Palestine question and the notion of a one-state Palestine encompassing Jews and Muslims as political utopia; and analyse the twentieth-century African writer Bessie Head's fiction in the light of utopianism.

In 'Utopia: Future and/or Alterity?' Miguel Abensour asks whether the transition from spatial projections to temporal projections, from imaginary journeys into space to imaginary journeys into time, is one of the distinctive signs of utopian modernity. His answer is in the negative. Instead, he argues, following Levinas, for a view of utopia as radical alterity. Attribution of time to utopia amounts to attribution of time to the Other. Abensour's view of utopia seeks not to control or domesticate it through insertion within a totality or within a dialectical game of totalities. Arguing that orienting utopia towards a future detracts from the radical other-ness of utopia, Abensour finds it important to discover affinities between the waking up of sleeping significations and utopian waking up. He draws on Richir's notion of the revolutionary utopian community which sees it swayed by a dream, and gives access, thanks to the suspension of all symbolic benchmarks, to an alterity and an alterity-content: an other time, an other space, and an experience of an energy which is not to relapse into Power. Abensour finds the fictional correlate for his philosophical argument in William Morris's *News from Nowhere* (1890), in which, introducing an original utopian hypothesis, the future society would experience at the outset an epoch of rest, a suspension of historical time, or a stasis of time. This is a time of rest, surely, but also a time when there is a heightening sense of disquiet, as the sign of the coming of a new and different history.

In 'Echo of an Impossible Return: An Essay Concerning Frederic Jameson's Utopian Thought and Gathering and Hunting Social Relations', Peter Kulchyski argues that Fredric Jameson's important reflections on utopian thought, particularly his *Archaeologies of the Future* [25] need to be critiqued in the light of the grounded utopian politics of indigenous communities in northern Canada. He argues that while Jameson has made an invaluable contribution to thinking about utopia through his readings of what he calls utopian fiction, he misses a whole category of utopian sociality by focusing on the imaginary futures of science fiction while ignoring both the utopian dimension of anthropological thought and the utopian social relations that still circulate in contemporary indigenous communities. The chapter stresses the urgency of contemporary struggles, particularly of Dene, Cree, Anishnabwe, and Inuit in northern Canada, as intergenerational communities of production, communities

---

[25] Fredric Jameson, *Archaeologies of the Future: The Desire for Utopia and Other Science Fictions* (London: Verso, 2005).

that deserve the name, communities that echo values from ancient times and may be able to propel them into the distant future.

In 'Radicalism in Early Modern England: Innovation or Reformation?' Rachel Foxley considers the nature of early modern English radicalism, using the concept of utopianism to interrogate the ways in which it was possible to frame demands for fundamental change within early modern English society. In her chapter, Foxley looks at the ways in which early modern writers presented their visions of social and political —and sometimes moral and spiritual—transformation. Comparing works which seem overtly 'utopian' in their framing, from Thomas More onwards, with the writings of the seventeenth-century Levellers and Diggers, she suggests that they share many strategies for imagining change without arguing explicitly for 'innovation'. Utopian pasts (whether classical as in More or English as in the Levellers and Diggers) and utopian elsewheres (as in More or Harrington) become vehicles for a transformative reinterpretation of the present, and it is that reinterpretation of the present which enables the demand for what might seem to us, and to shocked contemporaries, to be 'radicalism' or 'innovation'.

The chapters by Abensour, Kulchyski, and Foxley speak particularly richly to the theme of utopia, history, time, and memory. Abensour engages in a reflection on whether alterity or chronicity is a more radical mark of utopia, and comes down on the side of radical alterity, in a way which proposes to move from historical forecast to radical phenomenology. Kulchyski argues that we have in our contemporary world grounded communities of hunting gathering peoples who challenge capitalism and its dystopia: such communities, as this introduction has argued earlier, show that utopian memories of the pre-capitalist past are not only memories. Rather, in communities such as the ones Kulchyski describes, economic, social, and cultural practices which appear to be utopian actually exist. Foxley's chapter shows how much seventeenth-century political radicals invested in memories of an inevitably reinvented past in order to frame their demands for socio-political change. The complexities and many possible configurations of relationships between the past and memory, the present, the future, and the utopian ideals are brought out by these parts of the present volume. Any singular notion of utopia as a reductive placement in the future is demolished. Reversals of progressist notions of time; interweavings of past, present, and future; and complexities of historical inflection in utopian writing mark out the analyses offered in the volume.

The relationship between utopia/dystopia and time and history, as reconfigured by politically radical creative works, is also in focus in 'Dystopia, Utopia, and Akhtaruzzaman Elias's *Khowabnama*' by Subhoranjan Dasgupta. He argues that the dividing line between utopia and dystopia gets blurred, perhaps even erased, when agents of the latter borrow and usurp elements of the utopian programme to attain their own objective. One such calculated usurpation took place in the 1940s in pre-partition Bengal in undivided India, when the Muslim League, determined to carve out a separate Islamic homeland/nation out of the Indian subcontinent, promised the abolition of exploitative feudal land relations to millions of poor and landless peasants. This promise of emancipation was, however, first articulated and put to practice by the architects of the historic Tebhaga movement in Bengal,[26] who under the direction of the Communist Party of India fought for the rights of the deprived peasants. Akhtaruzzaman Elias, perhaps the greatest novelist in Bengali literature after Manik Bandopadhyay,[27] has explored this contradiction and conflict between the dystopic illusion propagated by the Muslim League and the utopian praxis spearheaded by the Leftists and the peasants in his classic novel *Khowabnama* (Dream-Elegy). His literary sensitivity and political insight have simultaneously explored the hypocrisy of the usurpation and the splendour of the genuine struggle, which, though defeated, preserved the impulse of liberation.

In his evaluation and textual analysis of this novel, Dasgupta shows how dystopia can come dangerously close to utopia, yet how incompatible and antithetical the two are in terms of practice. He attempts to unravel the dialectic with the help of a creative–historical text where, in spite of the depiction of betrayal and defeat, the vision of emancipation refuses to die.

---

[26] The Tebhaga movement was a peasant movement in Bengal, waged by sharecroppers who demanded two-thirds of the produce for themselves. It took place principally from 1946 to 1947, and did not die out till 1950. *Tebhaga* literally means three shares of harvests. On this movement, see, for example, D.N. Dhanagare, 'Peasant Protest and Politics: The Tebhaga Movement in Bengal (India), 1946–47', *Journal of Peasant Studies* 3, no. 3 (1976): 360–78.

[27] Manik Bandopadhyay (1908–56), one of the finest writers in Bengali, was known for his searing, psychologically and socially experimental, realist fiction. He was a left-wing, Marxist writer who struggled as a professional writer with poverty, alcoholism, and epilepsy. Utopian and dystopian themes are prominent in his work, for example, in his novels *Padma Nadir Majhi* (*The Boatman of the River Padma*, 1936) and *Ahimsa* (*Non-violence*, 1939). In both of these, he showed communities which are simultaneously utopian and dystopian, where criminality, lust, and evil are present in utopian islands and ashrams.

In 'Palestine: Land of Utopias' Sonia Dayan-Herzbrun argues that the geographical area of mandatory Palestine, having been a privileged ground of Orientalist fantasies, then became from the late nineteenth century a place of utopian projections that brought together strange and sometimes conflicting eschatological visions, national aspirations, and feminist or socialist ideals. The impasse of the present situation conjures up a new political project—that of a single state where citizenship and equal rights are accorded to all, irrespective of religion or ethnicity. Insofar as this project involves living together in plurality and the sidelining of identititarian antagonisms, it works as mobilizing utopia. It can be seen in its different versions as fully realistic and, at the same time, as revolutionary.

In Part II, 'Engendering Utopia and Dystopia', we start with Theresa Moriarty's chapter '"One Darling Though Terrific Theme": Anna Wheeler and the Rights of Women'. Moriarty analyses the life and career of a formidable and charismatic utopian and feminist thinker and activist, Anna Wheeler, whose argument for the rights of women dates from the 1820s. It was first published within the *Appeal of One Half of the Human Race, Women, Against the Pretensions of the Other Half, Men, To Retain Them in Political, and Thence in Civil and Domestic Slavery* by William Thompson,[28] in 1825. Anna Wheeler was born in Ireland, where she married and bore five children, of whom only two survived. She left Ireland with her two daughters after 12 years of marriage. She lived in Guernsey and France, and after 1827 she remained in London. Anna Wheeler kept in contact with major utopian writers and actors such as the Saint-Simonians, Charles Fourier, and Robert Owen. In London, she met and networked among continental revolutionary refugees from Italy, Poland, and France, as well as the emerging political working-class movements in France and England. Moriarty analyses her continental connections, as well as influences within the British political movement, which placed her at the centre of the emerging political claims of women.

---

[28] William Thompson (1775–1833) was an Irish political economist, philosopher, and utopian socialist, principally known for his contribution to the workers' cooperative movement. Although he worked closely with Robert Owen, by 1832 Thompson disagreed with Owen's position that the government and the stock exchange needed to invest in cooperative communities. Thompson believed that the workers' movement needed to generate its own resources to develop and sustain such communities. See Richard Pankhurst, *William Thompson (1775–1833): Britain's Pioneer Socialist, Feminist, and Co-operator* (London: Watts, 1954).

In 'A Parliament of Women: Dystopia in Nineteenth-century Bengali Imagination', Samita Sen discusses the vision of a dystopia described in a Bengali (vernacular) nineteenth-century popular tract named *Meye Parliament ba Dwitya Bhag Bharat Uddhar* (Women's Parliament or Second Part of Rescue of India). The chapter draws on the considerable scholarship on nineteenth-century Bengal, exploring how emerging literati perceived, in the rapid social change brought about by colonialism, a breakdown of the traditional social order. This perception led to deployment of prolific, occasionally powerful, images of *Kaliyuga*, the dystopian fourth age or time period conceptualized in Hindu cosmology, to describe processes of modernization. One major element of the popular discomfort with the times lay in attempts at social reform, a move spearheaded by a group of progressive elite Bengali men, but prompted and backed by European missionary and British official critique of Indian social practices. Much of this turned on gender relations within Indian society and the spotlight was on the marriage system. Gender thus became a major source of social contestation in the period, among the missionary and officialdom, among reformist Indians and the so-called conservatives, and among those who sought to define 'Indianness' in terms of elite (Brahmanical) arrangements of caste, family, and property relations. Vernacular literature, proliferating as a result of the introduction of print technology, and giving rise to modern forms such as the novel, focused on gender relations. Among these, a variety of lowbrow tracts generically often referred to as *bat-tala*, became known for their sharp satirical commentary on the breakdown of established hierarchical caste and gender relations, thus leading to a complete collapse of the social and moral order. The text under discussion falls into this category of Bengali literature. It is not constructed as a linear narrative, but rather as a collection of snapshots from discussions of specific issues in the parliament and associated committees. There are two remarkable features of this tract. First, it speaks of a reversal of gender equations in the polity and in the wider social sphere; this is not a land of women, but one ruled by women in which men were suppressed and subordinated. Second, the women actively seek to address some of the chief elements of their subordination. The author focuses on two aspects of what he perceives to be women's concerns: marriage and motherhood. In a heavy satirical vein, he outlines the ways in which the women seek to reverse the order of sexual morality by assertion of female promiscuity and the rejection of female chastity and monogamy. In the last vignette, the author sketches in the terrible consequence of this dystopia, a prostitute colony in the outskirts of Calcutta, with men as service providers and women as clients.

In "'Empire Builder": A Utopian Alternative to Citizenship for Early-twentieth-century British "Ladies"', Martine Spensky analyses the periodical *The Imperial Colonist*, a women's review—written by women for women—which first appeared on 1 January 1901 with the main object of encouraging the emigration of British women 'of the right sort', that is, 'respectable' women, to the colonies. A white supremacist ideology of empire building was upheld by *The Imperial Colonist* and impregnated the journal. Nonetheless, the women who wrote in it and selected the chapters and correspondence for publication did not share this restricted vision of womanhood and women's role. Their utopia is a world of equality and respect—not similarity—between men and women, a world in which the rigid class hierarchy prevailing in Britain would become softer without disappearing and where respectability and hard work would promote individual women to a much better position than the one they would have been able to reach on the soil of the motherland, while her work would have contributed to building the Empire. This society of 'natural'—if not 'social'—equals, the 'citizenry of the Empire', all of whose members would be geared towards its development and glory, would not, however, include all the inhabitants of the 'new' country. The original inhabitants, whatever their country of origin was, would remain attached to their low status, that of dependent children who would remain so for centuries until maybe one day they might became 'equal' to their British co-subjects, thanks to the Christian teaching and the good example set for them by 'imperial colonists'. Feminism, imperialism, colonialism, and utopianism thus intersect in uneasy and contradictory ways, as brought out by Spensky's detailed textual analysis.

In 'Ladylands and Sacrificial Holes: Utopias and Dystopias in Rokeya Sakhawat Hossain's Writings', I analyse the oeuvre of Rokeya Sakhawat Hossain, a supremely adept writer in the utopian and dystopian modes. This South Asian, Bengali Muslim feminist, educator, social worker, and polemicist (1880–1932) published one classic female utopian narrative, *Sultana's Dream* (1905), in English; I have translated another novella by her, *Padmarag* or 'The Ruby' (1924; my translation and edition 2005), and have argued that this is another feminist utopia, with realist contours, based on Rokeya's own school and women's organization, represented as located at the heart of a patriarchal, dystopian society. My chapter places these utopian narratives in juxtaposition with powerful essays and sketches by her which delineate, often with black satire, the real-life dystopia that Rokeya sees millions of women inhabiting, in pieces such as *Baligarta* (The Sacrificial Hole). I bring into comparison with these Rokeya's bold fables-cum-political allegories, *Muktiphala* (The Fruit of Freedom) and *Jnanaphala* (The Fruit of Knowledge). I argue that Rokeya posits an emancipatory socio-political public domain of action, with utopic contours, led by women, holding out the promise of resisting colonial and patriarchal dystopia.

In 'Utopia in the Subjunctive Mood: Bessie Head's *When Rain Clouds Gather*', Modhumita Roy argues that in looking at South African fiction in the 1960s and 1970s, one would be hard-pressed to find experiments with utopian fiction. In fact, apartheid fiction is full of dystopian narratives that capture with force and accuracy the unfolding horrors of a police state. The fiction of apartheid felt its first duty to represent the realism of dystopia, leaving implicit/unspoken the desired future. In her chapter, Roy argues that Head's *When Rain Clouds Gather* is a lonely and notable exception to the fiction of apartheid. Published in 1968, the novel opens with Makhaya's exit from a nightmarish world of barbed wires, violence, and destruction to a settlement of people who have all gathered together to make a 'new' world. The Golema Mmidi of the novel is based on a village in Botswana to which Head herself had fled.

Roy analyses the particular version of utopian fiction that Head is able to create—one which is ambivalently poised between the 'vicious clamour of revolution' and the 'horrible stench of evil social systems'. Among the most notable features of the novel is the making of a 'feminist' hero, Makhaya—long before the feminist movement had articulated such a possibility. Roy's point is not to argue that the novel is a straightforward imagined utopia. Golema Mmidi is not heaven on earth, nor has it been brought into being through revolutionary change. It is not the futuristic world of science fiction, nor a world from which pain and suffering have been effectively eliminated. It is, in fact, a novel experiment in creating what might be seen as a contradiction in terms—a 'realist utopia'.

In 'Globalization, Development, and Resistance of Utopian Dreams to the *Praxis* of Dystopian Utopia', Marie-Claire Caloz-Tschopp argues that critical work on modernism, and on totalitarian domination in the twentieth century and its long genesis (colonialism, imperialism, and 'total war') have battered the optimistic doctrines of progress present in theories of development, and have made us question the 'natural' link between war and revolution. Based on the works of Hannah Arendt, Cornelius Castoriadis and Rada Ivekovic, and on Caloz-Tschopp's own work, among other topics, on citizenship and immigration policies of Europe, Caloz-Tschopp identifies a way of questioning, and finds, tentatively, a new place: (post) topos, between utopia and dystopia.

Ralph Pordzik has argued, studying postcolonial utopia from countries such as India, Australia, New Zealand, and South Africa, that postmodern, postcolonial utopia depict heterotopia, or

> ... the view of a world in which fragmentation, discontinuity, and ambiguity determine the course of action and the striving of the protagonist/reader to make sense of what he or she is given to understand is constantly undermined by the introduction of new perspectives and points of reference that cannot be integrated into a meaningful whole.[29]

The reader of this book will realize that sensitively inflected studies of utopia and dystopia written globally and across historical periods show that this mode is inherently paradoxical, contradictory, and oscillatory. Whether in colonial India or white colonial New Zealand or seventeenth-century England or twenty-first-century indigenous Canada, utopian and dystopian modes of writing succinctly bring together oscillations between possibilities, dreams, fantasies, and impossibilities. Such writings, thoughts, practices, and movements are heuristic. It is perhaps a mistake to spend too much time thinking about whether and in what way exactly they are realizable: they offer us some of the most intricate and innovative experiments, whether thought experiments, creative experiments, or real-life experiments, in the unfolding process of open-ended human growth. Utopia and dystopia show us the human brain capturing infinite possibilities for development in finite form.

---

[29] Ralph Pordzik, *The Quest for Postcolonial Utopia: A Comparative Introduction to the Utopian Novel in the New English Literatures* (New York: Peter Lang, 2001), 3.

PART I

Utopia and Dystopia: Debates and Resonances

2

Utopia

Future and/or Alterity?*

Miguel Abensour

I

Would not transition from spatial projections to temporal projections, from imaginary journeys into space to imaginary journeys into time, be one of the distinctive signs of utopian modernity, as mentioned by Doren and cited in *Ideology and Utopia* by Karl Mannheim? Two names come to mind in relation to this metamorphosis: on the one hand, Thomas More who describes the utopian island with the help of the travelogue by the sailor–philosopher Raphaël Hythlodaeus and, on the other, Louis-Sébastien Mercier, author of *L'an 2440* (The Year 2440, 1770) which bears in epigraph a sentence of Leibnitz: 'The present is pregnant with the future.' Louis-Sébastien Mercier seems to have gained widespread acceptance in his transition from utopia to uchronia. There are, in fact, various utopias which attempt to outline the future society as arising, freed from the evils of the present society, but also as a way of maintaining in a different manner the ambiguity of the term brilliantly conceptualized by More who, as we know, perpetually oscillates between the land of nowhere and the land where everything is fine.

Even though Mannheim underscored the significance of this odyssey of utopian consciousness—in its affinity with the time of its birth and its passage thenceforth—as a sociologist, he could not remain content with this change of motif, especially since he failed to construct a social–

---

* Translated from the French by Trinanjan Chakraborty. Edited by Barnita Bagchi.

historical presentation of forms of the modern consciousness, in keeping
with the confrontation between social groups. Once this articulation of
utopia in time was recorded by him, the work of Mannheim proceeded
to elaborate a differentiation of temporal utopian forms between millenarianism, liberal–humanitarian utopia, conservative utopia, and social-
ist-communist utopia.[1]

To tell the truth, if we want to gauge the exact dimension of this new
orientation of utopia towards a passage through time and, therefore,
towards the future society, it would be proper to turn our attention towards
the philosopher Ernst Bloch. Following the example of Doren, he spells out
in a recorded interview with Theodor W. Adorno in 1964, titled '*Something Is Missing... Metamorphosis of Utopia*':

> At the outset, for Thomas More, utopia was the identification of a place on an
> island, in a South Sea. Afterwards, this identification got transformed: it came
> out of space to enter into time. The utopists, particularly those of the 18th
> and 19th centuries, Fourier and Saint-Simon, thereby located the dream-land
> into the future, transforming simultaneously the *topos* itself of utopia which
> moves into time from space.[2]

Only in *The Spirit of Utopia*, a pioneering work of the twentieth century, and in *The Principle of Hope*, he succeeds in attributing to this new
articulation of utopia all its philosophical import. And to that extent, he
could ground this articulation of utopia in time into ontology, more precisely into a doctrine of the unfinished being. The articulation of utopia
in time is plural. According to Bloch, utopia would originate from an
ontological site, a site pertaining to being. Being is thought of at the
same time as a process, unfinishedness and tension towards the perfection. So a multiplicity of dimensions is drawn into utopia, since utopia
and its persistence would come within the scope of the economy of the
being. Now this philosophy of utopia falls in with the dominant strain of
contemporary philosophy which foregrounds the future as the essential
of temporality. How does Bloch manage to resolve all this? He sets out
from the ontological category, the negative category of Not (*Nicht*) as in
the expression 'Not Yet'. The Not is origin. It is at the beginning, it is

---

[1] Anne Kupiec and Karl Mannheim, 'L'utopie et le temps', *Mouvement*, 45–46 (2006):
87–97.

[2] Ernst Bloch and Theodor W. Adorno, 'Il manque quelque chose' (Radio interview
between Ernst Bloch and Theodor W. Adorno hosted by Horst Krüger in 1964), *Europe* 86,
no. 949 (May 2008): 39.

the beginning. A double movement is perceived in the Not. If the Not is Emptiness, it is at the same time the drive, anxious to escape from emptiness. This is why the Not is what puts the beings in motion, in form of drive, need, tension. Bloch pays a particular attention to a form of Not, which is a 'Not having' and which is nothing other than hunger. The Not ought to be carefully distinguished from Nothing: the act of Not is to set going, the act of Nothing is destruction. Within the hunger, Emptiness manifests as *horror vacui*, as the aversion of the Not towards the Nothing. The hunger which is a 'Not having' is at the same time, movement outside this 'Not having', movement towards a having which is yet to come, towards the creation of a having in the future.

Bloch advances one more stage leading explicitly to temporality while he moves from the *Not* to the *Not Yet*. The *Not Yet* is 'what characterizes the tendency in the material process', the tendency of the origin in search of its exit. The struggle of the hunger to come out of the deprivational state is conceptualization, construction of the means of production to come. Within this movement towards the exit, the *Not Yet* is the experience of unfinishedness of being. Within the unfinishedness of being, within *Not Yet Being*, utopia would locate its eternal source and it would locate its most certain principle within the tension oriented to the perfection situated in the future. It is as if utopia, the utopian impetus, had to achieve, through its intent for Excess and the essential, the perfection of being, as if it were set going towards the perfection of being. This is how utopia—somehow carried, brought up by this ontological tension between the present unfinishedness and the forthcoming perfection— revives incessantly. 'The *Not* as *Not Yet*,' writes Bloch, 'passes straight through Becoming and beyond it: the hunger becomes the force of production on the repeatedly bursting Front of an unfinished world.'[3] And this declaration is essential for defining utopia as the place of maximal tension between future unfinishedness and perfection. 'The *Not* as *processive Not Yet* thus turns utopia into the real condition of unfinishedness, of only fragmentary essential being in all objects.'[4] Utopia would thereby be exit, escape from being, not as being, but only as becoming and unfinished within its becoming. Within this unfinishedness of being, within its continual shift with respect to unfinishedness—the essence— resides the secret of persistence of utopia, the driving force of its

---

[3] Ernst Bloch, *Le principe espérance* [The Principle of Hope], vol. I, translated from the German by Françoise Wuilmart (Paris: Gallimard, 1976), 371.

[4] Ibid., 371.

enigmatic revival, which all conservatives of the world pretend to con-
fuse with 'the eternal utopia'.

The surprising relationship of Emmanuel Levinas and Ernst Bloch has
not been sufficiently attended to. Thus, for one who wants to reach the
true dimension of this orientation of utopia to time, it is not sufficient to
locate utopia within this between-the-two, between the incompleteness
and the tension oriented to completeness, and derive simply from that
the orientation of utopia towards the future. Yet, it is necessary to take
note, as urged by Levinas in the lectures on *La Mort Et Le Temps* (Death
and Time), of the 'Blochian revolution' with regard to relationships
between time and death, which appear as a veritable *counter-Heidegger*.
'In fact, Bloch deliberates on death from the vantage point of time and
no longer, as in Heidegger, on time from the vantage point of death.' That is
a determining philosophical move which leads to various and significant
consequences. First, this is about rejecting, by going against Heidegger,
the identification of the originary time with being-for-death, with finitude,
in order to think thereupon of time in the light of utopia. This is to Bloch's
credit: 'The way (he) separates time from the notion of nothingness
in order to re-link it with utopian perfection. Time, here, is not pure
destruction—just the contrary.'[5]

This is the move, more precisely, this is the choice of a new site from
which one will have to identify the originary time which allows us to
move away from tropism towards death and conceive not only an attribution of utopia to temporality, but a fundamental outcome—overlooked
by Mannheim—*an attribution of time to utopia*. Such is the new identification of time propounded by Bloch, interpreted by Levinas. 'The
utopianism of hope is the patience of the concept moving along with
time. Time as the hope of utopia is no longer time thought of on the basis
of death. The first ecstasis, here, is utopia and not death.'[6] Insofar as
utopia is the expression or manifestation of the principle of hope, the
new attribution of time to utopia can be thought of.

> Time is pure hope. It is even the birthplace of hope. Hope for a completed
> world where man and his labour shall not be merchandise. A hope and a utopia,
> without which the activity that fulfils being—that is, humanity—could
> neither begin nor continue with its long patience of science and effort.[7]

---

[5] Emmanuel Levinas, afterword to *La mort et le temps,* by Jacques Rolland (Paris: Le
Livre de Poche, 1992), 119.

[6] Ibid., 114.

[7] Ibid., 110.

From there emerges a new perspective along with a new gaze. Thinking of death from the perspective of time, the utopian future, does not annul the infamy of death, nor does it dilute its power of destruction. Rather it removes from death some of its 'sting', insofar as henceforth it can be viewed with a different gaze. Death, far from being the exclusive meaning of time, or the inalienable possibility of *Dasein*, or the path towards authenticity, is dealt with and felt otherwise, although it is comprehended as a function of the time of utopia, in a perspective that somehow includes it and disrupts its internal economy.

> For Bloch, it is not death that opens the authentic future; on the contrary, it is within the authentic future that death must be understood. This is the utopian future as the hope of realizing that which is not yet. Hope of a human subject who is still a stranger to himself...[8]

It entails emergence, formation of another subjectivity, which is no longer a subject seized by *conatus*, 'which does not amount to the concern for being'—rather a subjectivity 'that is like a dedication to a world to come'.[9] It is at this distance from the self that the utopian future emerges and it is within the relationship to the Other that we can understand what allowed Levinas to perceive the Blochian revolution—no longer thinking of time from death, but thinking of death from time—as per theses conceived since 1946–47 in *Le temps et l'autre* (Time and the Other). Thinking of death from the perspective of time, from the utopian future, amounts to thinking of death from the yet-to-be-realized Other. This is because this dedication to a world to come is a dedication to the Other, insofar as, according to what is written in 'Time and the Other', the future is the Other. The relationship with the future is the relationship with the Other. 'The relationship with the future, even the presence of the future within the present seems to come about as a face-to-face meeting with those others.'[10] Our relationship with the Other is emboldened by the term 'utopian future', since the move by Levinas, when he thinks of utopia, consists in dragging the utopia out of the universe of understanding and knowledge, and assigning it to the order of encounter — a situation in which the I encounters the You—to turn it into a form of thought 'otherwise than knowledge' which has its source around

---

[8] Ibid., 114–15.

[9] Ibid., 115.

[10] Emmanuel Levinas, *Le temps et l'autre* (Paris: Presses Universitaires de France, 1983), 64 and 68.

the corner. From there, a new place is attributed to utopia: intermediary link, passage directed towards completion, towards the 'for-others', which confers meaning to the Blochian formulation. Thinking of death from the perspective of time signifies thinking of death from the perspective of the perfect world to come, as a view from the Other. Levinas attributes to utopia that which, as hope, is anticipation—the function of connecting two poles with differential potential, the unfinished and the completed, thereby also performing a function of short-circuiting temporality, and thus of disruption of the orientation of time. Attribution of time to utopia amounts to attribution of time to the Other. 'This utopia (of an absolute habitation) short-circuits time, but it is at the same time an agent of the human dimension and the work of humanity. This short-circuiting of time is the condition of the revolutionary consciousness.'[11]

II

The attribution of utopia to time and the attribution of time to utopia were so powerful as concepts that both of these spread out even to critiques of utopias, the one of Marx, for instance. Marx hailed the greatness of the grand utopias of the nineteenth century—the Saint-Simon, Fourier, Owen triad. In contrast to Proudhon, they offered not 'the shadow of the present society' but 'the imaginative expression of a new world'. Marx's work consisted not in proclaiming the end of utopia, but in devising salvage for utopia by transferring it within a concept of historicity, that is, into a dialectical ontology. It follows that at the level of form and not thematic content, a distinguished relation exists between the orientation towards the future of grand utopias and the 'morphological forecast' of communism, the forecast of the re-appropriation of human community, as this can be found in the work of Marx, provided that we reinstate its real temper of critical communism. Truly speaking, Marx's work on the corpus of grand emancipatory utopias is complex: it can be defined, on the one hand, as an injection of utopia into the text of Hegel, into the Hegelian concept of history, so that the philosophy turned into praxis could know the future, and on the other, an injection of Hegel and the concept of history into the field of utopia. Thanks to this intervention, Marx came to the point of transforming the classical question on the origin of private property into a new and unusual question: that of the relation of alienated

---

[11] Levinas, *La mort et le temps*, 114.

labour to the path of human development.[12] The passage from 'crude communism' to critical communism can be located, very precisely, there. Simultaneously, Marx de-reifies private property and transplants utopia into another element—that of dialectical ontology. The concept of labour as an ontological category, thenceforth defined 'as reproduction of man by himself' is the core of this ontology. If, within a classical utopian perspective, we set out from the institution of private property—a condition or a substance external to man—this will be pitted against communism as a 'condition which must be created', or as an ideal on the basis of which reality would have to be shaped. It is evident that this is really a word-to-word correspondence between two sides, between property/communism, between human labour alienated as objective substance, and the production of man by himself. This new conception of history, as formulated by Marx, sets forth a new question and provides a new answer. A crucial sentence of *Economic and Political Manuscripts of 1844* underlines it: 'For when one speaks of private property, one thinks of dealing with something external to man. When one speaks of labour, one is directly dealing with man himself.'[13] This is about understanding how the universal movements of private property, on the way of becoming world historical force, or rather, the movement of estranged labour, produces its self-withering and tends towards a positive re-appropriation of the human community. In relation with this movement, we can henceforth know the shape of the new *Wirklichkeit*. Once this salvage through transferring is ascertained, it remains only to know whether the transformation of utopia or its revival shaped by 'morphological forecast' fully renders justice to utopia, to its will to absolute difference, whether it does not urge us to dissolve the submission to alterity into the orientation towards the future.

III

If we observe this attribution of utopia to time, its dedication to a world to come, it would appear that utopia, in the wake of the revolutionary event, would have taken a decisive plunge, as if this would unquestionably become simultaneously a seed and an inevitable moment of modern emancipation. Thanks to this new orientation, far from repeating these 'escapist' attitudes of the past, utopia would come closer to history to

---

[12] Karl Marx, *Manuscrits de 1844* (Paris: Editions Sociales, 1962), 68–69.
[13] Ibid., 69.

lead its struggle within it and would be proved to be capable of bringing about a new praxis. As this praxis would be more productive, utopia
would make its place in the imaginary, in that which Marx called 'the
poetry of the future'. In addition, modern progressism wants to recognize in this orientation of utopia towards the future a progress of the human spirit. Does utopia not work in unison with the most contemporary
philosophy by turning the future into the necessary dimension of temporality? Bloch in *The Principle of Hope* hails the forward dream. 'No
dreaming may stand still, this does no good. But if it becomes forward
dreaming, then its substance appears absorbing in a quite different
way.'[14] This articulation to the future takes almost an anthropological dimension: 'Here almost all men are future, they rise above the life that has
been granted them.'[15] This rising above turns the inadequate—everything
that produces discontent—into a barrier and not a habit which is natural and accepted as it is. A barrier that is an obstacle will have to be
overcome and surmounted, so that the dominant emotion would be the
hope which entails the invigorating action, not the fear which destroys
humanity. Hope is capable of bringing about and embracing the revolutionary consciousness: 'It can climb into the carriage of history without
having to leave behind what is good in dreaming.' A place is thus granted
to 'the waking dream of perfect life' capable of putting an end to the
'dreamlessness'. Yet, a doubt arises immediately against these certitudes
of progressism, however enhanced by Bloch's lyrical style. Could this
articulation in time, in future, entail a loss? Could this be a regress under
a cloak of progress? Does this forward dream not hide another form of
dreamlessness, an altogether new and unprecedented dreamlessness? Indeed, the price to be paid for catching up with history, the praxis, to climb
into the carriage of history could appear to be too high, since this forward orientation, if it is not brought under a critical examination, could,
unwittingly, lead to an unwanted collapse, even to the withering of the sense
of alterity. As if the utopia, child of absolute difference, were exposed,
in the name of orientation towards the future, to merge with what is not
utopia, either with scientific forecast (Comte), or with sympathetic forecast (the Saint-Simonians), or with morphological forecast (Marx). As if,
in the name of the interface with history, utopia renounces, unknowingly,
the search for what is different, as Adorno would have expressed it—in
short, the quest for otherness. The *lack of dreams* in this case would

---

[14] Bloch, *Le principe espérance*, vol. III, 547.
[15] Ibid., 547.

become qualitative, as it is the substance itself of the dream, its heterogeneity, which would be hit, if not destroyed. Von Cieszkowski declared in 1838, in *Prolegomena to Historiosophy*, that the future does not belong to Fourier, but that the system of Fourier belongs to the future, thus heralding the Marxian transformation, according to which the social movement revolves no longer around utopia, rather thenceforth it is the utopia which revolves around the social movement. But the question remains: from this opposite gravitation, does the utopia of Fourier come out unscathed? Moreover, is it legitimate to wonder whether the externality of the spatial utopia—'utopian space games'[16]—does not preserve remotely but in a more effective way the alterity of the utopian society?

One cannot be astonished by such a mode of interrogation. Let us come back to the Marxian move, the salvage of utopia through transfer to a dialectical ontology, through immersion in a dialectical paradigm. We noticed that utopia succeeded there in catching up with history, and confronted it, but to what extent? Did it not pay the price for this access to history by domesticating or vulgarizing its most fierce breakthroughs, all the more fierce since these are posited external to history? Did the absolute difference not get converted into relative difference? Did the majestic image of man that Marx recognized in Fourier not quieten down? Did Marx not favour labour to the detriment of the game? It is not true, as claimed by the Marxist critique for a long time, that one should always judge utopia by the Marxian standard. Why not judge Marx by the utopist standard? To tell the truth, the position taken by Marx on this subject appears to be complex. On the one hand, he critiques the utopian substitutionism whereby an 'inspired' utopian consciousness intends to substitute for the social movement, for the logic of class struggle. On the other hand, he does not hesitate to recognize in some of the utopias at least, the quality of imaginative expression of a new world. Thanks to the flight of imagination, to the poetry of the future, these would have succeeded in escaping the reproduction of the same; these would have succeeded in welcoming the Other. If we look into it closely, it is this game between the same and the Other, the identical and the non-identical, which constitutes the spirit of the Marxian critique of utopias, by condemning those which succumb to the domination of the same (the shadow of the present society) and by conversely hailing those which let access to the new, allow the Other to get the better of the same. But doesn't this critical

---

[16] Louis Marin, *Utopics: The Semiological Play of Textual Spaces*, translated by R.A.Vollrath (Atlantic Highlands, NJ: Humanities Press International, 1984).

framework apply also to Marxian labour, the salvage through transferring of utopia? Does the immersion of utopia into the dialectic, into the dialectical paradigm help retain in utopia its quality of novelty, radical alterity? This can be legitimately doubted when one refers to the well-known dialectical framework according to which the negation of negation brings forth a new affirmation. Now, it is precisely this framework which is at work in *Economic and Political Manuscripts of 1844* when it comes to transform the question of origin of private property into that of the relation of alienated labour to the path of human development, when it thereby makes utopia emigrate in between critical communism and its dialectical ontology. 'Communism', Marx proclaims, 'is the position as the negation of the negation, and is hence the *actual* phase necessary for the next stage of historical development in the process of human emancipation and rehabilitation'. He adds immediately that explanation, too often forgotten or neglected: '*Communism* is the necessary form and the dynamic principle of the immediate future, but communism as such is not the goal of human development, the form of human society.'[17] But on other occasions, we encounter in *Economic and Political Manuscripts of 1844*, it is true, in a more discrete and interrogative style, a distinction between an affirmation originating from the negation of negation and a true affirmation which arises out of itself—and not through the detour of the negation of private property.

> If we characterise *communism* itself because of its character as negation of the negation, as the appropriation of the human essence through the intermediary of the negation of private property—it is because it is not yet the true, self-originating position but rather a position originating from private property.[18]

In the same direction, Marx gives credit to Feuerbach for his critique of the negation of negation

> ... which claims to be the absolute positive, the self-supporting positive, positively based on itself....Feuerbach thus conceives the negation of the negation *only* as a contradiction of philosophy with itself....The positive position or self-affirmation and self-confirmation contained in the negation of the negation is taken to be a position which is not yet sure of itself, which is therefore burdened with its opposite, which is doubtful of itself and therefore in need

---

[17] Marx, *Manuscrits de 1844*, 99.
[18] Ibid., 107.

of proof, and which, therefore, is not a position demonstrating itself by its existence—not an acknowledged position; hence it is directly and immediately confronted by the position of sense-certainty based on itself.[19]

Does this not acknowledge that the concept of negation poses difficulty? Is it not recognition of the fact that the affirmation coming out of such a process, far from being true, is extremely problematic, from the viewpoint of the game of the same and the Other? This acknowledgement has been reviewed, clarified, and developed by Marcuse in the text *The Concept of Negation in the Dialectic*. Eager to demonstrate, contrary to Althusser, continuity between the dialectics of Marx and that of Hegel, Marcuse blames the materialist dialectics for staying in the orbit of idealist reason, as long as 'it does not annul the conception of progress according to which the future is already implanted within what exists'.[20] In order to radicalize the concept of passage to a new historical stage, Marcuse submits the concept of negation to a critical examination. It follows that all transformations of the totality offer 'the unfolding of an essence which already exists by itself but cannot become reality within the framework of the established order'.[21] Whether it is about time or manifestation of a phenomenon, the new seems to be exorcised, as if all future manifestations ought to restrict themselves to the expression of an already-there. If we are to believe the Leibnizian phrase 'The present is pregnant with the future', which implies that the future necessarily contains something of that which was a present then the future would not loosen its grip on dialectical thought. Within the path opened by Marcuse, the concept of negation of negation can also be subjected to critique, in the sense that the affirmation produced by this concept continues to be subjugated to the same insofar as the affirmation carries within itself elements of what it negates. This is a weakness, as we saw, already noticed by Feuerbach and Marx, who attempted to conceive an affirmation which would shun the game of negation and which would arise and come up from itself and not from its opposite. As much in the essence that unfolds, as in the second affirmation, reactive in some way, as in the way to conceive the future still caught in the past, one observes the

---

[19] Ibid., 127–28.

[20] Herbert Marcuse, 'Sur le concept de négation dans la dialectique' [The Concept of Negation in Dialectic], in *Pour une théorie critique de la société* [Towards a Critical Theory of Society], translated from the German by Cornelius Heim (Paris: Denoël/Gonthier, 1971), 213.

[21] Ibid., 214.

influence of the same, of the identical which threatens the expansion of the Other, the non-identical. This is why Marcuse directs his research towards the elements external to the totality. But as an unrepentant dialectician, he engages in reducing immediately its externality, by elaborating antagonistic relationships between partial totality and global totality, as if the externality within a dialectic would have to be necessarily deliberated upon, whereas, the idea itself of externality entails an exit out of the totality and thus out of the dialectic. Nevertheless, the critical effort of Marcuse, even though it retreats before what it inaugurates, has at least the merit of suggesting, unknowingly, that another path is possible, even if he refrains from going along it.

This new path is no other than the path of utopia, according to which, one admittedly thinks of the exterior as it is, without seeking to control or domesticate it through insertion within a totality or within a dialectical game of totalities. It is constituted by three specific moments: difference, exit, and negation. We have *Difference* in the form of absolute difference cherished by Fourier, prince of the utopists, that is, in the most moderate form of exploring the lateral possibilities, as shown by R. Ruyer in his book on utopia. We have *Exit*, in the form of exit out of totality, or in the form of exit out of becoming, the incomplete being going in the direction of the completed being, but exit out of the being as being. Lastly, we have *negation*: Levinas, in his lectures on *La mort et le temps* (Death and Time) suggests that 'nothingness of utopia is not nothingness of death', for nothingness of utopia is the one of the Not, or the Not yet—experience of lack or the negation of this lack—in order to overcome, thereby, this vacuity put in motion, whereas nothingness of death is Nothing, pure annihilation. Besides, in the case of utopia, this negation of the same by the Other, negation of the control by the same over the Other, in order to liberate the alterity, completes the rift or the rupture of the utopia. The twentieth century has experienced unprecedented historical trauma, unheard-of catastrophes. It would be improper to attempt relief from all this. There are in fact sufferings and deaths which resist the dialectic and their insertion into an 'all significative', and therefore, which force the dialectic to a halt or a stop. Dialecticizing, or intending to dialecticize, Auschwitz is an offence as much from the ethical point of view as from the political. Refusing relief from such events does not mean conniving at them, even less, succumbing to them. The rupture is so strong, intense, and irreversible that a single exit-point is left, highlighting the disaster and its non-integrable nature. Now, utopia can respond to this disaster, to the perseverance of the intolerable. For this event, however paradoxical this may appear, contains not the loss of utopia, but *a utopian warning* of a new kind, as if utopia, in its exteriority, were appearing to be the barrier against the repetition of such events, as if heading for utopia would be the only serious way to confer meaning and content to the phrase 'never ever again the same'. Utopia which inflects in plural, (evolves) either (as) exit out of the (false) whole, or by taking 'lines of flight' (Adorno), or by opening the cracks (Walter Benjamin). Hence many faces of utopian exteriority are possible, coming to terms with itself as such, seeking not to inhabit a new dialectic of the external and the internal. We are then present before an act of distancing which renders vain all efforts to blend and articulate utopia and dialectic under the name of concrete utopia. For, by following this trajectory, the consciousness about an essential and irreducible opposition between utopia and dialectic has been achieved. From this it emerges that the attribution of utopia to the future, far from being a progress, can, in some circumstances, appear to be a retreat inso-far as it makes utopia degenerate into a forecast, even worse, into futur-ology, as the eyes could not be kept fixed on the compass of alterity.

Let us examine the exit glimpsed by Adorno under the name of 'lines of flight'. It is in the number 100 of *Minima Moralia: Sur l'eau* (At sea)— that Adorno critiques some of the representations of the emancipated society, still under control of the model of production and in search of, really speaking, a predatory plenitude. 'If one thinks of the emancipated society as one emancipated precisely from such a totality, then align-ments become visible, which have little in common with the raising of production and its human mirror-images.'[22] The nature of negative dia-lectic consists in freeing the dialectics from an affirmative essence; in blocking somehow the process in accordance with which the negation of negation would produce a new affirmation, bring about a positive. Contrary to the tradition, the negative dialectic turns the negativity into its own living room, in the form of a negation determined by what is, so that the possibility of what is different by itself would be initiated. Trans-posed into the field of utopia, such a movement ends up in not conceiv-ing utopia as a step towards what ought to be, towards a new positive. It is evident that utopia can either be leeched off by the dialectical frame-work, or can assert itself as a process radically external to the dialectic and its adventures, as a utopian paradigm opposed to a dialectical para-digm. Although negative at the outset, utopia would continue by diverse

---

[22] T.W. Adorno, *Minima Moralia,* translated from the German by Eliane Kaufholz and Jean-René Ladmiral (Paris: Payot, 1980), 148.

means; eventually, the lampoon to a negation of what is, a destruction of what is, is about to block the path of a repetition of the same. This choice of negativity is but a preliminary, for it is all about substituting another intrigue for a dialectical process, a move for escape that Adorno calls 'lines of flight'. Something other than a dialectical process could emerge as if out of the living room within negativity. How is one to name this something other? A sidelong step, a movement, a shift, exploration of lateral margins, an impulse for extravagance, for being off the already beaten path, an exit, an escape, a move towards someplace else, a flight? As if, it were important to turn away from the dialectical framework in order to become simultaneously ready for another intrigue, to be oriented— thanks to the exit, the flight—towards *a someplace else*. In that case, the locking of dialectical process, instead of being perceived as weakness, can be seen totally otherwise, can be welcome as an opportunity leading to a sort of novel scenario which would put an end to the reproduction of the same, which would let the alterity rise. Here, it would be appropriate, on the one hand, to re-open the debate between Adorno and Ernst Bloch, and, on the other hand, to turn towards the untold exchanges which Walter Benjamin would have attempted, between Fourier and Marx.

To the new utopian spirit can be attributed philosophical consistency by integrating the resurgence of the utopia of 1848 to our time, as a form of specific intervention against the dialectic of emancipation, that is, its reversal into its opposite, the birth of new forms of domination and barbarism. It is for utopia to locate the sites responsible for the process of reversal and to investigate these sites for bringing about breakthroughs which, due to their laterality and marginality, would alone be prone to open unbeaten paths. In this context, one can cite the exemplary work of Walter Benjamin in its last text *On the Concept of History*.[23] In order to have identified, in the work, one of the sites of reversal of the emancipation and its acritical glorification, Benjamin, in the wake of Fourier, attempted to imagine a path different from the domination of nature, by allowing for the hypothesis of a joyful relationship to it, in the form of the second technique, so that the phenomenon of domination would cease to continue, and so that work would turn into play.

What does it mean to think of utopia by privileging within its theorization alterity, by giving the former priority over temporality, the

---

[23] Walter Benjamin, *On the Concept of History* (1940). http://www.marxists.org/reference/archive/benjamin/1940/history.htm (accessed 22 June 2010).

orientation towards the future? Even, by turning the access to alterity into the condition of possibility of reflection about the future, at the level of the pure human being, 'the utopian human being'? The work of Levinas answers this question, all the more so since it liberally accommodates utopia within the field of philosophy. In fact, to someone who admits that Levinas has attempted to think of *utopia otherwise*, away from classical preconceptions, from established thought, it appears that he has been able, by taking into consideration the negation proper to utopia, its specificity, to furnish a reply to the domination of the same, by choosing, at the outset, to conceive utopia under the sign of the alterity. In the Preface to *Utopie et socialisme* (Utopia and Socialism), it is acknowledged that utopia 'in a world where, since the century of the Enlightenments and the French Revolution, the sense of eschatology had been lost' is the only way 'to wish for the "totally other social"'.[24] *Totally other social* will have to be understood in a two-fold sense; either this clearly affirmed that alterity is related to a revival, a regeneration of man, 'with what is not yet in the least visible', or the *totally other social* points out the social as something that is totally other than the political and posited within a radical alterity with respect to the political. From a reified contrast between the civil society and the State—as argued by Buber who somehow sets about a reversal of Hegel—a separation and a strict contrast between the social and the political are simultaneously expounded. The social refers as much to a being-together of man, to the presence of man for man, close at hand—to the phenomenon of the fellow man—as the political refers to all that is prone to undermine the spontaneity of the social and to destroy the same, for instance, coercive powers, domination, and government muzzling the people. It would be up to socialism to take the task of eliminating the political, through a regeneration, a reviviscence of the social fabric as the being-in-the-society or the living-together of men. In this perspective, emancipation is conceived as a destruction of the political—of the government of the people—which would bring about an administration of society by itself, a self-management, from which would have disappeared all domination of man by man. This alterity of utopia as *totally other social* is all the stronger since it is rooted within the philosophical anthropology of Martin Buber, that is, within the opposition between two types of relationship: the I/that (objective and practical experience) and the I/You. Utopia can rightly be called the *totally*

---

[24] M. Buber, preface to *Utopie et socialisme*, by Emmanuel Levinas (Paris: Aubier Montaigne, 1977), 8.

other social because it concerns first the social as totally other than the
political, but also because it originates from the Encounter, the originary
place and condition of the advent of the ethical. Even though Levinas
distances himself from the anthropology of Buber, by introducing into it
a dissymmetry where symmetry reigned, he, nonetheless, strains out of
this fundamental opposition and implements it so that the utopia may
be posited more clearly. Also utopia has to be transported from places
where it is straying—the sciences and knowledge—and recovers for it its
first element, the inter-human relationships—more clearly, the human relation. Utopia has to be attributed to man relating himself to the concern
for contemporary philosophy in order to liberate man from the categories
suited to the objects. Utopia belongs neither to the order of comprehen-
sion, nor to that of knowledge—laws of society or laws of history intended to allow for forecasts about the future in accordance with these
laws—rather it belongs to the level of Encounter. It follows that utopia
is a form of thought 'otherwise than knowing', more than feeling or affect, a thought-affect, brought about from the vicinity, which has a philosophical meaning insofar as the Encounter is a relationship to the Other
as such, within its unequaled uniqueness and not to the Other as a part
of the world. Utopia, under the sign of alterity, is strengthened insofar as
it is unquestionably posited on the side of the I/You relationship, whose
goal includes, among others, keeping away the threatening connections
between knowledge and power. Alterity gets emboldened, for within the
deformalization to which Levinas submits the anthropology of Buber
and particularly, the concept of Encounter, by substituting dissymmetry
for the reciprocity within the relationship between the I and the You, by
building a pathway to ethics, utopia becomes the *thought for*, enlivened
by the *concern for, the others*. This transfer simultaneously blocks every
movement that seeks to reduce the Other to the same and supports the
negation proper to utopia as triumph of the Other over the same.

> In ethics in which the others are, at the same time, higher than the self, and
> poorer than the self, the I distinguishes itself from the You, not by its ordinary
> 'attributes', but by the dimension of height which breaks off the formalism
> of Buber.[25]

For one who wants to fully think of utopia from alterity, utopia as
totally other, it is essential to take into account the fact that the thought

---

[25] Emmanuel Levinas, *Noms propres* (Paris: Fata Morgana, 1976), 47.

about utopia unfolds within a 'philosophy of escape', as it has been located by Levinas in the study *De l'évasion* (On Escape) (1935). Philosophy which places in the core of its trajectory the 'category of exit, cannot be assimilated to the task of renovation, nor to that of creation'.[26] Levinas comes at this philosophy through alteration and radicalization of literary trends marked by the motif of escape. Levinas works for recapturing a deeper theme touching upon the root itself behind these motives. Moreover, he undertakes emphatically to demolish the gap between literary thematization and philosophical conceptualization: 'For these (motives) do not question being, and submit to a need for transcending the limits of the finite being. These reveal the horror about a certain definition of our being and not about the being as it is.'[27] On the other hand, being itself is put into play by the escape as conceived by Levinas. The modern sensibility would come upon a paradoxical situation: this appears to be torn between the revival of ontology and its contrary, as if the feeling contained by being, at the root of this return of ontology, were, at the same time, bringing about 'the most radical denunciation of the philosophy of being by our generation'. At the core of the contemplation of 1935 comes about the opposition continually taken up anew between, on the one hand, an experience of limitations of being, relating uniquely to its feature and properties, and on the other, an experience of an altogether different magnitude—the experience of being itself, on account of the fact that there *is* being. To the first experience corresponds the need for going beyond the limitations of being, transcending them, and to the second, a new need which would tend not to transcend these limitations, but to be liberated from being, from its gravity, in a word, to come out of it. This is the need for escape for which Levinas introduces a neologism, the need for 'excendance', in order to mark its implacable originality. What is the escape all about? This lies in the fact that there is being, but not its limitations. For what is imprisonment or enchainment is being itself. The most acute defect that the modern sensibility could perceive is about existence itself, the being of that which is and that which is not. And Levinas insists on the philosophical specificity of the need for escape, 'the fundamental event of our being'. It is not about going someplace, but only about coming out. '... in escape, we aspire but to come out ... an inimitable theme is urging us to come out of being.'[28] Now, at the end of

---

[26] Emmanuel Levinas, *De L'Evasion*, with introduction and annotation by Jacques Rolland (Paris: Fata Morgana, 1982), 73.

[27] Ibid., 71.

[28] Ibid., 17.

this contemplation, attempting to fathom the disruptions that such a philosophy can bring about, Levinas writes on the originality of the escape:
'this is about coming out of being by a new path at the risk of turning
upside down certain ideas which, for the common sense and the wisdom
of the nations, seem to be the most obvious'.[29] This is a reversal of the
obvious in the philosophical tradition along with the inherited thought.
Is it not precisely within this disruption delivered by such a philosophy
that Levinas could find the force to reply to all obvious philosophical en-
tities and to every attempt at reducing utopia and its alterity to the knowledge of the laws of society and history, in a way that different forms of
forecasts could be brought about. His is a complex reply which includes
various levels. Firstly, Levinas replies to the utopian modernity, not because
he returns to an earlier state, but as someone who is conscious and know-
ledgeable about deadlocks encountered by a conception of utopia oriented principally towards the future. He sets about a complexification of
the issue, through his efforts to go beyond an alternative between future
and alterity—by what seems to be a self-evident device—that is, by substituting the complexity of an articulation for the simplicity of an alternative. By doing this, his concern appears to be directed towards the
preservation of the negation of the utopia, the struggle against the domination of the same endangered by an acritical orientation towards the
future, particularly when it takes its inspiration from Leibnitz's saying,
'the present is pregnant with the future'. Since, in accordance with that
saying, continuity is laid down between present and future. The future
would contain within itself features, vestiges of the bygone present, and
leave the field free for the reproduction of the same. As the preface to
Totalité et infini (Totality and Infinity) brilliantly bears testimony to this,
it is essential for Levinas to rescue 'the extraordinary phenomenon of
the prophetic eschatology' which, in a secularized context, would be
related to utopia, to the utopian inspiration. It is important for him not to
subject this eschatology to all too obvious philosophical facts, to a thought
about the totality, to an ontology.

Eschatology is not a teleology which would naturally possess knowledge about history. 'It (eschatology) does not offer a teleological system
within the totality, it does not teach the orientation of history.'[30]

By being exterior to ontology, eschatology is exterior to a thought
about the totality, history as totality, and thereby to an acquaintance with

---

[29] Ibid., 99.

[30] Emmanuel Levinas, *Totalité et infini* (The Hague: Martinus Nijhoff, 1961), XI.

the future. 'Eschatology connects to being, *beyond the totality or the history* and not to being beyond the past and the present.'[31] Escape, if there is any, leads to an exit, not to an exit out of becoming, beyond past and present, but to an exit out of the being as it is, that which implies an exit from the totality and an exit from history in a parallel manner to the formation of relationship to an exteriority to the totality.

As eschatology forms a relationship to a surplus beyond the totality, utopia forms a relationship to the totally other social—totally other than the political—to the totally other temporal—totally other than a synchronic or dialectical time.

> It is a relationship to *a surplus always exterior to the totality*, as though the objective totality were not filling out the true measure of the being, as though another concept, the concept of *infinity*, were needed to express this transcendence with regard to the totality, non-encompassable within a totality and as primordial as the totality.[32]

It follows that Levinas, without openly considering the issue, could not accept Marxian intervention which, as we think, consists in salvaging utopia through transferring within it a dialectical ontology. Does it not amount once again to subject utopia to philosophical facts? To turn down a form of thought 'otherwise than knowing' about acquaintance and knowledge, by transforming the breakthrough towards alterity into the prediction of superior social form? Does it not amount to utopia within history, while one portion of itself aspires to be held outside the history? Here, an essential divergence between Levinas and Ernst Bloch certainly appears. While the author of *The Principle of Hope* seeks to explore, with the help of an ontology of incomplete being, all connections between utopia and dialectics, Levinas re-affirms, by situating utopia on the side of the Encounter and ethics, its exteriority with regard to every dialectical process.

From its relationship to a philosophy of escape, the Levinasian thought about the utopia can draw another advantage. This thought on escape, as noted, helps to distinguish between an exit out of the limits of the being and a much more radical move, an exit out of being itself. Here we come upon one of the differences that separates Bloch from Levinas, since one conceives of utopia as an exit out of becoming, as the being is within its historical limits, in the form of a tension of incomplete

---

[31] Ibid., XI.
[32] Ibid.

being oriented towards the completed being, while the other allows us to conceive of an unparalleled move, namely, the exit out of being as being. Now, this distinction is not meant eventually to allow us to differentiate two forms of utopia or utopian sequences. With regard to utopia, one could in fact distinguish between two quests for alterity, the one—relative—which describes or proposes *a being otherwise*, that is, another organization of *conatus* and relationships between these, and the other—absolute—which would aim at nothing less than coming out of the being as being, in order to achieve *an otherwise than being*. Another drama would be initiated for utopia: this would no longer be about regulating *conatus*, but postponing its exercise—the unfolding—in order to achieve the strongest sense of the term *désintéressement* (disinterestedness). Thus, Levinas, in the preface to Martin Buber, pays attention to unheard-of utopian moves in the context of *désintéressement*, in which new ethics, not alien to socialism, can be glimpsed. These utopian moves are all totally inspired by such *désintéressement*.

> In face of some of the audacious acts of resistance and martyrdom in our world in the name of the pure human—the utopian human—against the efficacy of *powers* and *mights*, this ethics asserts its objective status, proves to be *Wirklichkeit*, efffective reality, and doesn't let itself be repressed amid impotencies of the beautiful souls or unhappy consciousness.[33]

Rather than forgetting time, or in this case, the orientation towards the future, it is essential to subordinate, subject this modern orientation to the utopia-alterity, preferably, to turn the alterity into the condition of the possibility of another future, different from what is; it is essential, by giving this the priority, of letting it shape, fill out, paint the orientation towards the future following the logic appertaining to it, as though the future had to display the signs of alterity within each of its manifestations, in short, establish itself as a pure future which succeeds in taking time away from the clutch of the same, from the repetition of the same through the negation of utopia. In this quest for alterity, it comes to attain *a totally other temporal*, that is a time totally other than the synchronic time of Husserl, or a time totally other than the dialectical time of Marx and Bloch, as both these times represent the control of the Other by the same.

---

[33] Martin Buber, *Utopie et socialisme*, 10–11.

Since he privileged the temporality as a living present and described it as a flux or a flow of sense-perceptible qualities, Husserl reaches a homogeneous conception of time that works to preserve the same. It follows that 'The category of the same which controls these descriptions is not put in question. The becoming is a constellation of identical points. The other remains another same, identical to itself, discernible from the outside by its place within this order.'[34] As for dialectical time, in spite of negations which constitute it and give it rhythm, the new affirmation which it leads to, carries within it an indelible relationship to which it has negated and out of which it originates. Time of an interiority—the dialectical contradiction is always inside a totality—develops and unfolds through a continuous play between continuity and discontinuity. This is the reason why dialectical temporality necessarily enters into conflict with the negation of utopia whose characteristic consists in destroying the same to the advantage of the Other. To these two times which remain, on several accounts, in the reign of the identical or the identical of the identical and the non-identical, is opposed a non-rest of time, 'that by which the time contrasts with the identity of the same', a time of disquieting of the same by the Other, time which undergoes the test of the exteriority and thereby forms a relationship to the infinite. What results is a totally other temporal, other than the identical, other in the sense that it knows how to welcome the non-identical of the utopia. The diachronic time becomes utopian time, as utopian time becomes diachronic.

In a sense, the path traversed by Levinas, thanks to attribution of utopia to the Encounter, with the help of escape, the category of exit, the difference between the exit of becoming (Ernst Bloch) and the exit of the being as being, leads somehow to a rehabilitation of utopia insofar as Levinas chooses to ignore the distinction, as put forward by Rosenzweig, between utopia and redemption. The one, utopia, in its march towards the completion would be confined to the interior of the historical time, and the other, redemption, within its messianic impatience, would exercise a violent rupture from the time of history and would let happen a radical alterity which would appertain to a symbolic time. Everything happens as though Levinas were granting utopia the possibility of reaching an absolute alterity disclaimed by Rosenzweig. Levinas, in his intention to strengthen further his position, rather than conceiving utopia on the model of a march within a continuous, linear time oriented towards the completion, has recourse to the image of a short circuit which

---

[34] Levinas, *La mort et le temps*, 124.

suddenly connects the incomplete and the completed, running the risk of incandescence, as though utopia, far from being a 'passage-way', were proving to be a 'springboard' towards the alterity.[35]

Without taking these philosophical detours, there is at least one utopia, that of William Morris, *News from Nowhere* (1890),[36] which has glimpsed, beyond *the being otherwise*—in the question–answer exchange of the first part—the possibility of an *otherwise than being* in the ascent of the river in the second part of the narrative. For William Morris introduced an original utopian hypothesis, according to which the future society, the post-revolutionary society would experience at the outset *an epoch of rest*. This implies a suspension of historical time, a stasis of time when one could give oneself enough rope, which Nietzsche calls, in the second *Untimely Meditations*, the faculty of feeling for a moment outside history. Time of rest, surely, but a time when for a visitor, strangeness gradually heightens a sense of disquiet as the sign of the coming a new and different history. From this *époché* which brings out 'the vaporous orb of non-history',[37] the sun of radical alterity—the sun of a new happiness—can rise, thanks to the rupture from the historical time, thanks to the exit out of the time of history. For 'in the smallest as in the greatest happiness, there is always something which tells that happiness is happiness: the possibility to forget, or to put this in more scholarly terms, the faculty of feeling for a moment outside history'.[38] As though to subordinate the future to the alterity, the historical time had to be arrested, suspended in order to let alterity hold its council and to be able, thereby, to bring out a pure future, taking flight not from a dialectical process but from itself.

One of the various signs of persistence of utopia is its presence within contemporary philosophy. One can find, in fact, great philosophical works of our time, those of Marc Richir, for instance, in which a utopian dimension is becoming more or less clear. It is as though philosophy were admitting or rediscovering an indestructible relationship to utopia, to utopian images recognized by Walter Benjamin. Can there be philosophy without utopia? Certainly not, according to Marc Richir. In this

---

[35] Stéphane Mosès, *L'ange de l'histoire* (Paris: Gallimard, 2006), 108–31.

[36] William Morris, *News from Nowhere* (1890). http://etext.virginia.edu/toc/modeng/public/MorNews.html (accessed 30 December 2011).

[37] Friedrich Nietzsche, *Considérations Inactuelles*, translated from German and with preface by G. Bianquis (Paris: Aubier-Montaigne, 1964).

[38] Nietzsche, *Considérations Inactuelles*, 205.

latter, one can perceive the revolution of thought—the phenomenological revolution—interlaced with the thought of revolution, in which
utopia, so to speak, has its place. Thus, the same goes for *Du sublime
en politique* (Of the Sublime in Politics) in which, from the analysis of
great revolutionary moments, in the wake of Michelet, one comes to
the emergence of 'the utopian community', when, within the revolutionary event, the social gets phenomenalized.[39] Without entering here into
the complexity and the richness of Richir's method, let us remember
that with regard to our interrogation at the outset, whether this may be
about revolutionary celebrations or days, what phenomenology adopts in
the first place is the suspension of symbolic benchmarks in current use,
along with a suspension of all Power, veritable *épochè* which the revolutionary event immediately leads to. One can notice in Marc Richir as
well as in Emmanuel Levinas an urge to think of utopia as *épochè*. As
though it were essential to discover through the ways yet to be explored,
affinities between 'the waking up of sleeping significations' (Levinas)
and the utopian waking up, affinities between phenomenology and
utopia, between 'era of repose' or utopian suspension and phenomenological *épochè*. Let us cite Richir:

> What Michelet gives us to understand, is, with these celebrations of the
> Federation ... all the symbolic benchmarks which *symbolically instituted
> the land* in a network of places and positions, status and social roles–turn pale
> and get shaken. And these form the subject, after the turmoil, of a veritable
> phenomenological *épochè*: not because these have miraculously disappeared
> ... but, precisely because, they prove to be ineffective, appertaining to a past
> era, put on hold by the ephemeral suspension of the celebration.[40]

No one doubts that this revolutionary utopian community, swayed by
the dream—which is not to be confused with a community transparent to
itself, nor with a fusional mass—gives access, thanks to the suspension of
all symbolic benchmarks, to an alterity, an alterity-content—other time,
other space, experience of an energy which is not to relapse into Power.
No one doubts that this utopian community would be the necessary passage, so that the ordinary world would look totally new. And against

---

[39] Marc Richir, *Du sublime en politique* (Paris: Payot, 1991), 135–42; Marc Richir,
'Y a-t-il du sens dans l'histoire? L'expérience collective du sublime', in *Critique de la
politique autour de Miguel Abensour*, ed. Anne Kupiec and Etienne Tassin (Paris: Sens &
Tonka, 2006), 521–36.

[40] Richir, *Du sublime en politique*, 19.

the backdrop of this utopian alterity, there is a possible opening on the future. The strengthened alterity—since the phenomenological suspension has replaced the dialectical negation—opens on a community which needs not to be phantasmagorically instituted; rather, which needs to 'install the positive and empirical political community in such a way that it would not come to suppress the first (utopian community) and lead it to extinction or death'.[41]

If the Aristotelian definition of man as a political animal is stretched into man as a utopian animal, it signifies that the revolutionary utopian community belongs to a different order from the political community. The latter is haunted, perpetually tormented by the former and its eschatological horizons. If we follow Richir who affirms that every attempt to institute the utopian community as such 'inevitably corrupts and turns it into its most determined opposite', we get a sign and not the least of this radical alterity: the utopian community is never realized in a sustainable manner, or rather, it keeps alive its quality of non-place which outreaches every place and anticipates simultaneously every attempt which intends to get settled over there, by melting into one the place of nowhere and the place where everything is fine.

---

[41] Ibid., 139.

3

Echo of an Impossible Return

An Essay Concerning Fredric Jameson's Utopian Thought and Gathering and Hunting Social Relations

Peter Kulchyski

Preface: Up the Redstone River/Stumbling towards Utopia

The water splashes over the edge of the precipice, foaming and spraying and dancing down the orange face of the cliff to the golden-terraced pools below, seeping and trickling through them and farther down to the river. The water is clean and clear and pure: Theresa says that this water has a healing power. The ledge beside the falls offers a glorious view of the Redstone River winding its way through valleys and canyons out of the Mackenzie Mountains towards another great river, the Dehcho (called by the maps of the settler colony the Mackenzie River), which carries itself at a more dignified pace out to the northern oceans.

To get here, Jaime and I drive for four days, from Winnipeg straight as a bullet into the wind westward to Calgary. From Calgary north and north-west, and north and north and north we drive our drives. The pavement surrenders to gravel as we turn off the Alaska highway on to the Liard highway and enter the Northwest Territories. We come to unbridged rivers and cautiously pick our way on to the ferries that take us across them. We visit friends in Fort Simpson, sitting and talking politics over tea. We finally leave our van with other friends in *Pedhzi Ke*, at the end of that long road, and split a charter flight, sharing it with a family of three, which takes us over the Redstone River and the Begade and the Dehcho to the foot of the sacred bear rock to the Dene village of Tulita.

The next day we get in the boat that Theresa has ordered up: her brother Michael Widow's boat, with her son James to share the driving, and a few kids to absorb the sights. We travel back south down the Dehcho, our eyes caressing a landscape more intimately than the flight allowed. We pass my old friend the Begade, and come to another river, one I have not travelled, one that no one apart from the Shutagotine travel, the Redstone. Our jetboat screams with delight as we whip up against the current and knife our way into the hills that pay obeisance to the mountains beyond. Hours and barrels of gas and tea breaks later we come to a narrow black-walled canyon that seems to mark something: a world apart, a world closer to the mountains, a world that still is as it once was.

In this world we will camp, we will find the giant steps that lead to the falls, we will see the elderly woman in the rocks, and will drink and wash in her water and clean our eyes with her view and regretfully begin the long journey back to places where the placid water groans around the contaminated sludge that hides in its murk.

Frederic Jameson's Utopianism

In the last few decades, arguably no thinker has played a greater role in insisting upon the necessity of the utopian dimension in critical thought than the Marxist literary critic Fredric Jameson. From his early interest in and studies of those thinkers who stressed a messianic (Benjamin) or utopian (Bloch) strategy of critique, through his concluding essay on the utopian and ideological in *The Political Unconscious* which provided the foundation for his more well-known work on postmodernism and finally, to his smaller (*The Seeds of Time*) study of utopianism and larger, more recent (*Archaeologies of the Future*) study of utopian and science fiction, Jameson has consistently maintained the relevance and continued urgency of utopian-oriented writing and reflection.

The category of utopia actually steeps through Jameson's thinking, informing his choice of cultural texts to interpret as much as the strategy or line of interpretation he follows. Witness for example his essay on Frank Gehry's Los Angeles house, indeed his broader interest in architecture itself, as a 'material thought' or embodiment of utopian desire.[1]

---

[1] Frederic Jameson, 'Spatial Equivalents: Postmodern Architecture and the World System', in *The States of 'Theory'*, ed. David Carroll (New York; Columbia University Press, 1990).

In his introduction to *Archaeologies of the Future*, the text that provokes the analysis which follows, Jameson argues that

> Utopian form is itself a representational meditation on radical difference, radical otherness, and on the systemic nature of the social totality, to the point where one cannot imagine any fundamental change in our social existence which has not at first thrown off Utopian visions like so many sparks from a comet.[2]

Utopian visions provide a standpoint for explicit and implicit critiques of capitalism, and therefore cannot be separated from a socialist project, as he goes on to argue: 'it is still difficult to see how future Utopias could ever be imagined in any absolute dissociation from socialism in its larger sense of anti-capitalism'.[3]

What follows is inspired by and profoundly steeped in the balm of Jameson's analysis. It does not perform a genealogical reading of the utopian dimension of Jameson's thought, but rather offers an elliptical critique: an appreciation nevertheless guided by a standpoint-based criticism. In effect, while the force and parameters of Jameson's understanding of the critical value of utopian visioning is an invaluable contribution to materialist politics and theory, his situating of the utopian within the realm of fiction, especially future-oriented and science fiction, surrenders the opportunity to position a much stronger critique through an analysis of grounded utopian forms. The latter can be found, not in future-oriented or science fiction, but in the anthropological descriptions of gathering and hunting peoples.

Archaeology of the Future

Archaeologies of the Future can be seen as a Jamesonian tour de force. The text is a culmination of many years of thought and reading, and clearly carries the project announced in his *The Political Unconscious* to a fruition delayed in part by his parallel work on postmodernism. While the analysis of postmodernism involves a dialectical reading that engages with both the utopian possibilities and ideological resonances of postmodern culture, the analysis of utopian fiction represents a strong

---

[2] Frederic Jameson, *Archaeologies of the Future* (London: Verso, 2005), xii.
[3] Ibid., 196–97.

attempt to posit the critical value of utopian thought, and it tends towards the appreciative mode of critique. The book begins by reading through several theoretical problems confronted in and through utopian thought—issues such as space, the body, knowledge, the collective and social difference—and then moves on to read a range of writers: Fourier from the utopian socialist tradition leading into a range of science fiction writers including Ursula Le Guin and Philip K. Dick (who occupies a central position in Jameson's thought).

In the opening chapter, 'Varieties of the Utopian', Jameson posits 'two distinct lines of descendency from More's inaugural text: the one intent on the realization of the Utopian program, the other an obscure yet omnipresent Utopian impulse finding its way to the surface in a variety of covert expressions and practices'.[4] As regards the latter, which reads much like his understanding of the 'political unconscious', he notes that 'we have identified the city itself as a fundamental form of the Utopian image (along with the shape of the village as it reflects the cosmos), perhaps we should make a place for the individual building as a space of Utopian investment'.[5]

Jameson is as interested in utopia where it emerges as an explicit political program, through manifestos, revolutions, intentional communities, and so on, as much as in utopias that are imagined, projected, and, especially, represented in literary form. He is, after all and on a fundamental level, a literary scholar. What he misses, however, and more strikingly never accounts for on any significant level, are utopian forms found in anthropological descriptions: a site for utopian thought fully as rich as anything that can be found in science fiction, architecture, and political visioning. His archaeology of the future is therefore, to my mind, haunted by past and present social forms of explosive power and would be far richer if he accounted for these.

Gatherers and Hunters in Jameson

It is not that Jameson has nothing to say about, for example, gathering and hunting social forms. However, in his early work he retains a critical ambivalence with regard to the issue of whether gathering and hunting

---

[4] Ibid., 3.
[5] Ibid., 4.

social forms offer a grounded example of emancipatory and egalitarian relations, or rather can be characterized as representing a romantic mirage. Read, for example, the following from his study of Adorno, *Late Marxism*:

> Whether this is inconsistent with the Marxian vision of modes of production, and in particular with that of tribal society or primitive communism—indeed, whether the Marxian conception itself implies nostalgia for some golden age (on the order of the tradition of Rousseau, as for example in Sahlins's extraordinary 'First Affluent Society')—remains to be seen.[6]

We can almost see him in effect throwing up his hands as if to say: 'What am I to make of all of this? It's clearly undecidable.' We will return to Sahlins' essay, actually called 'The Original Affluent Society'. For now, let us compare the view he articulates in his book on postmodernism:

> A nostalgic-Utopian triad thus emerges which is handily identified as the Marxist 'vision of history': a golden age before the fall, that is to say, before capitalist dissociation, which can optionally be positioned where you like, in primitive communism or tribal society, in the Greek or Renaissance polis, in the agricultural communes of whatever national or cultural tradition before the emergence of state power: the 'modern age' or in other words capitalism: and then whatever Utopian vision can be appealed to replace that. But the notion of a 'fall' into civilization … is rather, unless I am mistaken, a feature of the right wing critique of capitalism ….[7]

It is my intent to show that he is indeed mistaken. The right-wing versions of these narratives do place their 'golden ages' in a variety of neolithic, agriculture contexts where social hierarchy was prevalent, and can be used to justify horrendous injustice. A materialist critique does the hard work of examining the evidence, which convincingly shows that gatherers and hunters produced socially egalitarian relations. To my knowledge, there are no 'right-wing' writers who can be found to endorse this latter view.

Hence, by the time of *The Seeds of Time*, he writes that,

> … third world societies were torn by a penetration of western modernization that generated over and against itself—in all the variety of cultural forms

---

[6] Frederic Jameson, *Late Marxism* (London: Verso, 1990), 99–100.

[7] Frederic Jameson, *Postmodernism or, the Cultural Logic of Late Capitalism* (Durham: Duke University Press, 1991), 337.

characteristic of those very different societies—a counterposition that could generally be described as traditionalism: the affirmation of a cultural (and sometime religious) originality that had the power to resist Western modernity and was indeed preferable to it.[8]

This leads him to conclude that all traditions are 'constructed' and 'what one wants to affirm today is that this second reactive or antimodern term of tradition and traditionalism has everywhere vanished from the reality of the former third world or colonized societies' and, finally, 'nothing but the modern henceforth exists in third world societies'[9]. Such sweeping pronouncements from the centre as characterizations of the margins are, always, to be suspected.

This egregious set of understandings is marked by a peculiar refusal for a Marxist like Jameson, for whom the category mode of production is a central analytic tool, positioned by none other than Jameson in his *The Political Unconscious* as the third and final horizon of interpretation.[10] Yet not only does he lump all Third World societies into a dubious catch-all (traditional), he goes so far in *The Seeds of Time* to argue that 'all the great precapitalist cultures prove to have been peasant ones (except where they were based on slavery)'[11]. Within a few short keystrokes, he effectively entirely 'disappears' the distinction between gatherers and hunters on the one hand and agriculturalists on the other, a distinction foundational to anthropological thought and one whose absence will come to trouble Jameson's otherwise supple cultural politics. In fact, the concept of mode of production is developed precisely by Marx to in part explain and understand this difference, as much as to explain and understand the difference between agricultural production and capitalism. It was certainly not developed to explain the distinction between modernism and postmodernism, which seems to be its main point of purchase for Jameson.

It is a particular problem for those of us concerned with the politics of gathering and hunting peoples in the world today, peoples who can be found in much of the American hemisphere, the South Pacific, Africa, and Asia. Jameson writes that,

---

[8] Frederic Jameson, *The Seeds of Time* (New York: Columbia University Press, 1994), 19.

[9] Ibid., 20.

[10] Frederic Jameson, *The Political Unconscious* (Ithaca: Cornell University Press, 1981), 88–102.

[11] Jameson, *The Seeds of Time*, 26.

... the genuine, radical difference that holds between Columbus and the peoples he encountered can never be articulated into a politics: at best an enslavement, at worst a genocide, and occasionally something like a compassionate attempt at an impossible tolerance (which is itself a form of patronizing condescension).[12]

So why is it that the imaginative differences projected by fictional constructors of utopias should present us with a politics, while the continually reinvented social differences built in daily interactions of indigenous gatherers and hunters does not? There is a serious problem here, and it has two levels. On the one hand, Jameson explicitly excludes the continuing struggles of contemporary gatherers and hunters for land and cultural rights from the very category of the political while on the other (which, as Gad Horowitz once wrote, turns out to be the very same hand), he forecloses the power of a whole additional set of utopian writings.

By the time he comes to write the *Archaeologies of the Future*, Jameson seems to have resolved his ambiguous position regarding gathering and hunting peoples even further, for example, deliberately equating medieval thought with that of 'tribal peoples': 'the unique conceptual resources of medieval theology ... in its primitive forms a kind of purely perceptual knowledge developed in the absence of abstract or properly philosophical concepts and conceptualities'.[13] Here we are fully in ethnocentric terrain, an ethnocentrism that does not recognize the fundamental breach between gatherers and hunters and agriculturalists, and that romantically implicitly asserts the superiority of 'modern', 'Western', 'abstract' reasoning. A strikingly undialectical endorsement of the notion of social evolution cannot be far behind, and we find it offhandedly deployed later in part two, chapter 2 of the book, which deals with science fiction writer Brian Aldiss. Here Jameson writes:

... that the destruction of less advanced societies is wrong and inhuman is no longer, surely, a matter for intelligent debate. What is at issue is the degree to which even benign and well-intentioned intervention of higher into lower cultures may not be ultimately destructive in its results.[14]

Actually, what is at issue is the question of whether it is possible to speak of 'higher' or 'lower' cultures, what is the political value of such

---

[12] Jameson, *Archaeologies of the Future*, 66.
[13] Ibid., 61.
[14] Ibid., 265.

a formulation, whose interest does such a hierarchy serve, and, if one begins to nuance an analysis in the manner that Marx did, which cultures actually occupy the ethical high ground?

Even on his own terms, as a literary critic fashioning a major reading of the utopian and science fiction genres, Jameson's dismissal of careful consideration regarding gathering and hunting peoples impoverishes aspects of his critique. The chapter on Ursula Le Guin, clearly one of Jameson's most important utopian writers, entirely neglects the degree to which her understanding of alternative social forms comes from her own studies of anthropology (not to mention her anthropological lineage). Hence, one of her major works, *The Word for World Is Forest*, is entirely neglected. He can have nothing to say about it. His reading of her masterpiece, *The Dispossessed*, becomes limited because he has no idea of from where she drew her inspiration. In fact, she is a utopian fiction writer who is arguably invested in and grounded in anthropological description, which pervades her fiction but has to be excluded from Jameson's reading.[15]

The Gatherer–Hunter Paradigm in Anthropology: Sahlins

It is not that Jameson does not have an understanding of anthropology (a criticism that can be made of significant currents in contemporary cultural theory; it is a critical problem, for example, in Agamben). *The Political Unconscious* ends with a well-considered response and riposte to Marshall Sahlins' criticisms of Marxist economic instrumentalism as articulated in his *Culture and Practical Reason*. What is striking is the degree to which Jameson, not generally an unastute reader, seems to miss Sahlins' point. Jameson's concern to defend Marxism leads him to argue that 'our own view of culture as the expression of a properly utopian or collective impulse [is] no longer basically functional or instrumental in Sahlins's sense'.[16] Sahlins' point is really about ways of knowing: that different social forms or modes of production involve differing loci of interpretation:

---

[15] Ibid., 267–80.
[16] Jameson, *The Political Unconscious*, 293.

...the cultural scheme is variously inflected by a dominant site of symbolic production, which supplies the major idiom of other relations and activities. One can thus speak of a privileged institutional locus of the symbolic process, whence emanates a classificatory grid imposed upon the total culture. And speaking at this still high level of abstraction, the peculiarity of Western culture is the institutionalization of the process in and as the production of goods, by comparison with a 'primitive' world where the locus of symbolic differentiation remains social relations, principally kinship relations, and other spheres of activity are by the operative distinctions of kinship.[17]

That is, each mode of production has a corresponding central organizing principle through which phenomena are interpreted. The very concept 'mode of production' emerges from the economic structure of thought endemic to capitalist society. Gatherers and hunters, for Sahlins, interpret the world through the lens of kinship. All of this, in my reading, is still framed within a notion of understanding the profoundest kind of social difference through the logic of modes of production.

That said, it perhaps would have been more useful for Jameson to engage with Sahlins' earlier text, *Stone Age Economics*, where the opening essay, 'The Original Affluent Society', which as we have seen Jameson himself describes as 'extraordinary' but does not engage in a strong reading of, inscribes a utopian vision of gatherers and hunters. In Sahlins' vision, gatherers and hunters created a social form that involved minimal needs and extensive leisure time. There in fact can hardly be found a more strongly and politically potent utopian text in the twentieth century: from it Delueze's concept of nomadism emerges, Baudrillard's critique of production operates in its shadow, and gathering and hunting peoples the world over have found an ideological justification for their varying struggles. Sahlins' studies in *Stone Age Economics* lead him outside the parameters of economic thought itself, so that *Culture and Practical Reason* is a logical conclusion or extension. Strikingly, both Jameson and Sahlins are Marxists and both are strongly influenced by Jean-Paul Sartre's *Critique of Dialectical Reason*; a stronger dialogue between the two would certainly play a role in dramatically strengthening Jameson's utopianism.

Sahlins is not the only anthropologist to celebrate gathering and hunting social forms. The life work of Eleanor Leacock was oriented

---

[17] Marshall Sahlins, *Culture and Practical Reason* (Chicago: University of Chicago Press, 1976), 211.

to illustrating the degree of gender egalitarianism that prevailed among gathering and hunting peoples. Richard Lee, Stanley Diamond, and a host of other anthropologists snapped back at a century of ethnocentric dismissals of so-called primitive peoples. In Canada, Hugh Brody is a leading figure among a wide range of anthropologists, often engaged in political advocacy work, who take seriously the difference between gatherers and hunters and agriculturalists, and whose descriptions of existing communities have dimensions that parallel the utopian fictions endorsed by Jameson.

Postmodern Critique: Hybridity and Boundaries

It is not that this work is uncontested. The political right continues to insist on the barbarity of gathering and hunting social forms, continues to accept notions of social evolution, and continues to push for 'modernization', 'progress', and 'development'. We will leave the critique of this body of thought for another time and place. Meanwhile, a segment of the theoretical left associated with postmodernism (though not Jameson's dialectical version of postmodernism) has come to criticize the notion of cultural boundaries itself. The concept of hybridity, deployed in varying ways by Homi Bhabha and James Clifford (out and inside of anthropology), is now commonly used to suggest that distinct cultures themselves are of questionable value. And there are those who have argued that 'there is no outside' of *Empire*[18].

Excursus: On production and community

Here is a paradox. The notion of 'blood and soil', associated with Nazi ideology, has been entirely discredited. Indeed the notion of cultural hybridity is positioned against notions of cultural or racial purity which underlie historical and contemporary forms of racism. And yet, the indigenous communities I work with in northern Canada found their claim to social justice on: 1. their ancient and continuing relation to a specific territory and, 2. their cultural distinctiveness as a specific community. Part of the substantive value of these communities is that they can be characterized as intergenerational productive communities and as such can teach us about community itself, about how

---

[18] Michael Hardt and Antonio Negri, *Empire* (Cambridge: Harvard University Press, 2001).

communities that deserve the name can continue to remake themselves inside and outside of the pores of capitalism.

Jameson actually provides invaluable theoretical tools for defending gatherers and hunters from these politically naive, ungrounded, and regressive formulations. His recognition of the value of the concept mode of production, his defence of the concept of totality, his conceptualization of the centrality of collectivity, and indeed, his understanding of the urgency of the concept of utopia—all line up closely with the contemporary politics of gatherers and hunters in northern Canada. It is, therefore, a significant containment of his own thought that limits the political power of Jameson's utopian project.

Hence, when Jameson writes 'as though the Utopians also were anamnesis, the deep recovery of what is both forgotten and known since before birth'[19], or in the following passage, also from *The Seeds of Time*, he is provides a description better suited to the social reality of gatherers and hunters than to a future only capable of being dreamed:

> A state of society that does not need history or historical struggle lies beyond much that is precious to us in individual as well as collective existence; its thought obliges us to confront the most terrifying dimension of our humanity, at least for the individualism of modern, bourgeois people, and that is our species being, our insertion in the great chain of the generations, which we know as death. Utopia is inseparable from death in that its serenity gazes calmly and implacably away from the accidents of individual existence and the inevitability of giving way; in this sense it might even be said that Utopia solves the problem of death, by inventing a new way of looking at individual death, as a matter of limited concern, beyond all stoicism.[20]

Materialist Utopian: Political Value of Gatherer–Hunter Position

A feminist materialism that looks towards the grounded utopian social forms found in contemporary gatherers and hunters presents an extraordinary wealth of intellectual resources in the struggle against capitalist colonial dominations. If we can accept, with a broad stream of critical anthropologists, not that the issues are undecidable but rather from the

---

[19] Jameson, *The Seeds of Time*, 96.
[20] Ibid., 123.

weight of evidence when read carefully and as free of ethnocentrism as our generation can construct itself, that gatherers and hunters thrived in sustainable communities for millennia in politically egalitarian and gender-egalitarian social forms where wealth differentials were relatively minimal, most property was owned in common, and where respect for personal autonomy was a fundamental base of the social order, we are then in a position to say that capitalism, rather than being an extension of some ancient and natural impulse, is rather a historical anomaly and probably an unsustainable mode of production. We can say, in fact, that capitalism appears possible in theory but has not really worked in practice. Socialism, or stateless communism, in fact worked in practice (and continues to subversively exist) for the vast portion of human history. And this is precisely the value for argument that Jameson ascribes to utopian thought.

Materialist Utopianism: Fighting with Gatherers and Hunters in the Present Conjuncture

Furthermore, situating utopian forms in gathering and hunting social relations also puts Marxism front and centre in a critical contemporary social struggle, particularly in the Americas. What are Marxists to make of the indigenous resistances taking place at the present conjuncture in Bolivia, Venezuela, Brazil, Chiapas, and Oaxaca? Do we have any specific insights? What about Australia, or new Zealand, or the so-called 'tribals' of India, or China, or that part of China called Taiwan, or much of Africa? My own political and theoretical work is directed to another margin that is central to anti-capitalist struggle, northern Canada.

Any political approach that does not see value in indigenous social forms leaves no room for the specificity of the political wars taking place over lands and communities in northern Canada. The future orientation of Jameson's archaeologies vitiates the value of an otherwise impressive and actually invaluable set of theoretical reflections.

Marx once argued that value is created by both labour and 'nature'. The working class, who are the creators of value through labour, are engaged in a shifting and continual struggle against capitalist exploitation: represented in this year (2009) by a new, monumental shift of resources from the poor to the rich. But land (Marx's 'nature') is equally important to capitalist so-called development. The Americas are a battlefield of indigenous land struggles, and the history is not entirely one of defeats. The adoption by the United Nations of the Declaration of the Rights of Indigenous Peoples is symbolic of the advances made by a broad resistance movement with its own internal dynamic and logic, which has made indigenous rights the core doctrine of defence. Those struggles are engaged in by indigenous peoples, who are on the front lines of anti-capitalist struggle because the voracious appetite for growth has pushed the frontiers to a confrontation for the last vestiges of uncommodified territory.

The Urgency of the Now with and against the Glacial Temporality of Utopia

As I write these words, Canada is engaged in the largest industrial project in the world: the extraction of oil from the so-called tar sands in northeastern Alberta. The project involves tearing up enormous swaths of hunting territory, producing massive tailing ponds, sapping rivers, constructing a grid of pipelines from the north and the west and to the south and the east, using the so-called clean natural gas to produce greenhouse spewing oil, importing workers from around the world, and pumping pollutants into once pristine rivers. The oil produced is to be sold as a 'secure' energy source to feed the voracious market of the United States for individualized transportation. From an ecological perspective, it is a kind of madness.

On the front line of the struggle against this project are the Cree and Chipweyan communities directly downstream, though the network of indigenous and environmental activists working to oppose the insanity name their annual gatherings 'Everyone Is Downstream'. Hence, the issues involved in this discussion are not merely of academic (in its pejorative sense) concern, and do not simply relate to questions of who can produce, for example, a stronger reading of Le Guin. If the Mikisew Cree are seen as 'traditionalists' romantically attached to an outmoded form of social organization, capitalism need not look back at what it leaves in its wake and can even praise itself for offering up a few 'jobs' to this backwater territory.

But what is at stake here is a larger, and what Jameson calls the 'glacial' standpoint of utopia[21] that is strikingly a part of this equation. If it can be shown that the Mikisew Cree might actually have something to teach the rest of us about how to construct intergenerational communities of

---

[21] Ibid., 123.

production, the threat they pose to global capitalism is twofold: as bearers of a land base that is required for capital accumulation, and as bearers
of a set of social relations that threaten the claims of capitalist society, of
modernism, to be the embodiment of progress. It is precisely at this point
that Jameson's words return us to the critical value of his work, as when
he writes in an evocative set of passages which I cannot quote in full,
that 'progress'

> ... is now seen as an attempt to colonize the future, to draw the unforeseeable
> back into tangible realities in which one can invest and on which one can
> bank, very much in the spirit of stockmarket 'futures'. ... Where Benjamin
> observed that 'not even the past will be safe' from the conquerors, we may
> now add that the future is not safe either, and that it is compared to the level-
> ing of the land speculators and builder-investors, whose bulldozers destroy
> all the site-specific properties of a terrain in order to clear it ....[22]

Postface: Colville Lake

In the late spring of 2007 I attended a meeting, the only *Mola* present, of
leaders from two Dene communities in the Northwest Territories: Fort
Good Hope and Colville Lake. About 30 people were present, and the
meeting lasted all day. The meeting was held entirely in the Dene language, with the interpreter present quickly realizing that I was the only
person present who needed interpretation, and providing it individually
for me since I was taking minutes for the use of the communities. It
began with each of the chiefs briefly speaking: one welcomed everyone to
his community, the other spoke about the purpose of the meeting. About
a quarter of the participants were female; the ages ranged from middle
age to elders. They did not speak around the circle, or follow Robert's
famous rules of 'order'. Rather, each person spoke at the point when
they were moved to speak. No one directly responded to anyone else, but
issues were contested, often by individuals who spoke much later in the
day. There were very serious issues on the table, involving potentially
millions of dollars in capital-value terms. Voices were never raised. No
one spoke longer than about 20 minutes at the most. By day's end, everyone had spoken. The most forceful speaker was a female elder from the
host community. No vote was held. No formal resolution was arrived at.

---

[22] Jameson, *Archaeologies of the Future*, 228.

But a discussion had been initiated, serious differences aired, and a certain kind of fragile solidarity established.

It struck me that such a meeting could not have been held in, for example, the universities I have worked my whole professional career in. A chair would be essential, and rules of order required. Dene from contemporary communities retain a whole set of skills that allows them an ethics of speech. In the dominant culture, where as Baudrillard notes, 'power is the spoken word', those skills and that ethic has been lost, lost in our very rush to speak and in our very inability to listen. In Dene terms, we are not polite or civilized people. We are rude and untutored in polite forms of address.

The road ends at *Pedhzi Ke*. Fort Good Hope, Colville Lake, and the falls on the Redstone River are all further north, well past the end of that road. What if all the other roads lead straight to global destruction, save this tortuous twisted difficult road towards small scattered intergenerational communities of gatherers and hunters? No, Fort Good Hope is not utopia: there are too many serious social problems there. But, yes, Fort Good Hope bears the traces of something that deserves to be called utopia, bears the traces of something that must not be forgotten by those of us concerned with these questions.

But of course, when faced with all of this, the cheerleaders of capitalism bray: you can never go back. You can never go back you can never go back you can never go back for all your tears and all your written words and all your life's blood and all your meetings your rallies your slogans your loves your anger patience energy creativity those glorious dreams of a justice that deserves the name and those explosive flashes of compassionate insight you can never go back in spite because as a result of for the reason for all....

4

Radicalism in Early Modern England

Innovation or Reformation?

Rachel Foxley

In this essay I will consider the nature of early modern English radicalism, using the concept of utopianism to interrogate the ways in which it was possible to frame demands for fundamental change within early modern English society. I will take utopianism, minimally, to mean the full imagining of a radically alternative society, often as existing in the present. The main part of this chapter will examine some seventeenth-century writings which are often described by historians as politically and socially 'radical', arguing that the ways in which these texts are and are not utopian can illuminate the problem of early modern radicalism.

The concept of radicalism is a difficult one for historians of this period to apply without an unhelpful degree of anachronism creeping in; some have argued against its use tout court in the absence of 'radicalism' or 'radicals' in the English language before about 1820.[1] More fruitfully, J.C. Davis has set out an influential case for a 'functional' identification of radicalism in this period, specifying criteria for the applicability of the term which include the requirement that the 'radical' thinker should propose a 'transfer mechanism' through which the projected political and societal transformation will be achieved.[2] This, according to Eliav-Feldon,

---

[1] Conal Condren, 'Radicals, Conservatives and Moderates in Early Modern Political Thought: A Case of Sandwich Islands Syndrome?' *History of Political Thought* 10, no. 3 (1989): 525–42. Also, *The Language of Politics in Seventeenth-century England* (Macmillan: Basingstoke and London, 1994), chapter 5.

[2] J.C. Davis, 'Radicalism in a Traditional Society: The Evaluation of Radical Thought in the English Commonwealth 1649–1660', *History of Political Thought* 3, no. 2 (1982): 193–213.

is something which classic utopias singularly lack, existing in an imagined present which, in its perfection and other-ness, is hopelessly isolated from the course of history and thus from the hope of applicability.[3] This does, indeed, seem a viable conclusion to draw from Thomas More's *Utopia*, which I will discuss briefly before turning to the works of some mid-seventeenth-century English radicals. These seventeenth-century thinkers, I argue, were in some senses profoundly utopian, but mapped their utopianism onto the past and present of England in such a way as to open up the feasibility as well as the imaginability of their visions.[4]

More's *Utopia* (1516) is the founding text of the modern Utopian tradition. The travel narrative that frames the description of the land of Utopia places that imaginary society, and the others which Hythloday mentioned in Book 1, in an 'elsewhere' of the present, carefully tied in to the real-life voyages of Amerigo Vespucci.[5] This 'elsewhere' is carefully taken beyond the real-life lands encountered by Vespucci, as the travellers journey on past the equatorial no-man's-lands into a new set of civilizations, distorting mirrors of those which are familiar to them. The journey is also drily distinguished from the more arrantly fictional travellers' lore: what Hythloday finds is truer but stranger:

---

[3] Miriam Eliav-Feldon, *Realistic Utopias: The Ideal Imaginary Societies of the Renaissance 1516–1630* (Oxford: Clarendon Press, 1982).

[4] Keith Thomas has similarly drawn a contrast between sixteenth-century Utopian writings which were 'no more revolutionary in practice than were the concepts of paradise or heaven', and the more 'action-oriented Utopia' which was to come in the seventeenth-century, albeit still encouraged by a millenarian as much as a political framework. See, Keith Thomas, 'The Utopian Impulse in Seventeenth-century England', in *Between Dream and Nature: Essays on Utopia and Dystopia* eds. Dominic Baker-Smith and C.C. Barfoot (Amsterdam: Rodopi, 1987). Chloë Houston argues that seventeenth-century Utopias could be rather gradualist and reformist, and conversely that the seventeenth-century figures who do deserve the label of 'radicals' might shun utopian forms as unhelpful and impracticable. See Chloë Houston, 'Could "Eutopian Politics [...] Never be Drawn into Use?" Utopianism and Radicalism in the 1640s', in *Cromohs Virtual Seminars: Recent Historiographical Trends of the British Studies (17th–18th Centuries)* eds. M. Caricchio, G. Tarantino (2006–07), 1–4, http://www.cromohs.unifi.it/seminari/houston_utopias.html (accessed 14 December 2011).

[5] Thomas More, *Utopia*, eds. George M. Logan and Robert M. Adams (Cambridge: Cambridge University Press, 1989), 10–11. Hythloday accompanied Vespucci on the last three of his four voyages, 'accounts of which are now common reading everywhere', and then travelled on separately with a few other men.

We made no inquiries, however, about monsters, which are the routine of travellers' tales. Scyllas, ravenous Celaenos, man-eating Lestrygonians and that sort of monstrosity you can hardly avoid, but to find governments wisely established and sensibly ruled is not so easy.[6]

It has also been argued, though, that Utopia's 'elsewhere' is intended as a rather precise mirror of England/Britain, an island of about the same size, cut off by a narrow channel (in Utopia's case, an artificial one), and perhaps with a similar number of cities. Utopia, then, is an elsewhere which is a distorting mirror of England, set very much in the present day. But it is also a vision of a utopian past, in its reproduction of elements reported of the classical states of Greece and Rome, and advocated in the works of classical writers. While the text itself describes Utopia as a society existing in the present, the marginal notes—added, it is supposed, by More's friends in the process of preparing the text for publication— contrast the practices of the Utopians with what happens 'now', as if they were reading a historical text about a classical republic. Of course, these placings of Utopia as a model, if not ideal, past, or elsewhere, are also accompanied by the numerous signals to us that Utopia is, as its name suggests, not so much an elsewhere as a 'nowhere'; or, as in the alternative name of 'Udepotia' which Guillaume Budé suggested in response to the text—it is a 'neverland'.[7] This apparently wistful placing of the island in the realm of impossibility is of course strongly influenced by Plato's Republic, in which Socrates acknowledged that the city he described was not so much an achievable earthly goal as 'a pattern ... laid up in heaven' on which the individual souls of the just, rather than the real societies of men, should model themselves.[8] What is most striking about *Utopia* is that the reflection it offers of England is the one which makes England not more, but far less apt for the needed social and political change than its readers may previously have realized. In spite of the complications of the text, which do perhaps allow (and intend) the reader to emerge with a commitment to gradualist, pragmatic reform, it is hard to read the text as suggesting that anything genuinely approaching 'utopia' could be achieved in that way. The idealistic and uncompromising traveller Hythloday (who is specifically compared to Plato[9]) is, on that point, in

---

[6] Ibid., 12.

[7] Ibid., 118–19, letter from Budé to Lupset.

[8] Plato, *The Republic*, eds. G.R.F. Ferrari and Tom Griffith (Cambridge: Cambridge University Press, 2000), 312, 592b.

[9] Ibid., 10.

agreement with the sceptical politician 'More'. The contemporary reader of *Utopia* should certainly have interpreted England differently by the time she or he put down the book, and perhaps have been brought to see for the first time some of the desperate faults of the nation; but the text offers no underlying positive message about the true nature of England for readers to take their motivation from. In the end, the text offers an aporia rather than a programme for action, and this is because it has essentially succeeded in showing how very unwise it would be, if you wanted to create an ideal commonwealth, to start with sixteenth-century England.

The radical social, economic, and political proposals which emerged in England in the civil war period more than a century later faced this problem of utopianism in fascinating ways. It is a paradox that the English Civil War of the 1640s, a set of events which unleashed the radicalism studied by Christopher Hill in 1972 under the title *The World Turned Upside Down*, was fought by both sides on the pretext (at least) of opposing 'innovation'. In the couple of years before the war began in 1642, the King and the Parliament became the cores of opposing parties who recruited armies to fight each other. The propaganda produced by these two increasingly clearly defined 'sides' took on a strange mirror-image quality, each side accusing the other of identical crimes of 'innovation'. John Pym, the great parliamentarian leader, famously asserted that among the evil counsellors of Charles I, there was a 'design to alter the kingdom both in religion and government'. A royalist document issued a year-and-a-half later retorted that it was the parliamentarian troublers of the kingdom 'whose Designe is, and alwayes hath been, to alter the whole frame of Government both of Church and State.'[10] On both sides, the assumption, for polemical purposes at least, was that any such alteration was to be resisted, and that the defenders of the status quo were morally in the right.

Years of bloodshed were to pass before the war generated the most striking religious, political, and social demands which have with hindsight been labelled as 'radical'. Some moves in that direction, however, were present from the start, especially in the religious sphere: the 'Root and Branch' petition of 1640 demanding the outright abolition of the episcopacy was a notorious example. The petitioners added to their list of

---

[10] John Pym, Speech of 7 November 1640 in Maija Jansson, ed., *Proceedings in the Opening Session of the Long Parliament, House of Commons. 7 vols, Proceedings of the English Parliament*, (Rochester, N.Y. University of Rochester Press, 2000), vol. 3, p. 35; *His Majesty's Answer to a Printed Book*, 26 May 1642, British Library, Thomason E.150[20], p. 2.

grievances against the bishops the fact that other churches had abolished episcopacy when they had rejected the authority of the Pope and the Roman Catholic Church.[11] This harking back to reformation, and the sense, common in England, that the reformation of the church was incomplete, reveal one of the most potent ways in which early modern English people could argue for radical change: they could frame it as 'reformation'. Against the invariably pejorative word 'innovation', used to describe the actions of opponents in the religious and political spheres, we may set the positive concept of 'reformation'.[12] While the word came gradually to be applied to the 'change of religion' of the sixteenth century which resulted in the Reformed and Protestant churches of Europe, it could also be used in much more open senses for attempts at change. In keeping with the religious reformers' understanding of their actions as restoring the original true Christian church, 'reformation' in spheres outside religion was also often understood as renewal or recursion to a past better state, rather than simply improvement without reference to the past.[13]

---

[11] Samuel Rawson Gardiner, *The Constitutional Documents of the Puritan Revolution: 1625–60* (Oxford: Clarendon Press, 1906), 137–44.

[12] For the parliamentary debate on the Root and Branch petition, in which the Root-and-Branchers were naturally themselves accused of seeking 'the greatest Innovation that ever was in England', while more moderate spirits 'desired a Reformation', see John Adamson, *The Noble Revolt : The Overthrow of Charles I* (London: Weidenfeld and Nicolson, 2007), 180ff. Even an advocate of 'innovation', Francis Bacon, argued that it should be undertaken gradually and imperceptibly, in the same way that time itself wrought change: J.C. Davis, *Utopia and the Ideal Society: A Study of English Utopian Writing, 1516–1700* (Cambridge: Cambridge University Press,1981), 135; significantly, Bacon was himself the author of a classic utopia, the *New Atlantis* (1627).

[13] The *Oxford English Dictionary* lists several early modern senses of the noun 'reformation' but does not include a sense of recurring to a past better state, but does list exactly these senses for the verb 'reform'. I believe that this was an important connotation of the noun as well, and one reason why 'reformation' was often used as a positive term where 'innovation' was always negative. To give a few examples derived from a title search on Early English Books Online (long titled cited, my emphasis): *A faithful memorial of that remarkable meeting of many officers of the Army in England, at Windsor Castle, in the year 1648. ...All which is humbly presented, as a precious patern and president unto the officers and souldiers of the said Army (or elsewhere) who are or shall be found in the like path, of following the Lord in this evil day; searching and trying their waies, in order to a through return and reformation* (William Allen, London, 1659); *X solid and serious qveries concerning the power of church discipline...: also an admonition to the Parliament to promote the restitution of true religion and reformation of Gods church to the abandoning of all popish remnants ...* (R. Gualter, T.B. & c, London, 1646); *Confirmation and restauration the necessary means of reformation, and reconciliation; for the healing of the corruptions and divisions of the churches...* (Richard Baxter, London, 1658); *A true reformation and perfect restitution, argued by Silvanus and Hymeneus; where in the true Church of Christ is briefly discovered here in this life in her estate of regeneration...* (J.G., London, 1643).

I will offer three case studies here: the Levellers, the Diggers, and the republicanism of James Harrington. All of them, I will argue, display a utopian reimagining of the present; but all of them give their visions practical purchase by rooting them in a reinterpretation of the past and thus allowing them to affect the course of history in the future. All of them also suggest, in some sense, the return to an idealized or even mythical past, national or human, avoiding the charge of innovation.

The Levellers offer an important case study here. The Levellers (the name was a hostile nickname) were a political pressure group who emerged at around the time of Parliament's victory over the King in the first civil war, and who demanded freedom of conscience in religion and a constitutional settlement which would abolish the veto powers of the King and Lords (if not the institutions of monarchy and House of Lords themselves) and ensure equality before the law for all, with a widened franchise. Debate among political theorists about the nature of their thought has tended to credit them with a critical role in the development of the idea of the social contract, seeing their proposed *Agreements of the People* as ways of refounding from first principles an English polity, after the dissolution of the old regime into a state of nature as a result of war and misgovernment. On this view, the Levellers, as well as being the civil war radicals who came closest to achieving real political leverage and influence on events, would also have been remarkably outspoken advocates of outright change. This change might also be seen as peculiarly systematic, if not utopian, if the *Agreements of the People* are seen as complete constitutions or blueprints for the functioning of society.

There are indeed, rousing moments in the Levellers' writings, which seem to suggest a shaking-off of historical burdens. The *Remonstrance of Many Thousand Citizens*, from July 1646, says that 'whatever our Fore-fathers were; or whatever they did or suffered, or were enforced to yeeld unto; we are the men of the present age and ought to be absolutely free from all kinds of exorbitancies, molestations or *Arbitrary Power*'.[14] At first glance, this seems to announce a new freedom from precedent and history, but when one looks closer this is not quite the case. The claim here is as much about the reinterpretation of the past and consequently the present as it is about cutting free from the obligations of the past. The clear suggestion is that in the past, people did not so much create binding precedents through their own free actions, as suffer unjustified encroach-ments on their freedom. Rather than announcing that a new standard of

---

[14] D.M. Wolfe, *Leveller Manifestoes of the Puritan Revolution* (New York and London: Thomas Nelson and Sons, 1944), 114.

freedom was to be won, the sufferings of the past are described not so much as due to what our ancestors 'did' as to what they 'suffered' or were 'enforced to yeeld unto', a phrasing which clearly suggests that any oppressive contracts which were made were in fact void, as they were made under force. Thus the present is not what we might think: we may have been living for a long time under the provisions of contracts which, legally speaking, were never actually made.

This reinterpretation of the present is a characteristic aspect of Leveller writing, and particularly that of John Lilburne. Lilburne tends to be regarded as the Leveller writer who uses the most old-fashioned, unradical modes of argumentation, crammed as his pamphlets are with legal precedents and appeals to Magna Carta.[15] However, his legalism actually offered him not only a highly effective means of demanding change, but a way of reinterpreting the past and thus the present. The 'common-law mind' that so many seventeenth-century gentlemen shared did come in different flavours, and the more radical exponents of the ancient constitution (discussed by Janelle Greenberg) could take the history of the English law as the history of constant struggles to vindicate and reassert traditional rights simply by exercising them, in the face of constant encroachments on those rights.[16] Soberer men and better lawyers than Lilburne had used such a view of the common law to produce tendentious accounts of the past, and Lilburne was clearly following his hero Sir Edward Coke, who used the law to systematically cut down the room for legitimate arbitrary or prerogative power in England. What Lilburne does, as I have argued elsewhere, is to use the common-law language in a novel way to build up a claim for the uniform and universal rights of 'free-born Englishmen' (this phrase was a recurring motif throughout Lilburne's writings). While English law, objectively interpreted, was full of 'privileges', 'immunities', 'liberties', and 'franchises' which applied to selected individual groups through grant rather than through right,

---

[15] Robert Appelbaum, *Literature and Utopian Politics in Seventeenth-century England* (Cambridge: Cambridge University Press, 2002), 133: 'Restoration, of course, was as prominent a goal as reinvention among many of the leaders of the Leveller movement, especially those like Lilburne to whom the idea of the Norman Yoke and the nationalistic implications of being "freeborn" were so attractive.'

[16] Janelle Greenberg, 'The Confessor's Laws and the Radical Face of the Ancient Constitution', *English Historical Review* 104, no. 412 (1989): 611–37; Janelle Greenberg, *The Radical Face of the Ancient Constitution: St. Edward's 'Laws' in Early Modern Political Thought* (Cambridge: Cambridge University Press, 2001).

Lilburne makes all of these into a package which belongs by right to all Englishmen simply because they are Englishmen.[17] One way in which he effectively expresses this reinterpretation of the present is his use of the term 'birthright', which comes to connote all that is due to a citizen. The force and idealism of Lilburne's reinterpretation of the juridical status of the English present is clear when he extends the grounds on which this 'birthright' is claimed from English law to higher authorities too: the 'inheritance of our Fathers, and the Birth-right of us and our children' is 'our Fundamentall Lawes and Liberties, Franchises and Priviledges, that God, Nature, and the just Customes of the Land in which wee live, hath given us'.[18] Even so, the term 'birthright' is an indicator of the crucial influence of the legal tradition and specifically of Coke's interpretation of English law. In the speech which he reports himself giving to the Committee of Examinations, Lilburne firstly declares: 'I am a free-man, yea, a free-borne Denizen of England', and he goes on to quote Magna Carta to justify his rights: 'Sir, the Priviledges contained herein is my Birthright and Inheritance.'[19] This follows Coke's assertion which itself followed Cicero that the law is 'the best birth-right the subject hath', which Lilburne quotes directly elsewhere.[20] The power (and, of course, perhaps also the weakness) of the language of rights is its appeal to the present, valid, unarguable existence of those rights. Polemics using the language of rights rarely argue that a right *should* exist or needs to be created. Lilburne's language of 'birthright' thus creates a reinterpreted present, in which his readers should suddenly see themselves as possessors of an English and human birthright which has immediate implications in the present.

Legalism, then, and particularly a radical version of common-law thinking, could be a powerful means of reinterpreting the past—the meaning and even existence of certain grants and rights—and through that, the present, as certain prescriptions were argued to be still in force, if not actually yet recovered in practice. Lilburne, for example, asserts that

---

[17] Rachel Foxley, 'John Lilburne and the Citizenship of "Free-born Englishmen"', *Historical Journal*, 47, no. 4 (2004): 849–74.

[18] Lilburne, *The Charters of London; or, the Second Part of Londons Liberty in Chaines* (London, 1646), 1.

[19] Lilburne, *The Copy of a Letter... to a Freind* (London, 1645), 2.

[20] Edward Coke, *The Second Part of the Institutes of the Laws of England* (London, 1797), 56; Lilburne, *Innocency and Truth Justified* (London, 1646), 64.

'by the antient, good, just and unrepealed laws of England' parliaments should be held annually; here it is only the fact that parliaments were clearly *not* held annually which tells us that 'unrepealed' does not mean 'effectively in force'.[21] For Lilburne, the currency of legal right is absolute, and has merely to be vindicated. This sense underlies the common trick in Leveller language of protesting not so much about the injustice embodied in current institutions, but about 'usurpations', 'exorbitancies', and 'encroachments' of the authorities on pre-existing rights. Of course, in the thinking of some Levellers, some of the time, one of the most important ways in which these usurpations had taken place was a literal usurpation: the conquest of England by William the Conqueror, and the violation or replacement of existing institutions by those associated with the invading power. This Norman Yoke vision, too, presents a view of the past which leads to a reinterpretation of the present; in this case, the more romantic and aggressive historical vision of ancient Saxon liberties currently crushed under the 'Norman yoke', but there to be recovered.[22]

Does this, then, take us in the direction of another view of the Levellers, one which undermines any claim they may have to radicalism? 'Revisionist' approaches to the Levellers have suggested this angle, stressing conservatism, nostalgia, and a reactionary localism in the Levellers, and thus suggesting that any 'radicalism' they display is of a romantic kind very far from the revolutionary ideologies of later centuries. Thus, John Morrill compared the Levellers with the Clubmen who attempted to keep the armies of both sides out of their localities and to restore what they perceived as the rightful pre-war order.[23] More recently, Condren has interpreted the Levellers as exhibiting 'an extremity casuistry of conservation—in extremis you may innovate to conserve'. Davis offers a similar, if more subtle and convincing, reading of the Levellers, arguing, that 'we can see them as attempting both to restore the political culture

---

[21] Lilburne, *The Resolved Mans Resolution* (London, 1647), 19–22.

[22] Christopher Hill, 'The Norman Yoke', in *Puritanism and Revolution: Studies in Interpretation of the English Revolution of the 17th Century* (London: Secker and Warburg, 1958).

[23] J.S. Morrill, *The Revolt of the Provinces: Conservatives and Radicals in the English Civil War, 1630–1650* (London: Allen and Unwin, 1980), 100–01; J.S. Morrill, 'The Army Revolt of 1647', in *Britain and the Netherlands: Vol. VI, Law and Society*, eds. A.C. Duke and C.A. Tamse (The Hague: Nijhoff, 1977), 55, says that both Levellers and Clubmen were 'earthed in the mythology of local community consensus government'.

of the unacknowledged republic, and seeking to achieve this by transformative means'.[24] Indeed, some support for this 'conservative' view of
the Levellers' ultimate aims might be found in the fact that the Levellers
themselves opposed the trial and execution of Charles I when it came, and
loudly proclaimed the illegitimacy of the new commonwealth regime.
They were not of a piece with the revolutionaries of 1648–49, who
were prepared to see constitutional change achieved by the sword, and to
justify it as 'Right and Might Well Met'.[25]

I would suggest, instead, that the Levellers should still be seen as
visionary, and that their reimagining of the English past, whether through
the tropes of the Norman Conquest or of the ancient constitution and
the common law, is simply one of the most powerful and natural means
available to them for imagining change. The imagination of that change
as in some sense already present, implicitly and ineradicably, in the fabric of English life, whether in pre-Norman liberties or the continuing
texture of the English law, is in a sense a utopian imagination, and all the
more powerful for that.

Something of the same quality, indeed, is present in the other strand
of Leveller theorizing, the argument from natural rights. It is this that has
been seen as the more radical Leveller strategy, and the one which led to
the supposed 'social contract' proposed in the Levellers' *Agreements of
the People*. However, the character of the Levellers' natural rights thinking has not been well understood, and the Leveller texts in fact suggest
an interpretation which makes natural rights parallel with and compat-
ible with English rights. We have already seen that Lilburne was prone to
citing English law and the laws of God and nature alongside each other
as grounds for his claims, with no apparent sense of discomfort. The
Levellers did not, then, appeal to natural law as a fall back to be called

---

[24] Conal Condren, 'Afterword: Radicalism Revisited', in *English Radicalism, 1550–
1850*, eds. Glenn Burgess and Matthew Festenstein (Cambridge: Cambridge University
Press, 2007), 317; J.C. Davis, 'Reassessing Radicalism in a Traditional Society: Two
Questions', *English Radicalism, 1550–1850*, 358; the idea that the traditional structures
of governance in early modern England were so participatory at the local level as to be
in some sense 'republican' was influentially expressed by Mark Goldie, 'The Unacknowledged Republic: Office-holding in Early Modern England', in *The politics of the excluded,
c. 1500–1800*, ed. Tim Harris (Basingstoke: Palgrave, 2001).

[25] The title of a 1649 pamphlet by John Goodwin. On the nature of the Levellers' split
with the new regime and its roots in the nature of Leveller thought, see Martin Dzelzainis,
'History and Ideology: Milton, the Levellers, and the Council of State in 1649', *Huntington
Library Quarterly* 68, no. 1 (2005): 269–87.

on once civil society had reverted to a state of nature, but as a foundational law which should animate and inform the lives of all polities, and to which one could appeal even from within civil society. I have argued elsewhere that both Lilburne and Overton present accounts not so much of the origin of government, as of corrupt, tyrannical government. These accounts imply that what is needed is, again, a return, a restoration of morally innocent, prelapsarian relationships, which can include government by consent.[26] Lilburne makes it clear that humans are capable of this, in spite of the corruption into which they have fallen, due to the redeeming work of Christ as 'the Restorer and Repairer of mans losse and fall'.[27] The Levellers did not talk about a 'state of nature', but only about the 'law of nature'; they wanted to reject any sharp split between nature and government, and to assert that we are still living under the law of nature, which we can appeal to even from within a polity. Again we see the urge to reinterpret the present, to assert that we live under laws we may not have considered, which bear on our rights and actions in ways we urgently need to identify through the use of our reason and our consciences.

The group of men known as 'Diggers' (again a hostile nickname; interestingly, they thought of themselves as 'True Levellers') were never as close to real political influence as the Levellers. Their leader, Gerrard Winstanley, published a series of writings justifying, initially, the actions of a group of men led by him who decided to cultivate the common ground on Saint George's Hill in Surrey, in fulfilment of their belief that the earth should be a 'common treasury' for all. While various 'Digger' experiments of this kind were attempted in 1649–50, none were successful, and by 1652 Winstanley is found writing a rather different kind of work. His *Law of Freedom in a Platform* presents a model for an ideal society, complete with a structure of magistracies and a minimal law code. While the ends and basic principles which it is meant to achieve are very similar to those of the earlier works which the Digger communes aimed at, the emphasis on human imperfection rather than perfectibility, and on the compulsion which is thus needed to achieve a functioning righteous society, have been pointed to as very significant departures from the argument and spirit of the earlier works.[28]

---

[26] Rachel Foxley, 'Problems of Sovereignty in Leveller Writings', *History of Political Thought* 28, no. 4 (2007): 642–60.

[27] G.E. Aylmer, *The Levellers in the English Revolution* (London: Thames and Hudson, 1975), 72–74 (quotation, p. 72).

[28] Davis, *Utopia and the Ideal Society: A Study of English Utopian Writing, 1516–1700*, 182.

Many major themes unite the works from the Digger phase and the later *Law of Freedom in a Platform*, and one of them is the familiar sense that what is needed is not innovation or revolution so much as reformation or even, in Winstanley's own words, 'restoration'. *The Law of Freedom in a Platform* has the subtitle 'True magistracy restored', and that theme of restitution runs through earlier Digger works as well. Webb has pointed to the very unexpected way in which these religious and social radicals reproached the commonwealth authorities by accusing them of breaking their promises—promises made in the 'Solemn League and Covenant' with the Scots which the parliamentarians had signed up to in 1643, in return for military aid against the King. While for Webb this displays a surprisingly contractarian side to the Digger thought, what I find particularly interesting about it is the very selective way in which the Diggers used the Covenant—a fact also pointed out by Webb, who notes that Winstanley's use of the document was limited to a mere 13 words of it.

The Solemn League and Covenant was negotiated with rather different ends by the Scots and the English, and was a clever mixture of the idealistic and the lowest common denominator. At its more cautious end was the promise to 'preserve and defend the King's Majesty's person and authority', studiously ignored by Winstanley and the Diggers. At its more idealistic end was the famous first clause, covenanting subscribers to 'the preservation of the reformed religion in the Church of Scotland', and, pointedly, 'the reformation of religion in the kingdoms of England and Ireland ... according to the Word of God, and the example of the best reformed Churches'.[29] What Winstanley picked up on out of this was the word 'reformation', and while in the Covenant this word was applied only to religion ('in doctrine, worship, discipline, and government [of the church]'), Winstanley used it to justify his enormously more radical programme of social, economic, political, judicial, and spiritual change. (Webb notes that all the other radicals of the time in fact rejected the Covenant as oppressive.) Webb argues that Winstanley needed a concrete referent, an existing promise, on which to hang his call for labourers to desert their landlords and come and work the common lands in fulfilment of a utopian vision, a vision which was otherwise expressed in the overarching eschatological terms of spiritual history, rather than the

---

[29] Gardiner, *The Constitutional Documents of the Puritan Revolution: 1625–60*, 268–69.

material developments of earthly history.[30] However, perhaps more revealing of the way in which Winstanley tried to make his vision of the future thinkable and doable for his contemporaries was not his grounding of his hopes on parliamentarian promises made less than 10 years earlier, but his sense that both spiritual and material history were undergoing a 'reformation' or 'restoration' to a state of righteousness which had previously existed. Taking the word 'reformation' out of the Solemn League and Covenant, and using the phrase 'according to the Word of God' to justify him in his exceptionally broad treatment of the idea of 'reformation', his call for reformation moved far beyond the narrow categories of organized religion, for which he had little but scorn, lumping clergy and lawyers together as mere tools of the oppressive Norman kingly power. Thus, in *A Declaration from the Poor Oppressed People of England*, he asserts:

> And this we count is our dutie, to endeavour to the uttermost, every man in his place (according to the nationall Covenant which the Parliament set forth) a Reformation to preserve the peoples liberties, one as well as another ... for if the Reformation must be according to the word of God, then every one is to have the benefit and freedom of his creation, without respect of persons.[31]

In the *Law of Freedom in a Platform*, the more 'utopian' work which sets out the grounds for a whole society—one to be built in England, by the carrying through of the logic of the revolution which had swept away the King—Winstanley's thinking was much the same, in spite of J.C. Davis' view that Winstanley's approach was no longer the 'perfect moral commonwealth' assumption that spiritual and moral renewal would make disciplinary regulation of society unnecessary. So Winstanley, even in 1652, assured Cromwell (to whom the work is addressed), 'The Spirit of the whole Creation (who is God) is about the Reformation of the World, and he will go forward in his work.'[32] So even when Winstanley moved on to drawing up more human plans for his ideal society, what was ultimately at issue was not a new way to regulate human flaws, but still the spiritual reformation which Winstanley had looked to in his earlier writings. This divine reformation—for in his vision, to reform anything

---

[30] Darren Webb, 'Contract, Covenant and Class Consciousness: Gerrard Winstanley and the Broken Promises of the English Revolution', *History of Political Thought* 24, no. 4 (2003): 577–98.

[31] Gerrard Winstanley, *Selected Writings*, ed. Andrew Hopton (London: Aporia, 1989), 30.

[32] Gerrard Winstanley, *The Law of Freedom in a Platform* (London, 1652), 4.

'according to the Word of God' was to reform much more than merely the practice of religion—was still evident in the society of the *Law of Freedom in a Platform* because that society still fulfilled the requirement that the earth should be a 'common treasury' to all (although, strikingly, without completely abolishing private property as the earlier pamphlets seem to suggest will eventually happen).

G.E. Aylmer has shown how Winstanley imagines a dual recursion, to an ideal past which is simultaneously pre-Norman and prelapsarian—something which, as we have seen, has parallels in the Levellers' dual justifications for the changes they advocate.[33] Winstanley wrote:

> The Reformation that England now is to endeavour, is not to remove the Norman *Yoke* only, and to bring us back to be governed by those Laws that were before *William the Conqueror* came in, as if that were the rule or mark we aime at: No, that is not it; but the Reformation is according to the Word of God, and that is the pure Law of righteousnesse before the fall, which made all things, unto which all things are to be restored.[34]

In some ways, the Digger strategy of self-presentation was very similar to the Leveller one. Like the Leveller authors, Winstanley used extensively the language of 'birthright' and 'inheritance', urging those in power to grant the people what was already rightfully theirs. As with the Levellers, Winstanley's work bridged the past, present, and future; by grasping the nature of society in the uncorrupted past, people would not only see their 'inheritance' in the present (the earth still *was* rightfully a 'common treasury' for all), but would be encouraged in the work of restoring it to reality in the future.

We find in James Harrington's *Oceana* of 1656 a model commonwealth which has many similarities to More's *Utopia*. Although written in English rather than Latin, *Oceana* shares the learned, classicizing quality of More's text. Like More, however, Harrington uses the classicizing place-names to depict a world which is in some ways very familiar: an

---

[33] G.E. Aylmer, 'The Religion of Gerrard Winstanley', in *Radical Religion in the English Revolution*, eds. J.F. MacGregor and B. Reay (Oxford: Oxford University Press, 1984). In his recent discussion of the issue of radicalism, mentioned in connection to the Levellers above, Davis puts forward a parallel explanation of Winstanley: that he wanted to restore the society of self-governing communities (the 'unacknowledged republic' again) by reconstituting society. Davis, 'Reassessing Radicalism in a Traditional Society', 359–60.

[34] Winstanley, 'To the Lord Fairfax', *Selected Writings*, 42.

archipelago where the nations of 'Oceana' and 'Marpesia' share an island, while to the west the isle of 'Panopea' presents a perpetual problem of culture and governance. Decoding these nations as England, Scotland, and Ireland is hardly difficult. Just as Oceana is an elsewhere which is also here, it is also a society of the present which strongly recalls the classical past. The Latinate geography is complemented by a Hellenic system of magistracy: the ruler of Oceana is an 'archon'.

All this closely recalls the devices of More's *Utopia*, and yet *Oceana* is a straightforward model, offered with the utmost seriousness for England's imitation. It is dauntingly, thoroughly programmatic. The historical out-line of the government of Oceana makes it clear that the work is set more or less in the present, a present in which the civil war has taken place, and Harrington's version of Oliver Cromwell, 'Olphaeus Megaletor', plays the leading role in government. Yet there is a strange overlap between present reality, an alternative present, and a possible near future. When Harrington narrates that the 'lord general' with the approval of the army deposed the parliament, we might see a fairly true representation of Cromwell's actions in 1653 in ending the Rump parliament, or, at the beginning of the next year, in accepting the power returned to him by the Little Parliament ('Barebones Parliament'). However, in Harrington's version of the events, the lord general is inspired to do this by reflecting on a passage from Machiavelli's *Discourses* (not Oliver Cromwell's accustomed reading) about the benefits to a people of a decisive law-giver like Lycurgus. And rather than being made Lord Protector, with a constitutional framework which balanced his power with that of a coun-cil and a parliament, Harrington's lord general is made 'Lord Archon, or sole legislator of Oceana'.[35] Harrington then takes us into a fictional future a few years hence, when the Archon, with the help of exception-ally complicated scholarly and deliberative mechanisms (certainly not resembling anything that was taking place in England, apart, that is, from Harrington's own work), has drawn up and implemented the ideal form of government for Oceana. This process, set out not as an abstract model whose parts are described synchronically and functionally, but as a series of the steps needed in time to bring this ideal constitution into existence, is both a fiction set in the past, bringing us up to an alternative present, and a proposal for the future. How literally Harrington meant that proposal to be taken is shown by his repetition of the steps needed

---

[35] James Harrington, *The Commonwealth of Oceana; and, A System of Politics*, ed. J.G.A. Pocock (Cambridge: Cambridge University Press, 1992), 66–67.

to create the commonwealth, edited down a little from *Oceana*, in a subsequent pamphlet.[36] In a sense, there is a slightly different time frame and fiction implicit in Harrington's work, too: in one light, the action of Harrington's *Oceana* begins at the moment when Oliver Cromwell finishes reading Harrington's *Oceana*—the work was of course 'Dedicated to His Highness The Lord Protector'.

In addition, *Oceana* continues the civil war tradition, which we have already seen, of insisting that it is, in a sense, not so much a proposal for change as a reinterpretation, a true explanation, of the existing state of the land. By 1656, with Charles I executed seven years earlier and England's only written constitution and republican government having come in the intervening years, there seems little need for this. But Harrington does not restrict himself to pointing to the events of the 1640s and 1650s, when the monarchy was overthrown, to make his imaginative case for an English republic. Instead, he suggests that 'the genius of this nation hath ever had some resemblance with that of ancient Italy, which was wholly addicted unto commonwealths'. Indeed, one of the grounds for his praise of the agrarian commonwealth spirit which he saw in England was that 'such an one [is] ... the least subject unto innovation and turbulency.' Recent years have seen the unignorable turbulence of the civil wars only because the 'foundations' of the property system had been changed without a concomitant change in the distribution of political power; prior to that, 'this people was observed to be the least subject unto shakings and turbulency of any'.[37] The innovative historical and theoretical analysis of the relationship between property and government on which Harrington based his political model has been the focus of much study; what concerns us here is the way in which this justified him in claiming that his extraordinary model for political change was in fact a mere alteration in the political superstructure, which would bring England into line with its pre-existing nature, as properly understood for the first time by Harrington himself.

To conclude, then, Harrington, in spite of the features of his Oceana which strongly recall More's *Utopia*, was in some ways in tune with the civil war radical pattern of utopian envisioning through reinterpretation

---

[36] James Harrington, 'Brief Directions, Showing How a Fit and Perfect Model of Popular Government May Be Made, Found, or Understood', in *Political Writings of James Harrington*, ed. J.G.A. Pocock (Cambridge, 1977), 583ff., with the model intended for present-day England starting p. 590.

[37] James Harrington, *The Commonwealth of Oceana; and a System of Politics*, 5.

of the past and thus the present. These authors aimed to leave their readers understanding themselves and their place in history differently—
indeed, the need for people to 'understand themselves' was a trope which
featured in Leveller writing, but one which could equally have been
echoed by Winstanley or Harrington. Harrington himself provided a suggestive epigraph to his work, directly challenging his readers to look for
themselves in the pages which followed. It is a quotation from Horace,
describing the cruel predicament of Tantalus, so near and yet so far from
slaking his desperate thirst:

> Tantalus a labris sitiens fugientia captat/ Flumina: quid rides? Mutato no-
> mine, de te/ Fabula narratur.[38] [Thirsty Tantalus keeps trying to capture the
> waters which flee his lips. Why do you laugh? If you change the name, the
> story is about you.]

This, too, was a sentiment which the Levellers and Diggers would
have endorsed. England was tantalizingly close to achieving true feli-
city; all that was needed was for people to recognize the rights which
they already possessed, and start acting on them. More had offered a
vision of an alternative England in the present day, but built on the past of
the classical republics. But the seventeenth-century radicals imagined an
alternative England so rooted in the English past and the shared spiritual
and moral past of humanity that it overlaid and started to displace or
transform the English present in the reader's mind.

An obvious, but difficult, question arises: how much of this was a
matter of rhetorical strategy? Surely these writers must have been conscious what a desperate distance separated their visions from the world
in which they actually lived? Are these declarations of the inherence of
the radical vision in the present *conscious* attempts to bridge the yawning
gap—for the sake of an instinctively conservative audience—between
seventeenth-century England and any kind of egalitarian or republican
utopia? Clearly these authors could be deeply conscious of themselves
as oppositional: Overton, the Leveller, could appeal to natural rights and
taunt his readers with the lack of precedent for what he was about to argue;
Winstanley and the Diggers were aware of themselves as 'stand[ing]
up against' the traditional hierarchy of power—lawyers, priests, and
the rest. But that should not lead us to lose sight of the power of these
ways of iterpreting the present, and the genuine force that they had. The

---

[38] Ibid., 1.

Tantalus motif used by Harrington is about being both so near *and* so far from what you desire, and these authors were conscious of both. The import-ance of the belief that what was necessary was for people to 'understand themselves', and that the rest—unlikely though it might seem—would follow, is underlined by the desperation and a near-contempt with which these authors reacted at moments when it seemed to them that the people were incapable of understanding themselves as they needed to, being, as Overton put it, 'bestiallized in their understandings'.[39] If only they did, everything else really might change. As for Harrington's unlikely claim that the English had always been of a rather republican frame of mind, this is saying little more than a wave of recent historians, keen to read the texture of English local and political life even under monarchy as deeply participatory and citizenly: the proponents of the 'monarchical republic'.[40] If it is not patently absurd for modern scholars to read England under Elizabeth and James in this way, why is it absurd for Harrington?

These reimaginings of the state of England by radical writers were powerful enough to sweep away, rhetorically, large and evident barriers, making them into not historical inevitabilities, or divinely sanctioned forms, but accidents or usurpations which English history, human nature, and divine order, if properly understood, should overcome. The first task was reinterpretation. The rest would follow. England's civil wars were, to a large extent, wars of interpretation. What is striking is that the radical works which grew out of them, even when framed in rather utopian ways, often also claimed to be mere interpretations, revelations of the true nature of England.

---

[39] Overton, *A Defiance Against All Arbitrary Usurpations* (London, 1646), 2.

[40] Patrick Collinson, 'The Monarchical Republic of Queen Elizabeth I', *Bulletin of the John Rylands University Library of Manchester*, 69 (1987): 394–424; see also John F. McDiarmid, ed., *The Monarchical Republic of Early Modern England: Essays in Response to Patrick Collinson* (Aldershot: Ashgate, 2007).

5

Dystopia, Utopia, and Akhtaruzzaman Elias's Novel *Khowabnama*

Subhoranjan Dasgupta

Life as a whole is full of utopian projections, mirrored ideals, dream-manufactories, and travel pictures. In literature there are the characters who stride out ahead into what is not yet manifest, from the wretched Zendelwald in Keller's Seven Legends ... to the incomparably powerful Don Giovanni and Faust.

Ernst Bloch[1]

Setting the Perspective

While releasing a series of audio cassettes entitled *Aitijhyer Angikar*, a Bengali expression which in approximate English translation reads 'Commitment of Heritage', and which records the uninterrupted flow of Bengali literature from the medieval *Charyapad* to Rabindranath Tagore, Shamsur Rahman, the most renowned poet of Bangladesh, who described the passage starting with the birth of separate East Bengal as part of Pakistan in 1947 and ending with the birth of Bangladesh in 1971 as, 'a journey from the actuality of false dream to the real home of emancipation'.[2] By 'false dream', Shamsur Rahman implied 'dystopia'. The ambivalent meaning of this term, dystopia, according to Michael S. Roth, combines a double negative. It does not merely invoke the original meaning as offered by its first user, John Stuart Mill, who employed it in 1868 to describe a situation or a government that would be the 'worst imaginable', but also etches that particular 'state of affairs (ironically enough) we

---

[1] Ernst Bloch, *A Philosophy of the Future* (New York: Herder and Herder, 1970), 88.
[2] Shamsur Rahman in an unpublished interview with the author in Kolkata in 1996.

might intensely desire'.[3] This critical second aspect, that is, 'dystopia is the utopia you must be careful not to wish for'[4] constitutes the false dream mentioned by Shamsur Rahman. And in this specific context, the false dream refers to the Partition of Bengal in 1947 that led directly to the formation of East Pakistan.

Nourished and sustained by political forces belonging to both the communities, Hindu and Muslim, this dystopia was welcomed by the majority of Muslim-Bengali writers who equated the establishment of Pakistan with the attainment of their cherished 'Islamic Homeland'. In fact, the intensity of their desire or aspiration was evident in the titles of their novels which treated the vivisection of the subcontinent and the birth of Pakistan as the theme. Abul Fazl's novel hailed the new homeland with the meaningful title *Ranga Prabhat* or 'Red Dawn' and Abu Rushd chose the reassuring noun *Nongor* or 'Anchor', denoting a stable shelter, as the title of his text. Incidentally, this explicit association of 'homeland' with utopia, positive or negative, is nothing uncommon. While Ernst Bloch, who condemned the Nazis, ended his classic exposition on *The Principle of Hope* by evoking the image of returning to one's Home/*Heimat* ('Once he has grasped himself and established what is his, without expropriation and alienation, in real democracy, there arises in the world something which shines into the childhood of all and in which no one has yet been: homeland')[5], the Nazis themselves harped on this sense of homeland—in their case, ever-increasing homeland—by repeating the term *Lebensraum*, that is, the space where you live.

But not all Muslim writers of East Bengal (East Pakistan from 1956) greeted their homeland with unequivocal fervour. Some, indeed, were critical and sceptical from the moment they began their literary careers, and of them two who deserve the reader's special acclaim are Akhtaruzzaman Elias and Kayes Ahmed. Like Ritwik Ghatak, that unforgettable film-maker on Partition, Kayes Ahmed, whose poignant texts were compiled and edited by Elias himself, condemned Partition as the 'freedom to be a refugee'. Plucked out from his soil in West Bengal and despairingly estranged in East Pakistan, his new address, Kayes Ahmed in his novel

---

[3] Michael S. Roth, 'Trauma: A Dystopia of the Spirit', in *Thinking Utopia: Steps into Other Worlds*, eds. Joern Ruesen, Michael Fehr, and Thomas W. Rieger (New York and Oxford: Berghahn Books, 2005), 230–75; here, p. 230.

[4] Ibid.

[5] Ernst Bloch, *The Principle of Hope*, Vol. 3, trans. Neville Plaice, Stephen Plaice, and Paul Knight (Cambridge, Massachusetts: MIT Press, 1995), 1376.

*Nirbasito Ekjon/*The Exiled One spoke through his protagonist, who raised the following tormenting queries:

> What is the meaning of refugee? *Udbastu.* That means he who has no home. But I do have a home. Still I am a refugee, because I am country-less ... So, this freedom that we have gained after driving out the English—this Hindustan and Pakistan—is it to produce refugees ... Is this the name of freedom? Freedom to be a refugee? Who are those who manoeuvred and manipulated to turn human beings into refugees after so many years?[6]

In his frantic quest to piece together somehow the broken fragments of his lost home in his mind, Kayes Ahmed rushed to the village of his favourite author, Manik Bandyopadhyay. But his experience in this village of Bangladesh deepened the wound and he had to conclude, 'The politics of this subcontinent has been directed by this divisive awareness. Though independent Bangladesh has been established on the base of Bengali nationalism, a strong, healthy, and firm humanism has not emerged as the challenger of the separatist communal attitude.'[7] No wonder, rootless Kayes Ahmed committed suicide in 1992 to end his agony. This is a situation 'worst imaginable', and hence, an overwhelming example of dystopia.

In contrast to Kayes Ahmed's reaction, primarily emotional and psychic, Elias's denunciation of the dystopia of Partition was prompted by his pronouncedly Marxian point of view. In a revealing interview published in 1992, he focused on the limits of this divisive aspiration by stating:

> My father like many other members of the educated Muslim middle class of that time earnestly wanted that Muslim boys and girls should keep pace with their Hindu counterpart, that they live with equal dignity. But, let us not forget, these boys and girls belonged to a particular class, to the Muslim middle class. It also needs to be underlined that only the progress of this middle class was aspired for. But the movement they unleashed in order to fulfil this aspiration simply cannot be endorsed. The Partition of 1947 was so catastrophic, so deplorable, so heartrending and meaningless that we are realizing it more every day.[8]

---

[6] Kayes Ahmed, *Kayes Ahmed Samagra*, ed. Akhtaruzzaman Elias (Dhaka: Mowla Brothers, 1993), 97.

[7] Ibid., 173.

[8] Interview with Akhtaruzzaman Elias in the literary magazine *Lyric*, in the special issue on him (Dhaka: 1992), 132.

This language of condemnation proves that he denounced Partition for that very reason, which made it so alluring, so 'intensely desirable'—to recall Michael S. Roth's words—for the members of his own class. He did not have to wait even for the 20-year-long exploitative domination of East Pakistan by West Pakistan to conclude that the promise of a free and fair Muslim homeland was meant to be broken. To him, as it appeared to other protesting leftist intellectuals of East Bengal like Badruddin Umar and Sirajul Islam Chaudhuri, Partition was the product of an orchestrated class collaboration between the Muslim League, on the one hand, and the Congress as well as the Hindu Mahasabha, on the other, with the colonial rulers fomenting the diabolic design in their own style. Those who dared to think and act otherwise, those who endeavoured to posit a redemptive utopia—for example, the peasant-fighters of Tebhaga, Tanka, and Telengana uprisings—were stamped out by the powers-that-be of both Hindustan and Pakistan.

When one seeks the source of this evaluation, one is pointedly reminded of Elias's adherence to his class-directed Marxian cosmovision. His close friend Syed Abdul Maqsud confirmed his unambiguous political position by noting, 'The little that I knew him, I can tell that he was profoundly influenced by Marxism in the late sixties. He was a Marxist and he remained Marxist till his death.'[9] More than anything else, this political commitment determined the contours of his utopia and dystopia and encouraged him to assert the following verdicts:

1. Muslim League's emphasis on Islam as the religion of socio-economic liberation was a well-designed ploy meant to deceive the masses, the bulk of the impoverished peasants in particular. As opposed to this betrayal, the Tebhaga uprising, which demanded two-thirds of the agricultural produce for the tiller and one-third for the owner, was an agrarian movement sprouting from the soil. It was based on the sacrifice and heroism of Hindu and Muslim peasants, as well as the tribals, and was directed to a large extent by the Communist Party.

2. The call for Partition was aimed to establish the authority of the Muslim middle and upper-middle classes who exhibited the same apathy towards the downtrodden as that shown by the Hindu exploiters. Hence, the new nation, new homeland, and new political dispensation left the majority exactly where it had been.

---

[9] Syed Abdul Maqsud, 'Akhtaruzzaman Elias-er Sange Anekta Path/With Akhtaruzzaman Elias, Traveling Together, For Quite Some Distance', *Ajker Kagoj/Today's Newspaper*, 11 January 1997, Dhaka.

The contours of dystopia and utopia received their full configuration in Elias's novel *Khowabnama*/Dream Elegy. This novel is unique in contemporary Bengali literature because no other creative text posits Tebhaga against Partition in binary opposition in so categorical a manner. While novelists of West Bengal concentrated on the plight of thousands of refugees who had crossed over from East Bengal to the West and their arduous struggle and rehabilitation, the novelists writing in East Bengal, though with certain misgivings, greeted Partition because it offered a separate homeland to the Muslims. By and large, they remained indifferent to rebellions like the Tebhaga and Tanka. Belonging to the middle class, they typified the analysis of Elias which said that Partition catered only to the aspiration of the Bengali middle-class Muslim. Hence, it was left to Elias to excavate the political message and worth of the Tebhaga embodied as utopia as antithesis and in opposition to Partition and its false promise. While the promise was enshrined in the very titles of the novels like 'Red Dawn' and 'Anchor', the falsehood struck with full force when the Language Movement erupted in 1951–52. Though the Language Movement led to the war of liberation in 1971, like Kayes Ahmed, Elias was not satisfied with the human condition as it prevailed in independent Bangladesh. Indeed, the class-ridden situation in Bangladesh prompted him even more to invoke the defiance and challenge of the peasants. The sociopolitical reality was nothing more than the continuation of the dystopia, in spite of the emergence of the sovereign republic of Bangladesh. The masters have changed, he asserted, but not the existential condition.

Desire for Dystopia

The crucial question that emanates from the previous section is: how could this dystopia turn out to be so intensely desirable? In his classic *Khowabnama*/Dream Elegy, Elias has given the answer by offering an imaginative transcreation of history. When the bigwig of the Muslim League, Ismael, promises the landless Muslim tillers and the sharecroppers a classless paradise in Pakistan where all produce will be theirs, we realize that the Muslim League has not only borrowed but also stolen and usurped the slogan of the Tebhaga. His treacherous words prove how instrumental and inflammatory politics can almost wipe out the division between utopia and dystopia by falsely imbibing the salvational essence of the former within the deceptive latter. The peasants listen spellbound as Ismael fumes:

> There is of course valid reason for the dissatisfaction expressed by the peasants here and there. The solution of this problem can be found only in Pakistan, where none will have the power to block the framing of laws in favour of the peasants. We have to examine what is the religion of these leaders who are directing the angry peasants. They are Hindus, though Hindu landlords have exploited the Muslim peasants from the start of the British rule. These Hindu leaders are sowing discord among Muslims by provoking you to fight. You can well imagine which community is gaining from all this. If the Muslim peasants abjure bloodshed and join the movement for Pakistan, their problem will be solved forever.[10]

That Ismael's demagoguery in fiction was an indispensable part of the Muslim League's divisive politics is borne out by the promise made by the prominent League leader, Giasuddin Pathan, who actually incited the Muslim sharecroppers in Mymensingh by saying that they should not waste time and energy for Tebhaga since, in Pakistan, they will be blessed by something even more fruitful—*choubhaga*. In contrast to Tebhaga which demanded two-thirds for the sharecroppers, the magical *choubhaga* promised all four quarters, that is, the entire produce to the sharecroppers.

In his remarkable text *Peasant Utopia: The Communalisation of Class Politics in East Bengal, 1920–1949*, Taj Ul-Islam Hashmi has analyzed the collapse of the Promise into Betrayal, of the dystopia absorbing the utopia with clinical precision. His critical exposition and Elias's creative text almost echo each other in substance and attitude, especially when Hashmi writes:

> The leaders belonging to the *ashraf, Ulama* and other non-cultivating classes mobilized the lower peasantry through the rural *ashraf* and rich peasants by sympathizing with the lower peasants' deplorable condition and justifying their demands for the redress of particular grievances. These leaders also assured peasants of imminent support from other quarters of society... which includes promises of a drastic land reform to grant more right to the tillers ... [they claimed] Pakistan stood for an egalitarian society, which would grant land to the tillers and higher socio-economic status ... a little push

---

[10] Akhtaruzzaman Elias, *Khowabnama* (Kolkata: Naya Udyog, 1996), 164.

[was needed] through the concerted action of all categories of peasants either by attending Muslim League meetings or by attacking Hindu landlords and moneylenders.[11]

Tamij, the fisherman-turned-peasant protagonist of the novel, like thousands of others, fondly believed that the politicians of the Muslim League would honour their oft-repeated promise. After the attainment of the separate homeland for Muslims he ruminated full of expectation, 'No there will be no landlords and moneylenders in Pakistan, Tebhaga will be implemented spontaneously.'[12] Only when he began reading expressions of silent denial on the faces of the politicians, he felt impelled to enquire. The reply he received from the Muslim League leader Abdul Kader struck him like a hit of the hammer. Laughing loudly and derisively, Abdul Kader told him, 'Yes there was that proposal for Tebhaga, it was raised in the State Assembly two years ago. The bill calling for the abolition of feudal ownership has been raised again recently but the sharecroppers' right based on Tebhaga has been excluded.'[13] This Great Betrayal directed Tamij towards the Land of Tebhaga, where the heroic battle doomed to defeat had entered its final phase. At this precise moment, Tamij became one of those characters highlighted by Ernst Bloch, 'who stride out ahead into what is not yet manifest'.

Tebhaga as Utopia

If the actuality, Partition, and the dystopia it evoked turned out to be spurious, what should we crave for? What could be the essence and content of the counter-narrative, of the liberating dream? This dream might perish like many other acts of stirring revolt (for example, the revolt of Spartacus and the peasant uprising in Germany), but the tragic termination would not deprive it of its aura. Indeed, it would be forged with all other abortive uprisings of the past and continue to inspire, transforming thereby the note of elegy into an echo of defiance.

---

[11] Taj Ul-Islam Hashmi, *Peasant Utopia: The Communalization of Class Politics in East Bengal*, 1920–1949 (Dhaka: University Press Limited, 1994).

[12] Ibid., 261.

[13] Ibid., 303.

In *Khowabnama,* the utopia of the vanquished Tebhaga is situated against the victorious Partition, though in end-effect Tebhaga and whatever it entails invokes the scenario of true redemption. It actualizes the Principle of Hope and, in the process, exposes the actuality of Partition as hollow and catastrophic. This is accomplished by Elias with enviable artistry because none else in the contemporary world of Bengali literature is able to transform a thwarted reality into an irresistible dream with more power and poignancy. Tebhaga does not occupy the centre stage of the novel, as Partition does. It wells up in the background from time to time like a rousing refrain, played at a distance. It recedes, advances, intervenes, and also disrupts the narrative of Partition with its corrective accent. Even when it is not physically present, its traces persist, like a signature that refuses to be erased. If Partition is what the world is, Tebhaga voices Michel Foucault's political intent 'To refuse what we are', and if the power of Partition 'is like a productive network which runs through the whole social body, it is much more than an agent and actor of repression', Tebhaga, to use Foucault's expression again, 'promotes new forms of subjectivity through refusal'.[14]

The first mention of Tebhaga, which coincided with the phase that led to Partition, occurs on Page 20 of the novel. In one revealing sentence, Elias condenses the essence of the movement, 'New and new waves are advancing from north and east. The sharecroppers are coming together to store the paddy in their homes.'[15] What is more striking is the impact of this single statement on the exploited villagers like Kulsum and Tamij. Kulsum is in the same breath amazed and excited but Tamij turns grave in wonder. The second mention occurs after 23 pages when the hapless Tamij begs the rising landowner Sharafat Mandal, who has stepped into the shoes of the Hindu landlord, to allow him to work as a sharecropper. While deliberations are on between the two, the elder son of Sharafat, Abdul Aziz, a staunch Muslim League activist, lambasts the audacity of the poor peasants who have demanded two-thirds of the produce they have cultivated with their own hands, and who will permit only a meagre one-third to be given to the landowner. Aziz's condemnation of Tebhaga is categorical:

---

[14] Michel Foucault, *The Foucalt Reader,* ed. Paul Rabinow (London: Penguin Books, 1991), 22.

[15] Elias, *Khowabnama,* 20.

Yes (they) can jolly well demand. You don't have to pay taxes to express your demand. But, one word, the land does not walk on its own to the landlord's house ... to acquire one tiny piece of land an ounce of blood needs to be released in the form of salty sweat from the body. Is the peasant aware of this sacrifice?[16]

These words of Aziz, and not the million promises made by Muslim League politicians (faithfully recorded in the novel) that the land will belong to the tiller in the Islamic paradise, exhibit the real attitude. They jar as a clashing counterpoint whenever politicians claim that Pakistan will ensure the eradication of landlords, landowners, and moneylenders.

Elias is determined to demolish this dystopia in his text. His objective is to posit his own idealized reality, and this he achieves by granting Tebhaga an elevated, aesthetic dimension. The chiseled prose of Elias resonates when he narrates the brave acts of the Tebhaga warriors. Challenging the thesis of Abdul Aziz on page 43 of the novel, Tamij recollects:

> The landowners, presumably, had spoken to the police. But to how many fields can the police possibly go ... Even the wives and daughters of peasants attacked with brooms, cooking spuds, kitchen knives. Had he not run through the paddy fields, leapt over sheaves of corn, one or two blows of spuds and brooms would have certainly hit him. Who knows if he had not suffered some hits? Who broadcasts willingly the news of being assaulted by women?[17]

Tamij, in this first phase of the novel, is a sullen opponent of the rebel peasant's temerity. Duty bound to be an obedient sharecropper himself, he says, 'The paddy is the dear life of the landowner. How can he possibly survive if this paddy is the object of pulls and thrusts?'[18] But the metamorphosis occurs at an unrelenting pace. Fisherman Tamij turns into the sharecropper Tamij, and after Partition when Tebhaga is actually crumbling, he decides to fight for it. Spurning the command of his political boss to go to Dhaka, he proceeds towards that undefined region where the paddy belongs to the tiller. By choosing his own course, not only does he challenge Engels' prediction on the progressive pauperization of the small peasant ('Our small peasant, like every other survival of a past mode of production, is hopelessly doomed. He is a

---

[16] Ibid., 43.
[17] Ibid., 44.
[18] Ibid.

future proletarian'[19]), but also etches the real consciousness, the real praxis, and the real utopia. The most inspired fragment of prose in the novel recreates this quest for emancipation:

> Though he is illiterate, for the first time in his life he is able to read the word 'Shantahar'. Going to Shantahar means, you go to Jaipur from there, to Akkelpur, to Hili … So many policemen are going, which means peasants are lifting the paddy into their barns, the cloth covering the arses of the landowners has fallen, the scoundrels are running, hiding in the arseholes of the police. And in the midst of all these the soil is being prepared … once the soil is ready the sapling will be brought and seeds will be planted in joyous abandon. Ah! It rained last night, the soil is as soft as butter, the moment the plough touches it, the plough delves deep down inside the earth, Tamij can even extract water from there. In the fumes of the Shantahar train you again inscribe the picture of paddy-fields. Ah what fields. The stalk flourishes in a flash, it bends below under the weight of the milk. Innumerable peasants have descended on the fields to thresh the thick clusters of paddy. The landlords have come with the police. Trains filled with police are spreading out in every station. They come down like cholera, like small pox. Peasants attack them with their scythes and sickles. The scoundrels gasping for breath cannot find the path to escape.[20]

Intrinsically linked with class struggle, this animated prose recreates the 'wish-landscape' of Ernst Bloch. It dramatizes a concrete moment in history and points towards an actual transformation of the material world. Its vibrant aesthetic quality is the creative correlative of Bloch's *Vor-schein* or 'Anticipatory Illumination', which is a pre-configuration of the Utopian Home.[21]

Elias is not prepared to view Tebhaga as an isolated eruption of emancipatory zeal. His worldview prompts him to regard it as one significant phase of the cyclic chain of rebellions linked to many others that have preceded it. In *Khowabnama*, the counter-narrative does not begin with Tebhaga but from the historic Sannyasi-Fakir uprising against the colonial rulers. The first half of the 1770s witnessed the spread of this challenge in Rangpur, Coochbehar, Bogura, Purnea, Mymensingh, and

---

[19] Frederick Engels, 'The Peasant Question in France and Germany', in *Selected Works of Marx and Engels*, vol. II (Moscow: Progress Publishers, 1975), 422–23.

[20] Elias, *Khowabnama*, 318.

[21] Ernst Bloch's seminal ideas on Utopia and its relation with Messianic Marxism is elaborated in his classic *The Principle of Hope*.

Dinajpur districts of undivided Bengal, though it proved to be abortive. The memory of the battles fought, especially the valour of its two leaders Majnu Shah and Bhabani Pathak, crystallizes into a series of exquisite lyrics whose mood sway from the warlike to the elegiac.

Once again, we note that by singling out this challenge in which the Muslim Fakirs and Hindu Sannyasis fought together against the British, Elias is denouncing the religious divide that is the very basis of Partition. While the air is thick with the smell of religious bigotry and hatred of one community for the other, Elias's simple protagonists in *Khowabnama* recollect the daring acts of the bygone heroes and emphasize their ideal communion. In chapter 37, though the Muslim-baiter Hindu gentleman Satish Mokhtar invokes Bankimchandra's *Anandamath* to claim that the Sannyasis burnt down the houses of Muslims, the low-caste Hindu toiler Kesto Pal drawing on his source of collective, redemptive memory stresses:

> No sir, the commander of our Bhabani Sanyasi was a Pathan. Majnu Shah was the king of Fakirs and Bhabani Sanyasi was the king of Sanyasis. They fought against the white soldiers of the Company. And that Muslim whose spirit dwells in the fig tree was with Majnu Shah. Moreover, Baikuntha says, that he was the commander of Bhabani's troops.[22]

This unadorned description of a united Hindu–Muslim revolt expressed in the dialect of an illiterate villager receives a heightened diction in the inspired chain of lyrics. Elias, the remarkable prose-writer, is at his poetic best when he writes:

> Majnu calls out Bhabani Sanyasi
> Catch the Whites and hang them straight
> Bhabani roars and the Giris flash swords
> They despatch the Whites to Yama's door.[23]

The lyric-chain, an abiding asset of this novel, includes the rousing songs coined by the village bard Keramat Ali in honour of Tebhaga. Keramat does not have to make any strenuous effort to compose these. They simply well up within him, as leaves come naturally to a tree, to use

---

[22] Ibid., 242.
[23] Ibid., 196.

the famous expression of John Keats on the process of poetry. Moreover, revealingly enough, even when the champions of Pakistan goad him to sing verses glorifying the new state, he returns irrevocably to Tebhaga:

> The truth is landlord is the enemy of peasants
> We demand an act which will abolish landlordism
> The landlord will get one third, and the peasant two third
> That is why we clamour for Tebhaga.[24]

Not politicians neck-deep in their calculation, but this bard laments the enmity between the Congress and the Muslim League, and when compelled to compose panegyrics to honour Pakistan, he feels positively uninspired. The listless eulogy that he somehow composes stands in sharp contrast to his animated songs on Tebhaga. For Keramat Ali, Pakistan is a forced idyll, a petty pastoral, while Tebhaga is the glowing counter-pastoral hardened by the protesting impulse. The bard of Tebhaga along with Cherag Ali and Baikuntha Giri, who are lyricist-preservers of the memory of Sannyasi-Fakir revolt, weave a chain of counter-pastoral challenging the falsehood of Partition in the pristine language of their poetry. They are the voices of what E.P. Thompson says 'rebellious traditional culture'[25]. The expression 'traditional' implies nothing retrogressive here because the age-old sanction dictates,

> Mine and Thine, were then unused
> All things common: Nought abused
> Fairly earth her fruitage bearing.

The string of poetry in *Khowabnama* inevitably reminds us of Raymond Williams who quoted these lines of George Chapman before explicating, 'This persistent and particular vision of the Golden Age, a myth functioning as a memory, could then be used by the landless, as an aspiration ... All things under Heaven only to be common.[26] Chapman's prayer, in point of fact, is stunningly simple. It focuses on the indispensable fulfilment of every single being's primary means, of the needs of millions of Tamijs going hungry in this world of abundance. It draws us

---

[24] Ibid., 163.

[25] E.P. Thompson, *Customs in Common* (London: Merlin, 1991), 9.

[26] Raymond Williams, *The Country and the City* (London: Paladin, 1973), 57–58.

compellingly to what Lyman Tower Sergeant defines as 'that most basic of all utopias, a full stomach, decent clothes and shelter'.[27]

Homeland for Elias and Bloch

We may now attempt to answer the question, what could have been Elias's political alternative to the Partition of 1947 within the perspective of the Indian subcontinent? What the Tebhaga uprising and the Sannyasi–Fakir revolt have already engraved in terms of a dream yet to be realized is given an explicit configuration in another passage in his first novel *Chilekothar Sepai/Sepoy of the Attic*. Truly talismanic in worth, this passage presents Elias at his unsurpassable best and offers his idealized alternative, which is an undivided classless subcontinent where destructive religion has no role to play. The subject is the death-defying struggle of the people of East Pakistan against Ayub Khan's military regime in 1969, and while narrating it, he merges the politics of the moment with the tumult of history in one unbreakable bond. The capital of East Pakistan, Dhaka, becomes a perennial battlefield where the uprisings of the past against the enemies of promise are resurrected. As the rebels and revolutionaries enact their impassioned defiance, Dhaka itself turns infinite and limitless. It is as if the two constituents of utopia, the temporal and the spatial, converge in this resurgence of history. It is as if the explosive *Jetztzeit* of Walter Benjamin[28] is ignited by the collective onrush of the past. Obliterating the borders between memory, legend, the past, the present, and the future aspired for, the particular text recreates a pageant of rebellions which floundered but did not fail to inscribe the promise of hope. Almost all critics of Elias have singled out this passage as the key to Elias's political aesthetic and creative assimilation of history. Here is an imperfect translation of this unique passage:

> This flow of people … Clothes of many and physiognomy appear unfamiliar to him. Who are they? Have the people of long, distant past also joined this march? There in the exact middle march the residents of Dhaka of Islam Khan's reign in their short dhotis! Even those of earlier times who used to go to

---

[27] Lyman Tower Sargent, 'The Necessity of Utopian Thinking: A Cross-national Perspective', in *Thinking Utopia: Steps into Other Worlds*, 1–14, here p. 10.

[28] Walter Benjamin, 'On the Concept of History', 1940; http://www.marxists.org/reference/archive/benjamin/1940/history.htm (accessed 22 June 2010).

Sonargaon in their boats filled with sacks of rice have come. The residents of Banglabazar and Tantibazar have emerged from the cold heart of the vanished canal? There stand the turbaned, dead soldiers of Ibrahim Khan's reign who battled with Shahjada Khusru. Osman trembles seeing the men who died of hunger in Sayestha Khan's days when the cost of rice was Taka 1 for eight maunds. They have not eaten for 400 years … Flying their waves of black hair they advance. This procession cannot be so massive unless all the battered are here … Battered by the Moghuls, by the Mags, by the company merchants. Breaking the dry layer of bricks of Racecourse Kalibari, the Maratha priest has come swinging his falchion, the fakirs of Majnu Shah have come; there throwing rings of finger-torn clenched fists the Muslim weavers come, their black bodies burn in the sun. The bone-all, starving naked bodies of weavers who weave jamdanis worth Taka 4,000 a piece are walking erect. The Imam, muezzins, musallis of Babubazar Mosque shot by the sahibs are walking, instead of muttering their ayat they are now roaring, 'We shall not let it go in vain.' The sepoys of Lalbagh Fort mangled by the beasts let loose by Nabab Abdul Ghani—Ruplal and Mohini Mohan—lackeys of the redfaced sahibs come. The sepoys of Meerut arrive after tearing down their nooses hanging from the palm trees of Victoria Park, sepoys of Bareilly, Sandwip, Sirajganj, Goaland. No, my friend, even that is not enough. The youths of Jugantar and Anusilan in their dhotis and banyans and devoted to their mother march, in their midst you can identify separately those two youths who were killed in Kaltabazar. Carrying the bloody waves of Dolai canal on his head Somen Chanda jumps out of Narinder Bridge. There is Barkat! His skull blown off … So many people, Dhaka's past-present-future is overflowing with the tide of new water, morning-afternoon-evening-night stand forgotten and dissolved, today it has no east-west-north-south, all the separation marks of seventeenth, eighteenth, nineteenth and twentieth centuries have been erased. Dhaka is intent to occupy limitless time and limitless space! Osman's heart trembles! How far can he go with this tidal surge? How far?[29]

Indivisible fragments of history and memory are woven here with the ongoing struggle to articulate the utopian message of the author. They read as related particles of some single immense story: the story of the class struggle as depicted in *The Communist Manifesto*. They excavate the political unconscious, so eloquently theorized by Fredric Jameson, and with their orchestrated surfeit of memory and myth, dreams and fantasies, and above all, actual battles and heroic martyrdom, prefigure the landscape of the future throbbing with the militant tremors of the

---

[29] Akhtaruzzaman Elias, *Chilekothar Sepai /Sepoy in the Attic* (Dhaka: Dhaka University Press Limited, 1995), 147–48.

past and present. These tremors embody, in the words of Ernst Bloch, 'humanity in action, human countenance coming to fulfilment'.[30] The two last queries of the passage—'how far … how far?'—echo the question with which Ernst Bloch's journey in *The Principle of Hope* began 'Where are we going … What awaits us?' And the answer we also read in the last lines of the same book, which is, 'homeland without expropriation and alienation'. This homeland is Elias's destination too, his *khowab* or dream.

[30] Ernst Bloch, *On Karl Marx* (New York: Herder, 1971), 21–23.

6

Palestine

Land of Utopias

Sonia Dayan-Herzbrun

To write about a land of utopias may seem quite paradoxical as the word utopia means precisely 'nowhere': a place out of time and out of location. Until the end of the eighteenth century, utopias were used mostly as critical tools against existing societies and political regimes. But, with the advent of modernity, radical transformations in society, and the conviction of many that the human condition was going to improve, utopias were linked to plans for the future. The 'nowhere' from which William Morris sent us 'news' in 1890 was aimed at becoming some sort of 'somewhere', if women and men first worked and struggled for that. As far as Palestine is concerned, it has been for a long time a land of utopias, as utopia is, or has been, linked in the Western vision, to messianism, with all the complex conceptions and connotations of this notion. From the nineteenth century some Western utopias tried to materialize in quite a strange mixture with colonialism. Colonized countries were described as empty places where experimentation of a new social order was possible, or places to bring in a better form of civilization: let us think of Robert Owen and his New Harmony (in Indiana, USA) or of the followers of Saint-Simon in Algeria. The authors who wrote about these attempts of settlement generally described the failures of the settlers, but they very rarely spoke about the colonial aspects of these adventures.

The Old–New Land

In a way, at least during an early period, Zionism can be considered as one of these colonial utopias. In the prologue of his manifesto, *The State of the Jews* (1896), Theodor Herzl, generally considered the inventor of political Zionism, speaks about his book as a philanthropic utopia. But he adds that this utopia is not a dream but a project that can be realized with the propelling force of the plight of European Jews. In 1896, he still hesitates between Argentina and Palestine for the location of this State. Argentina, he says, is one of the largest and richest countries in the world, with a small population. But Palestine 'is our unforgettable historic homeland'. He adds, 'We should there form a portion of a rampart of Europe against Asia, an outpost of civilization as opposed to barbarism. We should, as a neutral state, remain in contact with all Europe, which would have to guarantee our existence.' In 1902, after he had visited Palestine and met the Sultan Abdul Hamid, he had made his decision, which then encountered British imperialism. The State of the Jews was to be founded in Palestine. In a novel called *The Old–New Land* (1902), he then imagined what life would be in what he called the New Society created in Palestine by 1923. This utopian narrative (with heroes and love stories) is quite a queer blend of disparate elements. On a political level it has anarchist and socialist aspects: there is no state, no army, and no authoritarian education in the New Society in Palestine. Women have the same rights as men. The economy is not private but mutualistic. Jews and non-Jews are equal citizens. As in the Saint-Simonian utopias or in Jules Verne's novels, technologies are highly developed and are an important factor for progress. But all those wonderful realizations could only take place in Palestine through the intervention of the European Zionists. Herzl's description is riddled with orientalist and colonialist tropes: apart from the happy few members of the local elite, the indigenous inhabitants of the country (Turks, Arabs, and Jews) are shown as poor, filthy, unable to cultivate the land, which looks like a desert. Here, as in other cases, class bias is intimately interwoven with colonial bias, as wealthy Arabs or Turks appearing in the novel do not have the same imperfections.

Theodor Herzl's Zionism, with its many sides (scientism, socialism, and orientalism) and all sorts of different formulations and stages, is only one form of Zionism. Zionism had a lot of aspects and very different formulations. There are so many studies on this issue that I do not need to insist on it. I just need to stress a point. As a utopia of the future (holding the dream of extraordinary technological developments and of changes in the connections between people—particularly women and men), and at the same time a utopia of the past (the revival of ancient Palestine), political Zionism became also the ideology of a national and nationalist movement. It cannot be reduced to a mere colonial fact. But this colonial–national utopia has always been coloured with messianism. Even a secular Jew like David Ben Gurion, the first Prime Minister of the State of Israel, wrote in his Memoirs:

> Without a messianic, ideological impulse, without the vision of restoration and redemption, there is no earthly reason why even oppressed and under-privileged Jews ... should wander off to Israel of all places ... The immigrants were seized with an immortal vision of redemption which became the principal motivation of their lives.[1]

From Utopia to Nightmare

This utopia, however, appeared to more and more actors as not a re-demption but a loss. The real Palestine replaced the fictional one, as the existence of previous inhabitants of this land of utopias became some-thing the Zionist immigrants and settlers could no longer deny. They, and with them the State of Israel, had to deal with it. Historians have told this long story of wars and political violence. Some of them today interpret these events as an attempt at ethnic cleansing which did not succeed completely until now. Through the Oslo peace process, which began in 1991, Palestinians have acquired a national identity but not statehood. The media go on speaking of peace negotiations in order to set up the two states side by side, but beyond these hollow words, there seems to be no solution (as there is no serious effort made to implement it) to change the painful reality, to Palestinians being deprived of elementary rights, and to the situation getting worse everyday. The journalist Ali Abunimah compares this situation to a tale from his childhood. It is the story of Caliph Umar ibn al-Khattab who came across an impoverished woman with no food to feed her children. So she placed rocks in a pot of boiling water and stirred them constantly over the fire. Each time the children asked when the soup will be ready, she answered 'soon, soon'.[2] Hope is certainly better than despair, but you cannot feed starving people with rocks cooking in boiling water.

---

[1] David Ben-Gurion, quoted in Jacqueline Rose, *The Question of Zion* (Princeton: Princeton University Press, 2005), 45.

[2] Laila Haddad, 'The One-state solution: My Interview with Ali Abunimah', http://gazamon.com/2007/04/the-one-state-solution-my-interview-with-ali-abunimah/ (accessed 22 June 2010).

The failure, not only of the peace process but of the Zionist dream of redemption through the creation of a Jewish State has been noticed on both sides: Israeli and Palestinian. Avraham Burg, former speaker of the Knesset (Parliament) and of the Jewish agency, wrote in an article, published in September 2003, in the French newspaper *Le Monde* that Zionism is dead.[3] In June 2007, he gave an interview in the (Israeli) *Haaretz Magazine*, where he said: 'to define the State of Israel as a Jewish State is the key to its end'. In the Jewish diaspora, a similar point of view has been expressed by the prominent historian Tony Judt, who was once a Zionist, in a paper published in *The New York Review of Books*; he argues that the problem with Israel is:

> ... that it arrived too late. It has imported a characteristically late-nineteenth–century separatist project into a world that has moved on, a world of individual rights, open frontiers, and international law. The very idea of a 'Jewish state'... is rooted in another time and place. Israel, in short, is an anachronism...[4]

... and a dysfunctional one. Zionism had a meaning at the time of imperial collapse, when subject peoples dreamed of forming 'nation-states'.[5] This time is over. Referring to Avraham Burg, Tony Judt argues that Israel became 'a colonial state run by a corrupt clique which scorn and mocks law and civic morality'.[6] Herzl's utopia has turned into a nightmare. 'Unless something changes, Israel in half a decade will be neither Jewish nor democratic.'[7] The article of Tony Judt summarizes the arguments which are to be found in the books and articles written by Israeli-Jews or Jews from the diaspora who share the same analysis. Although this way of thinking has been expressed since the beginning of the Zionist movement on a very wide spectrum, from religious positions to secular ones, it gained popularity since the collapse of the Oslo peace process, and all the obvious violations of human and international rights

---

[3] Avraham Burg, 'La révolution sioniste est morte', *Le Monde*, 11 September 2003. http://www.mafhoum.com/press5/159C73.htm (accessed 28 December 2011).

[4] Tony Judt, 'Israel: The Alternative', *New York Review of Books*, 23 October 2003. http://www.nybooks.com/articles/archives/2003/oct/23/israel-the-alternative/?pagination=false (accessed 28 December 2011).

[5] Ibid.

[6] Ibid.

[7] Ibid.

which went with it. Of course, ideally, as the so-called moderates pretend to think what is actually possible, Israel could, or should, dismantle all the settlements on the Palestinian territory and come back to the borders of the pre-war of 1967 situation—that is to say 23 per cent of the mandatory Palestine (the Palestine under the British mandate). But facts on the ground show that it is far too late. There is now a permanent presence of the Israelis on the Palestinian ground, and Israelis, very well armed and protected, are there in growing numbers. So, even the creation of a mini-state is impossible.

Facing the Sad Reality

This reality is precisely what Palestinians are now acknowledging. Israelis and Jews deplore the collapse of their ethical and political values. Palestinians speak of their everyday life becoming more and more oppressive with no hope of an internal political solution. In his last two books Rashid Khalidi came to nearly same conclusions: 'The inexorable cementing of Israel's hold over occupied West Bank and East Jerusalem has rendered moot the possibility of establishing what could legitimately be called a Palestinian state.'[8] On the contrary, the departure of the Israeli settlers from the Gaza strip, which gave occupation the new face of a siege, did not change anything. So what Rashid Khalidi wrote in 2004 is even more relevant in 2008 as the number of settlements and settlers kept growing:

> It may be that the settlement since 1967 of well over four hundred thousand Israelis in the occupied West Bank, Gaza Strip and East Jerusalem—a process that was always ultimately aimed at ensuring permanent Israeli control over most of these territories and making the creation of a viable, sovereign Palestinian state alongside with Israel impossible—means that a completely new approach will have to be found.[9]

A lot of prominent Palestinian intellectuals and scholars who had played a part in the 'peace process' at one stage or the other, can be quoted

---

[8] Rashid Khalidi, *The Iron Cage: The Story of the Palestinian Struggle for Statehood* (Boston: Beacon Press, 2007), 207.

[9] Rashid Khalidi, *Resurrecting Empire: Western Footprints and America's Perilous Path in the Middle East* (Boston: Beacon Press, 2005), 151.

sharing similar points of view, making public declarations or writing papers or books, as the debate is expanding. In an interview given in Jerusalem to Akiva Eldar and published in the *Haaretz* (16 August 2008), Sari Nusseibeh, the highly respected president of Al-Quds University, who has been over years the advocate of the two-states solution, and the co-signatory of a peace plan with Ami Ayalon, former chief of the Israeli secret services, made a striking declaration: 'I still favor a two-state solution and will continue to do so, but to the extent that you discover it's not practical anymore or that it's not going to happen, you start to think about what alternatives are [there].' So here we are again, facing what Freud has called 'the reality principle'.

The only choice lies now between total despair and utopia. The new dream emerging from a new collective drama, this time lived by Palestinian people for 60 years, is still not an official political agenda. Although it is discussed in various circles, it takes now the form of an appeal to a 'one-state solution', what Tony Judt calls 'an unpromising mix of realism and utopia'. It is realism because it demands that what is happening on the ground should not be concealed. And political discourse, at the international level as well as at the national one, does conceal it. It is utopic, because everything has to be invented if this new configuration has to be built one day. It is utopic also because it can be difficult and painful to accept. On both sides, people would have to renounce having a State of their own. It looks, according to Sari Nusseibeh, like the solution of an 'ideal world' where 'people really want to be together'. Thus, there are many different directions and proposals for this one-state solution. In some narratives of Palestinian writers, it begins with the memories of some golden age where, in Palestine, before the creation of the state of Israel, Arabs (Christians and Muslims) lived happily and peacefully together. So something of this nature could be restored, if only colonization could come to an end. We are then in the same narrative structure as in the classical utopias. Others are preoccupied with legal, political or cultural aspects of such a solution.

Old–New Utopia

Nevertheless, on both sides, the idea of only one State on the territory of Palestine, as defined by the British mandate, is not something completely new. It existed already in the pre-state Zionist movement and was represented by a prominent group of Jewish intellectuals who were convinced that founding a Jewish state could only have very negative consequences. Their arguments went from deeply religious convictions to secular, ethical, and political positions. Among the most famous defenders of this idea, we find Judah Magnes, the founder of the Hebrew University of Jerusalem, and the philosophers Martin Buber and Hannah Arendt, the latter of whom wrote, in her essay 'Zionism Reconsidered' that the erection of a Jewish state within an imperial sphere of interests might look like a very neat solution to some Zionists, though to others it looked like something desperate but unavoidable. She wrote that in the long run, there was hardly any course imaginable that would be more dangerous, or more adventurist.[10]

Jacqueline Rose published in 2005 a very important book, *The Question of Zion*,[11] in which she carefully explains all these different positions. One of the main actors of this debate, swept off by the creation of the State, was the philosopher Martin Buber, who supported the same idea of a single state, conjoining the Arab and Jewish communities, with 'complete equality of rights between the two partners, disregarding the changing numerical relationship between them, and with joint sovereignty founded upon these principles—such an entity would provide both people with all that they truly need'. Immediately after the creation of the state of Israel, Martin Buber advocated for a covenant of two independent nations with equal rights and common development. This pattern re-emerged in the 1980s, with the encounters of the so-called pacifists of both sides, calling for mutual recognition. Although this pattern became the motto of the peace process, it failed completely, as seen before.

On the Palestinian side, the call for a single state 'secular and democratic' in all Palestine, emerged in the 1960s, inside the Palestine Liberation Organization (PLO). The original and unrealistic goal formulated in the PLO's charter has been first to eliminate Israel. It has been amended to the establishment of a secular democratic state in Palestine, replacing Israel, for Muslims, Christians, and Jews. But this goal was related to the dominant view in the Palestinian resistance movement, which was the armed struggle, in line with the many anti-colonial and liberation movements throughout the world and with a strategy of alliances with segments of the Israeli population. It looked more like revolutionary rhetoric,

---

[10] Hannah Arendt, 'Zionism Reconsidered', *Menorah-Journal* 33 (1945): 162–96.

[11] Jacqueline Rose, *The Question of Zion* (Princeton: Princeton University Press, 2005).

which meant 'that the PLO never developed a clear and persuasive vision for a democratic state that could present a credible challenge to Zionism's insistence on the necessity of a Jewish monopoly'. On the Israeli side, it was commonly perceived as a plan to drive, or to throw, the Israeli Jews into the sea.

The present situation is totally different as the call for a one-state solution comes from both sides, in permanent dialogue. Certainly, from a sociological point of view, these two parts do not have the same social basis. In the Palestinian Occupied Territories, and more precisely in the West Bank, and in Gaza, the domination of Hamas prevents the expression of this opinion, even though conviction in the one-state option is shared by a large part of the population. They have to experiment everyday with the trap in which they have been caught. They are starving not only of food (and water, as far as Gaza is concerned), but also of freedom and citizenship. There is also the problem of the Palestinian citizens of Israel, who, although citizens (with the right to vote), are second-class citizens (with less rights than the Jewish citizens), and who could (with the one-state solution) then be recognized as full citizens and as Palestinians. In the special case of the Palestinian inhabitants of East Jerusalem who are not legally recognized as Palestinians or Israelis, the situation is even more complicated. They are compelled to live a schizophrenic existence, described by Sari Nusseibeh thus:

> ... the fact [is] that these people speak Hebrew, and listen to Hebrew songs, go out with Israeli girlfriends, while at the same time they live in Arab neighborhoods and under the influence of Muslim culture. There are contradictory forces pulling at them.[12]

That is why an association like Adalah (The Legal Center for Arab Minority Rights in Israel) made a shift from a call for equal rights for Arab-Israeli citizens to a call for a one-state solution, presenting, like a 'dream', the project of a supranational state in Palestine, which could also help to solve the problem of the Palestinian refugees.

So what looked at first like a feeling or an opinion that had prevailed among ordinary people in Palestine has been articulated by more and more intellectuals and by some politicians, such as Azmi Bishara, who

---

[12] Sari Nusseibeh, Interview with Akiva Eldar titled 'We Are Running Out of Time for a Two-state Solution', *Haaretz*, 16 August 2008.

had been a (Palestinian) representative at the Knesset, but had to secure exile in Egypt. On the other side, the political establishment goes on expressing its opposition to this 'realistic' withdrawal, as it contradicts the official-nationalist discourse by which it still tries to legitimize its privileges. Some members of the Palestinian establishment or of the Palestinian Authority refer to it only as a threat towards the international community. According to Agence France Presse, Ahmed Qorei, at that time the Palestinian Prime minister:

> [T]he Palestinians could call for a bi-national state which they would share with the Israelis if diplomatic channels for creating a state of their own lead nowhere. Israel's continued policy of building the wall [blocking certain Palestinian territories] means that talk about a Palestinian state makes no sense. If this Israeli policy continues, we are going to come back to the option of a single, bi-national democratic state.

Back and towards Canaan

On the Israeli side, only intellectuals and activists defend this position in a struggle for justice and human rights. In a sense, this minority is developing a utopia. But some of them intend also to sell it as a feasible and realizable project. This utopia has been manifested in a common appeal for 'sharing the land of Canaan' and for the creation of the 'United States of Canaan'. This appeal, which has been published in July 2004, is called the Olga appeal, as it has been written in a place called Giv'at Olga. It takes the form of an appeal 'For Truth and Recon- ciliation For Equality and Partnership'.[13] Of course, the obvious model for this process is South Africa. So the appeal, undersigned only by Israeli-Jewish intellectuals (there were a hundred first signatories), demands on the one hand 'the immediate annulment' of all laws, regulations, and practices that discriminate between Jewish and Arab citizens and the dis- solution of all the institutions based on such laws, and on the other, an immediate end to the state of occupation, so that the people of the coun- try can live together. The material form of living together could be one or two states, or even a confederation. And actually, after the appeal has been published, a passionate debate has developed on bi-nationalism.

---

[13] The Olga Appeal, June 2004, http://qumsiyeh.org/theolgaappeal/ (accessed 22 June 2010).

It is still going on, in the newspapers and on the internet. It allowed the breaking of a taboo.

The South African experience which put an end to apartheid has also been one of the main arguments used by Edward Said in articles and interviews published from the 1990s. Edward Said had a visionary and extremely courageous attitude about this issue. 'We should look', he wrote in March 2001, 'to provide a solution to the conflict that would assert our common humanity as Jews and Arabs',[14] using exactly the same terms as Nelson Mandela in his anti-apartheid campaign. That meant, 'Two people in one land. Or equality for all. Or one person, one vote. Or, a common humanity asserted in a binational state' The Olga appeal says:

> We are united in the recognition that this country belongs to all its sons and daughters—citizens and residents, both present and absentees (the uprooted Palestinian citizens of Israel in 1948)—with no discrimination on personal or communal grounds, irrespective of citizenship or nationality, religion, culture, ethnicity, gender.

For the past few years, there have been different versions of this political utopia, in connection with the development of a new post-national ideology. Some assert a 'republican' conviction (one citizen, one vote) without any reference to ethnicity, but that seems quite uncommon in the Middle East. Others are in favour of a more classical version, such as Azmi Bishara, who thinks of a federal or confederate state, including two ethnonational communities. All that is yet to be discussed. What would be the legal code of such a state? Ali Abunimah pleads for a uniform legal code, which could be a guarantee for different rights, and first of all for women's rights, always in danger when personal 'status' is concerned. The Israeli music conductor Daniel Barenboim, who lives in Germany and has been a close friend to Edward Said, accepted in January 2008 a Palestinian passport, when it was offered to him. In a statement published in *The Guardian* he concluded, 'After all, in the sense that we share one land and one destiny, we should all have dual citizenship.'[15]

This one-state solution can be called a utopia, as it seems unthinkable to all those who asked for years for a Palestinian state. It means renouncing the ideology or the motto of a Jewish state, which in the

---

[14] Edward Said, 'The Only Alternative', March 2001, http://www.mediamonitors.net/edward9.html (accessed 22 June 2010).

[15] Daniel Barenboim, 'Passports to Progress', *The Guardian*, 30 January 2008.

actual historical conditions, could be realized only through a complete ethnic cleansing. It means also the recognition of the impossibility of a Palestinian state. Further, it leads to a new vision: the end of the nation state, this heritage of Western Europe, imposed on most regions of the world. It means imagining some sort of separation between citizenship and nationality, between nation and territory, in order to integrate the diasporas in the nations, or to establish some sort of a link beyond the borders. But it leads also to the possibility of multi-belongings, as expressed in the statement of Daniel Barenboim. Palestine is not the only part of the world where we have to think of post-national solutions. Of course, activists may think that at this very moment, with many sufferings and daily violations of elementary human rights, such a utopia is not the main point and a waste of time. But it is also important not to stick to necessity, and to take time to dream and imagine. This is so even if imagination involves, in this situation, taking seriously the legal aspects. What is fascinating with utopias is that they open paths to a world of hopes, and to a space for human agency. This new political utopia developed in and from Palestine, could help us fight against the trends of ethnicity and against all the closures and separation of walls.

PART II

Engendering Utopia and Dystopia

7

'One Darling Though Terrific Theme'[1]

Anna Wheeler and the Rights of Women

Theresa Moriarty

In the following pages you will find discussed on paper, what you have so often discussed in conversation—a branch of that high and important subject of morals and legislation, the condition of women, of one half of the human race, in what is called civilized society.[2]

When William Thompson wrote his 'Introductory Letter to Mrs. Wheeler' at the start of his 1825 *Appeal of One Half of the Human Race, Women, Against the Pretensions of the Other Half, Men, To Retain them in Political, and Thence in Civil and Domestic Slavery*, it was an unusual attribution. Few women were published at this time, especially under their own names.

Thompson's authorship of arguments for women's rights, was a deliberate effort to raise the voice of women in their own cause, and to promote the reasoning of one woman in particular. 'The days of dedication and patronage are gone by.' Here Thompson acknowledged his 'debt of justice' in framing the *Appeal*, 'especially in its bolder and more comprehensive views'. 'I wish to give everything to its owner.' In this book,

---

[1] William Thompson, 'Introductory Letter to Mrs. Wheeler', in *Appeal of One Half of the Human Race, Women, Against the Pretensions of the Other Half, Men, To Retain Them in Political, and Thence in Civil and Domestic Slavery*, Virago edition, with an introduction by Richard Pankhurst (London: Virago, 1983), xxii (hereafter the *Appeal*). All subsequent citations are to this edition.

[2] Thompson, 'Introductory Letter to Mrs. Wheeler', *Appeal*, xxi.

'To separate your thoughts from mine were now to me impossible.' He included some of her writing in the book, 'the produce of your mind and pen, written in your own hand. The remainder are our joint property, I being your interpreter, and the scribe of your sentiments.'[3]

Anna Wheeler, whom he addressed, was a woman in her middle years, in 1825, a single parent with two daughters, both in their early twenties. She had escaped her husband some years earlier, with the help of her family. By law she was a widow since her husband died in 1820.

She was born, Anna Doyle, in Ireland, in the 1780s, the eldest daughter of a country rector of the Church of Ireland. This relatively modest middle-class origin belied the status of her family within the social and political Protestant Ascendancy to which her family belonged. Her father died when she was still young and she married, aged 15, the heir of a landed family, Francis Massy Wheeler, in County Tipperary.

Anna Wheeler bore six children, all but one of them girls. The required son and heir to a landed family died in infancy, adding to the difficulties between herself and her husband. Only two of her daughters survived.

Country life had few outlets for women of her class. Her husband was said to have followed countryside pursuits. She found an escape in books. Reading could still be transgressive for women, but the English literary canon attests to the advantages of being a clergyman's daughter, in learning the accomplishments of both reading and writing.

Her daughter Rosina, later Lady Lytton, remembered Anna Wheeler's intellectual engagement at their home in the Irish countryside.

> ... my mother would be stretched on one sofa, deep in perusal of some French or German philosophical work that had reached her translated via London (and who was unfortunately deeply imbued with the pernicious fallacies of the French Revolution, which had then more or less seared their traces through Europe, and who was besides strongly tainted by the corresponding poison of Mrs. Wollstonecraft's book).[4]

This pen picture, designed to show her mother's distance from her family, and the subversive content of her reading, illustrated how Anna

---

[3] All quotes from *Appeal*, xxi–xx.

[4] Louisa Devey, *Life of Rosina, Lady Lytton* (London: Swan Sonnenschein, Lowry, and Co., 1887), 7–8.

Wheeler began to shape her intellectual challenge to women's social position.

She fled Ireland and her unhappy marriage, with her two daughters and her sister, after 12 years, with the help of her family. From then her main home was with her uncle, Sir John Doyle, first in Guernsey, where he was Governor, and later in London.

Anna Wheeler seems to have led a peripatetic life for some years after the Doyle household left Guernsey in 1816. Her first biographer, Richard Pankhurst says

'She sailed with her family to London, where she met her god-father Henry Grattan and resided a few months in a Jermyn Street hotel before paying a brief visit to Dublin. Soon after she found her way to Caen....'[5]

In Paris and Caen, one account says, 'She indulged in the society of freethinkers and socialists.'[6] Elsewhere her daughter said that her mother lived in a Saint-Simonian community in Caen. Pankhurst dates her first meeting with Charles Fourier in Paris, in 1823.[7]

In London in the early 1820s, Anna Wheeler was drawn to the circles of Jeremy Bentham, the English utilitarian philosopher and reformer. Here many of her lifelong friendships and associations began. Bentham played host to a large circle of European reformers and radicals, and it was probably here that she first met William Thompson. This son of Cork's mercantile classes was beginning his critique of the emerging capitalist society, embodied in a series of works, some of the most influential texts among the Owenite co-operative movement.[8]

Thompson stayed with Bentham for five months in 1822–23, to follow up his interest in Bentham's educational ideas. His visit coincided with the return to London of Marc-Antoine Jullien, the former Jacobin and editor, since 1819, of the *Revue Encyclopédique*. Jullien, who shared Thompson's interest in education, was on his way home to Paris from a

[5] Richard K.P. Pankhurst, 'Anna Wheeler: A Pioneer Socialist and Feminist', *Political Quarterly* 25, no. 2 (1954–55), 132–43.

[6] S.M. Ellis, *Unpublished Letters of Lady Bulwer Lytton to A.E. Chalon, R.A., with Introduction and Notes by S.M. Ellis* (London: Eveleigh Nash, 1914), 12.

[7] Pankhurst, 'Anna Wheeler', 134–35.

[8] William Thompson, *An Inquiry into the Distribution of Wealth* (London: n.p., 1824); the *Appeal* of 1825, *Labour Rewarded* (n.p.: Hunt and Clarke, 1827); and William Thompson, *Practical Directions for the Establishment of Communities* (London: n.p., 1830).

visit to New Lanark, to see for himself Robert Owen's industrial community and its innovative programme of schooling for both child and
adult workers.

Bentham introduced both men, and Anna Wheeler's friendship with
Jullien probably began here as well. Bentham was already associated
with Robert Owen as an investor in New Lanark. His household was not
limited to influential men at this time. Frances Wright, who went on to
found the community for freed slaves in Tennessee, held levées at his
home.[9] Here Anna Wheeler met women and men who formed the emerging ideas of socialism, and among whom she was associated throughout
her life.

In Bentham's home Anna Wheeler may have also learnt the strength
of networking, one of his lasting contributions to radical circles in
London. She would mirror this practice throughout her active life. She
retained the 'pursuit of happiness' as a guiding principle of her intellectual commitment to the rights of women.

In London, the friendship—intellectual and personal partnership—
between William Thompson and Anna Wheeler took root, which he
acknowledged in his 1825 book, and which lasted until and beyond his
death in 1833.

The *Appeal* was written from within these utilitarian circles. Thompson
wrote to refute the Scottish utilitarian James Mill's assertion that
women's interests were looked after by their fathers and husbands. In
his 'Article on Government' in 1820, Mill dismissed women's political
rights, whilst arguing that a citizen's only protection against tyranny was
the vote. Women, as daughters or wives, could rely on fathers or husbands
to look after their interests.

The *Appeal* asked three questions of Mill's claim: Why should all
women without husbands or fathers, and adult daughters living with
their fathers, or married women's interests be excluded from political
rights? And he also asked, 'Are the interests of women in point of fact
involved with men?'

Thompson argued in each case for adult women's individual protection through political rights and equal laws. Women's civil rights were
only guaranteed by possessing political rights. The book went further
than this to answer Thompson's questions. The *Appeal* looks at the relations of power between men and women, and rejected any identity of

---

[9] Cecilia Morris Eckhardt, *Fanny Wright: Rebel in America* (Cambridge, Massachusetts: Harvard University Press, 1984), 64.

interest between men and women, arguing rather that women's equal political and legal rights are essential.

Its extensive critique of women's lack of rights within marriage is where Anna Wheeler's voice is the strongest. Dolores Dooley, who has written extensively on both William Thompson and Anna Wheeler, points out, 'There is considerable textual evidence to claim that Anna Wheeler wrote substantial parts of the Appeal',[10] not only from her circumstances, 'in the situation you have been, to suffer from the inequalities of sexual laws',[11] but also from her style of writing. The *Appeal*'s concluding section headed 'Address to Women' shares both this style and passion.[12]

Thompson presented his book as a self-conscious development of Mary Wollstonecraft's *Vindication of the Rights of Women*, and the writing of her friend, Mary Hays from the 1790s.

Anxious that the hand of a woman should have the honour of raising from the dust that neglected banner which a woman's hand nearly thirty years ago unfolded boldly, I hesitated to write.[13]

Such a banner had been raised within the working-class reform movement of 1816 to 1819, but had been lowered by repression, censorship, and crisis by the 1820s.[14] The employment of the word 'slavery' in the title, and the many comparisons with the West Indian slave system in the *Appeal*, drew on the anti-slave trade agitation of the early 1820s to illustrate to readers the plight of married women in their society.[15]

The *Appeal* looked forward to new forms of society, where the rights of women could only be met within new forms of mutual association where equality among members could guarantee women's equality. The principle of association is posed against 'the whole basis of competitive society'.[16] Only in co-operation could human happiness be practically as well as theoretically pursued.

---

[10] Dolores Dooley, *Equality in Community: Sexual Equality in the Writings of William Thompson and Anna Doyle Wheeler* (Cork: Cork University Press, 1996), 179.

[11] *Appeal*, xxi.

[12] *Appeal*, 187–213.

[13] *Appeal*, xxiii.

[14] Dorothy Thompson, 'Women and Nineteenth Century Radical Politics: A Lost Dimension', in *The Rights and Wrongs of Women*, eds. Juliet Mitchell and Ann Oakley (Harmondsworth: Penguin, 1976), 112–38.

[15] *Appeal*, 85–89.

[16] Sheila Rowbotham, *Hidden from History: 300 Years of Women's Oppression and the Fight against It*, 2nd ed. (London: Pluto Press, 1974), 40.

The *Appeal* could be read by the women and men of the Owenite movement through their reading rooms and in their newspapers. French readers could get it in translation, and sections were reprinted in the United States.[17] Thompson and his *Appeal* gave Anna Wheeler a public authority on the 'Rights of Women', but it was a few years before she took to both platforms and press to amplify her views.

Personal matters sapped her energies and activity. In London, in 1825, five years after her husband's death, she was still hoping to win some settlement from her husband's will in Ireland. By the autumn she was living in Paris. There she and her daughter Henrietta threw themselves into the struggle for Greek independence. The Wheeler women lived a modest existence in Paris, in close touch with Marc-Antoine Jullien and his family, and were visited there by Jeremy Bentham. Henrietta, only in her early 20s, fell ill and died in September 1826.

At the end of August 1827, Anna Wheeler's second daughter, Rosina, married Edward Bulwer, 'and the match will, I hope console the mother for her sad loss', Bentham wrote to Lafayette.[18] In 1828, Anna Wheeler was in London. Perhaps she returned for the birth of her first grandchild, Emily.

Shortly afterwards, Anna Wheeler moved into a new public forum by unprecedented contributions to and correspondence with the Owenite press in England. She was now settled in London.

Anna Wheeler's letters frequently mention her ill health. Yet she seems to have lived a life of intense social networking. From London she maintained her links to Paris, often sending letters with travellers who moved between both cities. Her list of contacts reads like a roll call of radicals and reformers in both cities. In these years London became a capital of refugees and here Anna Wheeler mixed with Saint-Simonian missionaries from Paris, Italian revolutionaries, and Polish exiles. Her surviving correspondence originated from her efforts to introduce strangers and sympathizers, within and between the English and French movements.

Anna Wheeler's public advocacy for women's rights adopted the practice of women in France and the United States, which encouraged

---

[17] Bonnie Anderson, *Joyous Greetings: The First International Women's Movement* (Oxford: Oxford University Press, 2000), 76.

[18] Jeremy Bentham to the Marquis de la Fayette, 2 September 1827, in *The Correspondence of Jeremy Bentham*, 12 vols, vol. 12, ed. Timothy Sprigge (London: Athlone Press, 1968), 379–80.

the public role of women. In Paris, Saint-Simonian women debated by lectures and publications. In America, Frances Wright lectured in New York. Anna Wheeler raised her voice within a rising chorus of complaints in the cause she advocated, the emancipation of women, amidst public distress and more private demands.

Paris, still her spiritual home, forever linked with the death of her daughter Henrietta, had a revolution in July 1830. In England the wide-spread clamour for reform came together in the general election of 1831. The rise in the political climate, encouraged by the overthrow of the French Bourbons and the election of the Reform Parliament at West-minster, opened space for a more public challenge to the existing order of patronage and corruption, which Anna Wheeler always linked with her critique of women's position in 'civilised' society. These tumultuous years were marked by more personal concerns that embraced the public political platforms.

In 1830, Anna Wheeler had Ireland and her perilous finances on her mind. 'The meagre resources which the civilized fraud has left me has not been paid to me, due to the current state of Ireland.'[19] Whatever income she was due from Ireland may have been imperilled by the mounting campaign in Ireland to halt the payment of tithes to the Church of Ireland clergy.[20]

She became a grandmother for the second time in 1831, when her surviving daughter, Rosina Bulwer Lytton, gave birth to a son, Edward Robert, heir to his father's estate at Woodcot and Knebworth. It was at dinner with the Bulwer Lytton's in January 1833 that Disraeli formed his impression of Anna Wheeler as 'something between Jeremy Bentham and Meg Merrilies, very clever but awful revolutionary'.[21]

A more immediate blow in 1833 was the death on 28 March of her friend and collaborator, William Thompson, from 'inflammation of the chest',[22] a condition he had borne through much of his adult life. It was his public outing of her in his introductory dedication to Mrs. Wheeler in his *Appeal* of 1825 that gave her views on women a public authority.

---

[19] A.D. Wheeler to Charles Fourier, 30 July 1830, in Dooley, *Equality in Community*, 72.

[20] Irish tenant farmers' resistance to pay tithes to the protestant Church of Ireland began in County Tipperary, where Anna Wheeler retained family and marriage links. This nation-al campaign was followed in the co-operative press, especially from 1832 in the *Crisis*.

[21] Benjamin Disraeli, Earl of Beaconsfield, *Lord Beaconsfield's Correspondence with his Sister 1832–1852* (London: n.p., 1886), 146. Meg Merrilies is a gypsy in Walter Scott's novel *Waverly*.

[22] Edward T. Craig, footnote to his report on Ralahine, *Crisis* (13 July 1833).

This was confirmed in 1829 by an invitation to lecture at the radical Unitarian chapel in the City of London, not long after her return to London. There she qualified her argument against the claims of men's superiority by her insistence that men also would benefit from women's rights. She saw these guaranteed by equal education for children of both sexes, along with the removal of all disabilities of the unequal 'Social Condition of Women'.

Her talk was published under the title of 'Rights of Women' by the *British Co-operator*,[23] a journal emerging within the newly energized social movement among working class and artisan men and women, who made up some of the audience at the chapel. This and her subsequent publications in the Owenite *Crisis*,[24] meant her views were being read far beyond her immediate political circles, extending to both the European continent and America.[25]

In Paris, women had moved onto a new and a more public terrain. Women among the Saint-Simonians raised their voices in their own newspaper from August 1832, edited by and for women.[26] Marc-Antoine Jullien saw the opportunity for Anna Wheeler to contribute to this discussion. In November 1832, Anna Wheeler wrote:

> In answer to your invitation to write an article for the 'Journal des Femmes' I perceive by the perusal of three of its numbers, that I could write nothing worthy of its pages, nor anything consistent with its principles, that it could receive. I cannot cut and carve my opinions to the taste of the day.[27]

But, by the following year, Anna Wheeler's life in London and her time in Paris began to come together. She overcame her reluctance to write. Perhaps the death of William Thompson at the end of March moved her into a more public space within the emerging debate on women among

---

[23] *British Co-operator, or Record and Review of Co-operative and Entertaining Knowledge*, 1830. Anna Wheeler's talk was printed in its first two editions, April and May 1830.

[24] *The Crisis, or the Change from Error and Misery, to Truth and Happiness*, weekly, 1832–34, changed its title to *Crisis, and National Co-operative Trades Union and Equitable Labour Exchange Gazette* in 1833.

[25] Anderson, *Joyous Greetings*, 68.

[26] The weekly paper changed its title frequently in its early issues. Its original title, *La Femme Libre*, gave way to *Women of the Future*. They eventually settled on the title *Tribune des Femmes*. Claire Goldberg Moses, *French Feminism in the Nineteenth Century* (Albany: State University of New York, 1984), 63.

[27] A.D. Wheeler to Marc-Antoine Jullien, 15 November 1832, Stephen Burke, 'Letter from a Pioneer Feminist', *Studies in Labour History* 1, no. 1 (1976) 22.

Owenites and their international associates. More immediately, from the spring of 1833, Desirée Veret, founder of the Parisian journal, working as a seamstress, moved to London, close to Anna Wheeler. Veret remembered their friendship as 'a second mother to me'.[28] They shared news about each other in correspondence with Charles Fourier.

In June 1833, Anna Wheeler opened a discussion on women in her own name in Robert Owen's journal, the *Crisis*, which combined such personal and intellectual commitments in both capitals. She submitted her translation of an article by Jeanne Victoire [Jeanne Deroin], published 14 months earlier in the Paris paper, for publication in the *Crisis*. She promised other extracts from the French journal if the *Crisis* 'accepted and approved' of this one, challenging the editor to publish.

> Should more pressing matter fill the columns of the Crisis and these extracts not be required, you will have the goodness to signify the same, that no time should be expended unnecessarily in translating them.[29]

The vocabulary of Jeanne Victoire's 'Appeal to Women' chimes with William Thompson—and Anna Wheeler's—1825 book, not just the referential echo of both titles, but also in alluding to women as 'half the human race'.

Although Anna Wheeler presented Jeanne Victoire's argument as a translation, Bonnie Anderson, points out that she had added 'her own passages to it'.[30] Jeanne Victoire's opening question,

> When the whole of the people are roused in the name of Liberty, and that the labouring class demand their freedom, shall we women remain passive and inert spectators of this great movement of social emancipation, which takes place under our eyes?[31]

was prefixed by the declaration, 'With the emancipation of women will come the emancipation of the useful class',[32] asserting the political

---

[28] Desirée Veret to Victor Considerant, 1890, in Jonathan Beecher, *Victor Considerant and the Rise and Fall of French Romantic Socialism* (Berkeley, Los Angeles, and London: University of California Press, 2001), 442.

[29] 'To the Editor of the Crisis', *Crisis* 2, no. 23 (15 June 1833): 182.

[30] Anderson, *Joyous Greetings*, 68.

[31] 'To the Editor of the Crisis', *Crisis* 2, no. 23 (15 June 1833): 182.

[32] This slogan appeared on the third and fourth issues of 'Women of the Future', Moses, 63.

agency of women. The *Crisis* article repeated Anna Wheeler's viewpoint that under the present system, women nurtured the conditions of their own slavery. 'Without our tenderness, our sympathy and care, they [men] could never grow up to be our oppressors....'

Women should '*reject as a husband any man* who is not sufficiently generous to consent to share with us all the rights he enjoys.... *We demand equal marriage laws*—preferring infinitely a state of celibacy *to one of slavery*'.[33]

Jeanne Victoire's call for women's rights proposed 'one solid union' among women of all classes. She claimed 'Universal association' against nationalism, peace against war, and ended with a republican evocation, 'We will weave wreaths of flowers to bind the brows of those moral and pacific men who shall lead on humanity in its social progress, and who shall enrich our globe by science and industry.'[34]

The editor's introduction to the article, explained, or warned, that the sentiments of the article were 'those of the St. Simonians', and set down some of the terms in which the debate on women was conducted from 1833. Many contributors argued for the relative strengths of the figureheads of their movements. Where the French women had respected, anonymously, their [leader] Propser Enfantin, English correspondents praised Robert Owen against Charles Fourier.

This dialogue was conducted under anonymity from Paris: Jeanne Victoire (Jeanne Deroin) and Suzanne (Voilquin),[35] and the London paper's correspondents, Concordia, Vlasta (Anna Wheeler), Justitia, Philia, and Vesta. The use of pen names to conceal the authorship of the writer was an accustomed practice at this time. It is most marked among women, although not exclusively.[36] The French Saint-Simonian women writers rejected their male surnames, from fathers or husbands, by dropping surnames altogether, such as Suzanne, or replacing them with suitable abstract nouns, such as Jeanne Victoire. English and Irish contributors to

---

[33] 'To the Editor of the Crisis', *Crisis* 2, no. 23 (15 June 1833): 182.

[34] Ibid.

[35] See Sheila Rowbotham, 'A New Vision of Society: Women Clothing Workers and the Revolution of 1848 in France', in *Chic Thrills: A Fashion Reader*, eds. Juliet Ash and Elizabeth Wilson (London: Pandora Press, 1992), 190–99.

[36] Among the best known examples of early-nineteenth-century women were the novelists such as the Brontës, George Eliot, and George Sands, who all employed men's names to publish.

the *Crisis* debate favoured more literary, historical, or classical references. In 1833 Anna Wheeler contributed as Vlasta, a legendary woman warrior.

In August a regular columnist to the *Crisis*, Concordia, took up the theme of women's equality with men in a long letter addressed to Robert Owen, about his proposed legal code 'for the human race, women as well as men'. Concordia argued men could not draft laws for women, '… you will not succeed in regulating properly for beings whose feelings and habits are so little known to any but themselves'. Concordia took women's difference from men as her starting point, writing of their 'own distinct moral peculiarities, and those men can never understand'.

Anna Wheeler replied as Vlasta. She insisted, 'women's best security for happiness depends on the mutual co-operation of both parties'. She proposed, against Concordia, the example of Saint-Simonian women who represented their sex, 'to make woman an independent legislator for other women would be to plunge both sexes deeper into that mire of legislative ignorance'. Vlasta distrusted a legal code based on prohibitions. Equality of laws and education should take special care that the interests of any one individual of either sex should not clash with the interests of any other. She wrote of love between men and women as 'a fearful thing', perpetuating the degradation of her sex and arresting the 'moral progress of man himself'.[37]

Vlasta displayed Anna Wheeler's intellectual antecedents. When she argued that 'legislation should confine itself to discovering the common wants of all', based on the 'greatest happiness principle', she echoed Bentham's fundamental formulation of utility. Her refrain against 'civilised' society resonates with a Rousseau ring. When she deplored women's education, Mary Wollstonecraft's reading of how female education diminishes women reverberated in Anna Wheeler's argument.

Concordia and Vlasta were not the only people arguing about women in present society and the future. That summer the *Crisis* announced a 'Plan for a Practical Moral Union of the Women of Great Britain and Ireland for the purposes of enabling them to attain a superior physical, moral and intellectual character', and others joined the *Crisis* debate through 1833–34.[38] 'Woman' became a frequent column heading in the *Crisis*, under the editorship of her friend, James E. Smith. Correspondents

---

[37] 'To the Editor of the Crisis', *Crisis* 2, no. 23 (15 June 1833): 182.
[38] See Barbara Taylor, *Eve and the New Jerusalem: Socialism and Feminism in the Nineteenth Century* (London: Virago, 1983).

returned to this theme in March, April, and June 1834. Once again an article from *Tribune des Femmes* prompted the 1834 exchange. There Suzanne commented on Concordia's letter the previous August.

Anna Wheeler may have maintained some of this dialogue between French writers and English readers. Suzanne began, 'We receive occasionally letters published in the Crisis by women', and went on to link the ideas of Robert Owen and Charles Fourier. She addressed all 'Legislators', and system makers, '*The complete emancipation of woman, therefore must be the principle on which should rest, to be successful, the new Social System, we are labouring to establish.*'[39]

Justitia wrote to the editor the same day, championing Owen against Fourier. Philia's reply to Justitia demonstrated a detailed knowledge of *Tribune de Femmes* and referred to the 1833 exchange of letters in the *Crisis*, including Concordia's contribution.

Anna Wheeler's public life in these few years was consumed by women's challenge for attention to their issues. From 1833 she was committed to the terms of William Thompson's will, where he left plans promoting co-operative communities. Anna Wheeler was one of the 13 trustees of his legacy. When Thompson's surviving sisters challenged this will in the Dublin courts, Anna Wheeler gave and collected funds to defend Thompson's bequest in this long drawn-out legal dispute to stop his estate coming under the direction of the co-operative movement.[40]

Anna Wheeler's personal and intellectual commitment straddled different systems of thought. They include eighteenth-century rationalism, garnered among her readings in Ireland; the utilitarianism of the 1820s; and the co-operative movement London as well as the association in Paris, with women and men who were reshaping views of a future society. Her contribution was always directed on a single theme.

Such contributions were conducted within the outlines of ideas associated with Robert Owen, Saint-Simon, and Charles Fourier. But they affirm the importance of women taking action themselves and raise the urgency of women becoming active in their own freedom. For the women writers to the *Crisis*, the Owenite women of the 'Practical Moral Union', and the French women of *Tribunes des Femmes*, these were not theoretical political debates, but raised intense practical issues about how to lead a life organized on beliefs for the future.

---

[39] *Crisis*, 3, no. 28 (8 March 1834).
[40] 'To Mrs Wheeler', *Crisis* 3, nos 22, 25 (January 1834).

All the contributors to this debate looked towards a new society. Their hopes for an egalitarian future were formed within the old 'civilised' world being buffeted by new forces. The shape of the new society was emerging, not formed. Divisions within it seemed sharper, not smoothed by industrialization and mass production. The old lines of separation between the idle and rich and the labouring and poor were more marked. Even more so when alternative ideas of how such social fragmentation could be avoided were already articulated and proposed, with a popular following in many countries.

Anna Wheeler and her associates struggled to describe the possibilities of new forms of living without a language to describe them. They were heirs of the French Revolution inheritance of rights, and their witness of the industrial revolution needed a new language as well as a vision. Harmony, system, community, and association—all stood for their new vision. They invented new words—social science, socialism, and solidarity, among them. When they employed the word socialism they did not prefix it with 'utopian'. That qualification would come later.[41]

Anna Wheeler's small written legacy, a handful of letters in a couple of collections, belies the influence she had. She was a link between the Owenites, Saint-Simons, and the Fourierists, and maintained the bonds between them. Even if there is no extensive body of literature to search her philosophy, her focus, always on the rights of women, provides a rich source of early international feminism. James Elishama Smith, a former disciple of Joanna Southcott, and former editor of the *Crisis* remembered, 'She writes always on one subject—the present conditions of women and their rights as members of society and the equals of men.'[42]

When Hugh Doherty, the Fourierist editor of the *Phalanx* whom Anna Wheeler knew in London, wrote to her from Paris in 1848 to encourage her to come, he wrote how the rights of women were debated in all the political clubs, to tempt her there. This letter, entrusted to Robert Owen survives in Owen's correspondence in Manchester, along with the French tricolour Doherty attached to it. It was never delivered. The day Hugh Doherty wrote to Anna Wheeler, she died in London. Owen kept the letter among his correspondence, perhaps as a legacy of the formidable woman he had known for more than 20 years.

---

[41] Discussions among the socialists in 1830s used the word 'utopian' in their debate, but this phrase is always attributed to Marx and Engels.

[42] W. Anderson Smith, *'Shepherd' Smith the Universalist: The Story of a Mind, Being a Life of the Rev. James E Smith, MA* (London: Sampson Low, Marston & Co., 1892), 48.

Anna Wheeler's brave life, of which this account is only a part, suggests a woman of formidable charisma, both beautiful and intellectual, as many remembered her. Through her extensive networking and correspondence, she kept men and women in communication with each other, encouraging contact, not difference.

She died in London, always hoping to return to France. Ireland, where she spent her formative years as a young wife and mother and avid reader, was where she learned the bitter lessons of married women's powerlessness, against her husband and the world, and where she shaped her resistance. Ireland, however distant, remained a shared territory with her friendships, like William Thompson and Hugh Doherty. Both shared the beginning and end of a public life, in which she declared in 1829, how she hoped she lived.

> To die and make no sign expressive of my horror, indignation and bitter contempt for that state of society called civilized,…would I feel complete the measure of my regret for having lived only to serve and suffer, in my capacity of slave and woman.[43]

[43] *British Co-Operator*, http://libsysdigi.library.uiuc.edu/OCA/Books2008-12/3461585/ 3461585_djvu.txt (accessed 14 July 2010).

8

A Parliament of Women

Dystopia in Nineteenth-century Bengali Imagination

Samita Sen

Meye Parliament or the Parliament of Women is an anonymous tract in Bengali, one of the many satires and farces targeting the so-called New Women, which were prolific in Bengal in the late nineteenth century. Some of these are well known—*Pashkora Magh, Kolir Bou, Harjalani Boubabu, Miss Bino Bibi BA, Abalabarrack, Koshtipathar, Model Bhagini,* and *Keyabat Meye.* The writers of these cheap and popular tracts were engaged in building a stereotype of the New Woman—independent, educated, focused on reading romances, uninterested and unskilled in housewifery, and sexually transgressive. This easy equation, endlessly repetitive, was emblematic of the fears and insecurities of the men of an emerging middle class confronted with social change.

The current of social reform in colonial Bengal, beginning with the abolition of sati in 1829, created an arena of bitter contestation between a group of progressive elite Bengali men, prompted and backed by European missionary and British officialdom, and those who clung to 'Hindu' (read Brahminical) arrangements of caste, family, and property relations. Much of the conflict turned on gender relations and the spotlight was on the marriage system. Vernacular literature too, proliferating as a result of the introduction of print technology, and giving rise to modern forms such as the novel, focused on these themes. Set apart from the self-conscious experimentations with 'high literature' of the emerging *bhadralok*, there was also a variety of lowbrow tracts (one subgroup was referred to as *battala*) which became known for their sharp satirical commentary on the breakdown of established hierarchies of caste and gender relations and a spirited defence of the established social and moral order.[1] The two classes of literature shared similar concerns, but the latter weaved in 'high' morality through a 'low' language, and achieved great success as a vehicle for popular discomfort with social reform—women's education, their entry into professions, widow remarriage legislation.[2]

The lowbrow social farce as a genre emerged in the 1860s and reached a peak of popularity in the next two decades. Usually printed as short pamphlets on cheap paper, they were composed in the form of short skits, read quite widely but rarely enacted. The common thrust was a critique of urban corruption. In part a response to the educated *bhadraloks'* attempts to marginalize the languages and cultures of other social groups, they offered a complex range of social commentary. Sumit Sarkar, in an influential essay, named these '*Kaliyuga* literature'. *Kaliyuga* is the fourth and most corrupt age of Hindu cosmology and became a prolific, occasionally powerful, metaphor, which the emerging literati deployed to condemn the processes of modernization wrought by colonialism.[3]

Meye Parliament shared much of the general features of *Kaliyuga* literature. *Kaliyuga* was a paradigmatic dystopia, according to Sarkar, a recurrent and powerful motif for voicing high-caste male anxieties. Hardik Brata Biswas argues that the commentator Nilkantha, the most significant in this regard, had defined *kaliyuga* in the figure of the transgressive woman.[4] Coming after the Mahabharata War, *kaliyuga* signalled oppressive rulers, corrupt and impure Brahmins, powerful Shudras, girls

---

[1] There have been a number of studies on this genre of literature. In the last few months, three publications have addressed the publication of farces and tracts—Hardik Brata Biswas, ed., *Prahasane Kalikaler Bangamahila, 1860–1909* [Bengali women of the Kali period as represented in farces] (Kolkata: Charchapada, 2011), 14; Sumanta Bandopadhyay, ed., Introduction to *Kaminikalanka* by Nabinkali Debi (Kolkata: Wild Strawberries Books, 2010)—and the meaning and definition of *battala* as well as early history of Bengali treatises/books. In his award-winning book, Gautam Bhadra argues that *battala* should not be equated with lowbrow publications.—Gautam Bhadra, *Nera Battolai Jai Kawbar* [How many times does the sucker go to battala?] (Kolkata: Chhatim Books, 2011).

[2] Anindita Ghosh, *Power in Print: Popular Publishing and the Politics of Language and Culture in a Colonial Society, 1778–1905* (New Delhi: Oxford University Press, 2006); Bhadra, *Nera Battolai Jai Kawbar.*

[3] Sumit Sarkar, '"Kaliyuga", "Chakri", and "Bhakti": Ramakrishna and His Times', *Economic and Political Weekly*, No. 27–29 (18 July, 1922), 1548–50.

[4] Biswas, *Prahasane Kalikaler Bangamahila*, 14.

choosing their own partners, disobedient wives having intercourse with menials, slaves, and even animals. The reversal of social order—caste and gender, with women asserting themselves and brahminism growing weaker—was the hallmark of this phase in the mythical cycle of time. From this range, nineteenth-century writers made their own selection, focusing on the New Women, the emerging power of the Shudras, modern/Western corruption, the 'modern' craze for money, and, most importantly, the breakdown of the marriage system leading to sexual anarchy. While, most of the other tracts carry traces of a dystopic vision[5]—of a world turned upside down, of a collapse of the traditional social and moral order—in *Meye Parliament*, we find the fully fledged vision of a dystopia, a land ruled by the New Women.

This text shares many of the classical features of utopia literature, organized around a visitor (as usual, the narrator) journeying into an unknown land. Krishan Kumar has emphasized the Christian moorings of the genre, arguing that far from being universal, utopia appeared in the West, drawing on classical and Christian heritage. He identifies millenarianism as the key link, and cites the absence of utopia in Chinese and Japanese literatures. In general terms, this is perhaps true of the Indian case too, there being few striking examples of a literary utopia.[6] In Bengali, the dystopic genre identified by Sarkar has a weak parallel in the construction of the Golden Age of ancient Hindu civilization, a project Kumar would perhaps dub the 'pre-history' or 'pre-echo' of utopia, not to be equated with utopia itself. Following Kumar's analysis further, one may discern in *Meye Parliament*, along with a dystopic vision, what he calls the temperament of anti-utopia.[7] On the women's question, the tract is explicitly dystopic with a depiction of a social and political

---

[5] Hardik Brata Biswas has collected and republished 20 of these farces addressing gender themes. Some of these were already known, but he has also traced a few relatively unknown tracts. This laudable effort gives researchers ready access to a rich source. A casual glance through some of these tracts will show how common and recurrent were some of the characterizations of new women and how acute were the underlying anxieties regarding the existing gender order.

[6] The rather better-known exceptions are the two feminist utopias by Begum Rokeya Sakhawat Hossain. *Sultana's Dream* is discussed in this essay. The other in Bengali, *Padmarag*, is part of a recent collection by Barnita Bagchi: Barnita Bagchi, ed. and part-translated, *Sultana's Dream and Padmarag: Two Feminist Utopias* (USA: Penguin, 2005).

[7] Krishan Kumar, *Utopia and Anti-Utopia in Modern Times* (Oxford: Basil Blackwell, 1987), 19–20.

reversal of the gender order. This text is, however, exceptional among this specific genre of dystopic literature, being organized around an explicit political metaphor, the Parliament, and including, apart from issues of caste, marriage, and the 'women's question', discussions on democracy, welfare, and inequality. The political discussions are sketched in briefly and quickly, but they set this text apart from the bulk of the social farces. In these discussions, one may discern Kumar's anti-utopia, a profound scepticism of the 'hopeful claims made on behalf of humanity by social prophets and reformers'.[8] In terms of literary form too, the tract is perhaps closer to anti-utopia. John Reilly, for instance, finds in the obverse of the literary utopia the dominance of a 'common sense', which mistrusts the power of rationality and colours its conservative motive with a tone of ridicule. According to him, anti-utopia is akin to satire, a description that fits to a nicety both *Meye Parliament* and its kindred literature.[9]

Meye Parliament ba Dwitya Bhag Bharata Uddhara (Women Parliament or Second Part of Rescue of India) was published in 1886 by Biharilal Sarkar from Bangabashi press. In the India Office Library (London, UK) catalogue, it is described as 'A satire on the measures being taken for bringing about female emancipation, being a sequel to the *Bharata Uddhara*.' The booklet bears no author's name. It may have been written by Indranath Bandopadhyay, author of *Bharata Uddhara*, given his close association with Bangabashi at the time of its publication. The style of writing is similar in some ways, though that is an uncertain criterion, given the tendency of writers of the time to copy each other's styles. There was a great deal of similarity in the construction of images and ideas, and in the mixture of 'high' and 'low' languages used by writers of farces in the three decades, 1860s to 1880s.[10] In *Bharata Uddhara*, as well as in *Meye Parliament*, we find a similar positioning of the author (akin also to Indranath's later writings as *Panchananda*) with complex and multiple layers of arguments, sometimes on both sides of a debate. Indranath's stock-in-trade was an exaggeration, which was used to nudge the reader to read beyond the obvious meanings of the arguments presented. There was also sometimes the use of coded language in

---

[8] Ibid., 100.

[9] John M. Reilly, 'The Black Anti-Utopia', *Black American Literature Forum*, 12, no. 3 (1978), 3.

[10] For a discussion of copy and copyright in early Bengali publication industry, see Bhadra, *Nera Battolai Jai Kawbar*, 138.

references to contemporary public figures and events. Indranath styled his own work as *bangya rachana* (satire) and used his pen in merciless attacks on political opponents.[11] However, none of this is conclusive proof that Indranath wrote *Meye Parliament*, though it seems highly possible. It is equally likely that others writing within a similar satirical genre may have chosen to style this tract as a sequel to *Bharata Uddhara*, given the latter's popularity. It was known, for instance, that Biharilal Sarkar often wrote the texts he published, so he too may have been the author.

The test is 65-pages long. The claim to being a sequel to *Bharata Uddhara* lies both outside and within the text. *Bharata Uddhara* was (written in 1876) and published in 1877, immediately after the establishment of the Indian Association; *Meye Parliament* was published in 1886, a year after the establishment of the Indian National Congress. The two organizations merged within the next year. While *Bharata Uddhara* is a clearly focused commentary on the protest politics of the mid-1870s and the constitutionalism of the Indian Association, *Meye Parliament* makes no direct reference to the Congress or nationalist politics. There is some gentle fun poked at the parliamentary style of politics and the political ideals of equality and liberty, but the butt of the joke remains social reform and 'female emancipation'. The imagining of a world turned upside down, women as rulers and men as their subjects, and a complete reversal of roles, women in administration and men doing the housework at home, followed in the dystopic tradition of *kaliyuga* literature, sounding dark warnings of a terrible resolution of the women's question.

Bharata Uddhara (The Rescue of India): Towards Dystopia?

While it is not very clear why *Meye Parliament* is styled as a sequel to *Bharata Uddhara*, there are enough and significant resonances to warrant a brief discussion of this latter text in relation to the former. There can be no question that *Bharata Uddhara* is by far the best known of Indranath's tracts. *Meye Parliament*, by contrast, does not seem to have excited

---

[11] It appears that on occasion he made such an attack on Bankim Chandra Chattopadhyay, but later apologized. Swapan Basu, 'Unish Sataker Byangapatrika' [Satire-Periodicals of the Nineteenth Century], *Sahitya Parishad Patrika* 113, no. 4 (2006), 4.

either interest or controversy. My limited search so far has uncovered no reference to this tract in discussions of nineteenth-century Bengali publications.

Bharata Uddhara (The Rescue of India) was advertised as a *byangakavir byangyakavya* (satirist's satire), and it was the author's third major publication. Indranath began his career in writing with *Utkrishta Kavyam* (date unknown) followed by *Kalpataru* (1873). He was also known for a collection of essays, poems, and satires written under the sobriquet *Panchananda* (beginning in 1878) and alternately carrying a vulgarization of the same name, *Panchu Thakur*. This collection reflected, more than any of his other writings, a sharp critique of contemporary social and political change, as well as of specific events.[12] He used light, often commonplace, humour to highlight some absurd excesses of the reformist discourse, generally underpinned by a disapproval of social change.

Indranath was born in 1849 and died in 1910. He wrote *Bharata Uddhara* when he was about 28 years old and practicing as a lawyer at the Calcutta High Court. In a brief autobiographical sketch included in his collected works, he described the writing of *Bharata Uddhara* in about three evenings in December 1876. It was published and became instantly popular.[13] Indranath, by then closely associated with Akshay Chandra Sarkar, gave him a copy for review in his immensely popular weekly journal *Sadharani*. Sarkar promptly published the entire text in that journal. About the same time, Indranath, influenced by Sarkar, was attracted to neo-Hinduism. Sarkar was associated with the social 'conservatives' who opposed reform in religion, caste, marriage, and the introduction of women's education. Indranath too was critical of much of these winds of changes, though his early writings were sometimes ambiguous and his satire seemed to be targeted at both sides on the social reform debate, often

---

[12] He began to publish this series in 1875 in Sadharani in collaboration with Akshay Chandra Sarkar and the first part was published at that time. After a break, it continued to be published in *Bangabashi* for many years. The collection ran into five volumes *Panchakande Panchu Thakur*. Towards the close of his life, other writers began to contribute to this collection. Gautam Bhadra makes a passing reference to Indranath and Panchu Thakur's style of humour and connection with *battala* (Bhadra, *Nera Battolai Jai Kawbar*, 217).

[13] Indranath Bandopadhyay, *Indranath Granthabali*, Collected Works of Indranath, containing a brief autobiographical essay (Calcutta: Natabar Chakrabarty, Bangabashi Electro-Machine Room, 1925).

inflected with acute observations of customs and practices. On the whole, he was resentful of 'Western' social influence, although in many of his writings he wrote scathingly of the rising tides of 'nationalist' or as he calls it—repeatedly—'patriotic' opposition to British rule.[14]

His social thinking crystallized in later life, when he became associated with *Bangabashi*.[15] This journal was associated with the defence of existing Hindu customs and practices against the attack of the reformers and especially the Brahmos. Indranath was considered the chief influence behind the *Bangabashi*'s (edited by Jogendra Chandra Bose) shift to a harder neo-Hindu position. As Indranath began to adopt in his daily life elaborate observances of Hindu rituals and ceremonies, so did *Bangabashi* become established as the chief vehicle of articulating a neo-Hindu ideology with an emphasis on the Brahminical core of *varnashrama*—the established Brahminical social order based on caste, gender, and generation. According to Amiya Sen, the social philosophy of Indranath and Jogendra Chandra was based on an 'unflinching belief in the rigid hierarchical ordering of Hindu society in which obviously the supremacy of the Brahman assumes a pivotal importance'.[16]

In common with many other thinkers now called 'cultural nationalists', Indranath did not believe in social reform by legislation. Much of his sharpest barbs were aimed at attempts to reform marriage laws. One common theme of the period was the glorification of discipline in existing social practices, underpinned by an ideological commitment to the social discipline of Brahminical Hinduism. Indranath believed, along with many of his contemporaries, that social change should come from within, that scholarship and wisdom would lead to heightened awareness of the purer principles of Hinduism and a greater observance of self-control and restraint. In his view, law, an imposition from above, could not change individual behaviour. Rather, law was an instrument in the hands of the state to selectively target individual or group transgressions. In the late nineteenth century, such views were neither novel nor extraordinary, but Indranath wrote with wit and style and to an established

---

[14] Amiya P. Sen, *Hindu Revivalism in Bengal, 1872–1905: Some Essays in Interpretation* (first published in 1993) (New Delhi: Oxford University Press, Paperback edition, 2001), 241–43.

[15] In 1881 Jogendra Nath Bose launched the widely circulated *Bangabashi*. Indranath's association with the journal came a few years later. *Sadharani* and *Bangabashi* shared a similar ideological space in the cultural politics of late-nineteenth century Bengal.

[16] Sen, *Hindu revivalism in Bengal, 1872–1905*, 257.

readership and, thereby, gained substantial popularity. He was attacked by self-styled 'liberals' and social reformers. Indranath wrote acerbically, if predictably, against the Age of Consent legislations, which polarized Bengal's society into those for and against social reform, marking a decisive victory, it has been argued by historians, of the anti-reform cultural nationalist lobby.

Even though *Bharata Uddhara* deserves the fullest possible discussion, we can, at present, merely indicate its relevance for a reading of its supposed sequel. First, a bare outline of the story: Bipinkrishna, the chief protagonist, was employed, probably as a clerk, by the British. He was dismissed for lying and could not find another job. He blamed the British for his misfortune and was attracted to the politics of patriotism. If only the British could be routed from the land, thought Bipin, and Bharat was independent, 'I would loot and plunder' at will. This thought was followed by the idea, 'I would like to go out just now' armed with a *bonti* (equivalent of kitchen knife, a curved blade attached to a thin wooden plank usually used by women who sit with a foot on the wooden plank leaving both hands free for chopping fish, meat, and vegetables). The *bonti* is a major motif in the verse, used in multiple and playful ways. The noun is made into a verb (explicitly following the poet Madhusudan Dutt's style) *bontaiba* (I will kill/strike with the *bonti*). The hilarity intended and much appreciated by readers (as evidenced in some of the reviews) arises from the heroic pretensions of an effete clerical/professional Bengali middle class. The choice of the *bonti* as a weapon of war underlines their emasculation because it is a kitchen implement associated with women's skills. Bipin represents the worst of the deracinated Bengali Hindu, depending on cunning rather than prowess, chased by the demons of his own fears, prone to tears, and tied hopelessly to the mundane.

After a brief prologue, the text segues into a verse narration alternating between the dream-like and the realistic, between wish fulfilment and fiction. Bipin assumed the leadership of a group of 'protestors' to lead them in a war against the British. The Bengali army, using gram flour, chilli powder, and the *bonti* (all items from the kitchen), was victorious; the British sued for mercy, and a peace was concluded.

There are at least two remarkable elements in this story that bear upon a reading of *Meye Parliament*. First, Indranath's affiliation is very unclear in this sometimes quite crude stylization of protest politics. The Indigo agitations of the 1860s had politicized the Bengali middle class. These currents led in 1876 to the establishment of the Indian Association by Surendranath Banerjee, who travelled across the country garnering support for constitutional protests against discriminatory practices by the British. *Bharata Uddhara*, written in 1877, was an immediate response to this embryonic nationalist protest. An association of patriots at which Bipin proposed the war against the British was meant to lampoon the Indian Association and its very new foray into modern/Western associational politics. Indranath's response to emerging nationalism was deeply negative, he was not just suspicious and doubtful, but dismissively derisory. He neither understood its language nor agreed with its objectives.

To elaborate his contempt for nationalism or 'patriotism', as he calls it, Indranath borrowed heavily from two well-known colonial characterizations of Bengalis, as 'effeminate' and 'unfit to rule'. This leads us to the second question—of gender—that this text raises. We know that questions of gender were centre stage in colonial and early nationalist discourses. The British used metaphors of gender to naturalize colonial authority, as many historians have shown.[17] Indeed, colonial discourse turned crucially on a construction of imperial masculinity vis-à-vis the effeminate colonized born to subjection. When the latter sought to assert themselves in a new language of rights, such rhetoric grew shriller. From this discourse emerged the 'civilising mission' and the white man's duty to protect the women and low castes from male brahminical torture and oppression. This was the ideological framework within which the British approached the question of social reform movement. How did Indranath make sense of this relationship? He rejected the latter but accepted the former. He was a declared social conservative, steering *Bangabashi* to declaim an anti-reform neo-Hindu position. But does the term 'cultural nationalism' help us understand Indranath's position? Was he seeking a 'resolution of the women's question',[18] accepting the reality of British rule while seeking to preserve Hinduism in the realm of caste and family? If he rejected political nationalism altogether, as he seemed to have been doing in *Bharata Uddhara*, could one argue that his critique of modernization and social reform was underpinned by a radical revisioning of the 'private' as the locus of autonomy, or that he sought to construct

---

[17] Mrinalini Sinha, *Colonial Masculinity: The 'Manly Englishman' and the 'Effeminate Bengali' in the Late Nineteenth Century* (Manchester, UK: Manchester University Press, 1995); Indira Chowdhury, *The Frail Hero and Virile History: Gender and the Politics of Culture in Colonial Bengal* (New Delhi: Oxford University Press, 1998).

[18] Partha Chatterjee, 'The Nationalist Resolution of the Women's Question', in *Recasting Women,* Kumkum Sangari and Sudesh Vaid, eds. (New Delhi: Kali for Women, 1989).

the woman as the site of a new nationalist enterprise?[19] Certainly *Bharata Uddhara* provides no answer to these questions. Issues of social reform and the women's questions were not addressed in this text. In his later writings, they do occupy the centre stage and they resonate in myriad ways in *Meye Parliament*.

Ruled by Women: The *Bhadralok* in Dystopia

Meye Parliament's claim to be a sequel of *Bharata Uddhara* was a purely extrinsic device. Except that both were constructed on imaginary lines, the dystopic character being more pronounced in the latter, and that both were on a satirical vein, there is little to link the two. However, the claim to be a sequel was made explicitly and at the very beginning. The prologue describes how General Bipinkrishna (the name of the leader of the battle in *Bharata Uddhara*), having defeated the British and rescued India, concluded a peace treaty. Bipin felt that *Bachanabartta* (the arena/ circumlocution of speech/words/utterances), a large region in Bengal, could not be left under English control. Indeed the English too realized that they could not quite rule this land. This area was left to Bipinkrishna, who established a *bhaginirajtantra* (Republic of Sisters). 'The Republic' Bipin established, the author wrote, was 'with the sisters; there was no trace of the brothers in this system; therefore, instead of a republic he named it '*bhagnitantra rajya*' (State under the Rule of Sisters). 'The improvement of womankind that even the American women had failed to achieve in all this time, he managed in a moment.'[20] The author then makes a sly dig at Bipin's self-interest: Bipin had hoped that his wife would be the president of this new republic, but the ungrateful sisters did not acquiesce and his wife too refused. Disappointed, Bipin returned to his village and took up agriculture. After these first two pages, Bipin does not appear in the text, there are no direct references to *Bharata Uddhara*, only tangential connections, linked by general discussions regarding the ideas of democracy, republicanism, welfare, and community. Another oblique reference within the text is to *Panchananda*, the sobriquet used by

---

[19] Himani Bannerji, 'Projects of Hegemony: Towards a Critique of Subaltern Studies' "Resolution of the Women's Question"', *Economic and Political Weekly* 35, no. 11 (11 March 2000), 902–20.

[20] Anon, *Meye Parliament ba Dwitya Bhag Bharata Uddhara* (Calcutta: Bangabashi Press, 1886).

Indranath for the bulk and most sustained of his writings in *Sadharani* and later in *Bangabashi*. The narrator is commenting on the supply of missionaries for 'civilizing' *Bachanabartta* to be sent from India, and wondering about the possibility of Panchananda visiting this novel land under that guise.[21]

The text is not constructed as a linear narrative, but as a collection of snapshots from discussions of specific issues in the parliament and associated committees. The author gives a quick sketch of some basic elements of this novel polity, the narrator being projected as an observer reporting on six of the sessions of the parliament. Each theme is organized as a session of the parliament; the debates focused on some contemporary social issues. These discussions can be divided under two broad themes: first, those related directly to the women's questions, such as reproduction, domesticity, and prostitution, and second, a set of questions around equality, class and caste divisions, welfare and the role of the community. I will discuss the first in greater detail and then touch upon some of the other arguments.

Before I embark on a thematic discussion, let me mention some striking features of the text. The women remained recognizably women: they were not at all masculinized or 'mannish'. In fact they were characterized by an excess of femininity in dress and speech; and they were exposed as ignorant, uneducated, shallow, and quarrelsome. The women's raiment was described at some length: some wore saris, some wore long skirts or gowns, most of them wore socks and shoes, most of them wore elaborate hairdos and some headgear; all of them were heavily ornamented. The referent was the movement for women's dress reform. The contrast was clearly drawn: 'There was no Hindu visible in the crowd except one, wearing white conch bangles and the vermillion in her parting, with bare body and bare feet....'[22] The reference to 'bare body' was not meant to be taken literally—it implied that the sari had been worn without a 'blouse' or 'jacket'. In a curious inversion of morality, bareness of women's upper body as a symbol of cultural tradition acquired a special virtue and by contrast, covering the body with elaborate upper garments, appeared more sexualized by its association with dress reform, women's public appearance, and 'western' mode of women's dress.[23]

---

[21] Ibid., 15.

[22] Ibid., 5.

[23] Himani Bannerji, 'Textile Prison: The Discourse of Shame (Lajja) in the Attire of the Gentlewoman (Bhadramahila) in Colonial Bengal', *The Canadian Journal of Sociology/ Cahiers canadiens de sociologie* 19, no. 2 (1994): 169–93.

Another counterpoint appeared in elaborate length in the text. As part of the civilizing mission of the new republic, the women proposed a comprehensive dress reform for men: 'The brothers are dressed indecently; often they expose their bodies and legs and appear like naked....'[24] The reforms suggested were to abolish all facial hair including the eyebrows, to shave the men's heads and force them to wear caps sewn by the women, to allow only a sack-like garment, and to introduce an accessory fashioned as a tail. This, the sisters concluded, would keep the men in their place. But consensus could not be reached. Some of the members baulked at such a mutilation of their own men—husbands, sons, and grandsons—and resisted the move. The proponent of this reform, a famous barrister, defeated in the House, wiped her tears and left, swearing to set up a dress reform association.[25]

The 1870s and 1880s witnessed a highly controversial current of women's dress reform. Deeming the traditional style of donning only a thin sari inappropriate for public wear, women who wished to appear in public, began to include blouses and petticoats adapted to the sari. Brahmo women led the way, Jnanadanandini Debi (wife of Satyendranath Tagore, ICS) is credited with the first innovations. After she travelled to Ahmedabad with her husband, she was said to have re-innovated the sari borrowing from the more decorous Parsi style. These innovations raised a storm in orthodox circles as not only was this 'westernization', its purpose was heinous, it augured a breach of segregation and women's entry into public spaces.

The so-called *purdah* system was at the centre of the 'women's question' in the nineteenth century.[26] Spatial segregation and distinct gender roles were inscribed within the ideology of *purdah*. Towards the later nineteenth century, however, some among the cultural nationalists began to distance themselves from the *purdah system*, arguing that *abarodh pratha*, as it was also called, was not part of classical Hindu tradition, but a later distortion introduced after the invasion of the Muslims. The ideology of women's seclusion and segregation were present in both Hindu and Muslim societies, though there were enormous variations in practice across classes, castes, and regions. In *Meye Parliament, purdah*

---

[24] Anon, Meye Parliament, 44.

[25] Ibid., 45–46.

[26] Dagmar Engels, *Beyond Purdah? Women in Bengal 1890–1930* (New Delhi: Oxford University Press, 1996).

was reversed. When the men rebelled against the onerous conditions of their subjection, explained the narrator, they were placed in confinement. 'From then on the brothers were *pardanashin*. It was said that when they had succeeded in proving themselves they would again be set at liberty.'[27] Does the author mean to imply that women were placed in segregation and seclusion as a check against rebelliousness? It appears at first sight that by the usual inverted logic used throughout the text, the author is critical of the argument that women have to be instructed and educated and released from *purdah* rules.

This passage invites comparison with the famous feminist utopia, *Sultana's Dream*, written by Begum Rokeya Sakhawat Hossain (first published in 1904).[28] She uses the same devise of a reversal of *purdah* to a completely different purpose. The male confinement is called *mardana* (a term usually used to denote manliness/masculinity) and is the solution to the problem of aggressive masculinity. In Ladyland, the utopia ruled by women, men are kept confined so that women may inhabit the public domain in safety: '[Y]ou do not think it wise to keep sane people inside an asylum and let loose the insane?' The resident of Ladyland asked the Sultana. In Rokeya's imagination, the removal of the men created harmony, productivity, and social order. In *Meye Parliament,* the confinement of men was intended as a dark warning against women's lust for power. In Rokeya's vision, women freed from subordination were capable of creating social order, indeed a better social order built on peace, preservation, and benevolence. In *Meye Parliament*, the condition of women's subordination was the key to social order.

In the nineteenth century, wrote Sumanta Banerjee,[29] the middle classes began to move away from an earlier amorphous urban culture and began to shape a distinctive language and culture of their own. This *bhadralok* literary project involved, at first, a distancing not only from the plebian culture of the city but also a designated 'women's' language and culture. Bandopadhyay suggests that women may have participated for longer in the shared culture of the city. The project to incorporate women into the middle class, to fashion the *bhadramahila* through appropriate education, became part of the social reform project of late nineteenth

---

[27] Anon, *Meye Parliament*, 16.

[28] Bagchi, *Sultana's Dream and Padmarag*.

[29] Sumanta Banerjee, *The Parlour and the Streets: Elite and Popular Culture in Nineteenth Century Calcutta* (Calcutta: Seagull Books, 1989).

century. At the same time, 'women', writes Anindita Ghosh, 'were convenient props' to build the image of a refined and educated middle-class culture.[30] The project assumed a separate sphere of women's language and culture to which Reverend James Long lent intellectual credence by collecting proverbs and idioms supposedly used by women in their daily speech.[31] This *meyeli bhasa* was actually a shared domestic speech system. Towards the later nineteenth century, as middle-class men identified more with a 'polite' culture, domestic speech became associated with women, particularly uneducated women. The *bhadralok* placed strict limits to culture and knowledge, stereotyping and stigmatizing whole bodies of their previous shared world as 'women's'.

In *Meye Parliament* we see a sharp distinction between *meyeli bhasa* used by most of the women, except a few specifically marked as 'highly educated' or professional. The latter used formal speech, which was also used by the narrator. The others shared the domestic speech system, across class and caste divide. Thus, a sharp distinction was drawn between *meyeli* and formal language.[32]

The strategy of deliberate feminization included the depiction of women members quarrelling over trivial issues, grabbing each other's hair, pushing, and shoving. Describing how the second session ended up in chaos: 'Like the unbridled energy of steam cannot be confined, it bursts out of the boiler, thus the members engaged in rushing, slapping, kicking, punching, pulling hair...'.[33] This scene was preceded by one member, Joymani, taking the Marshall by her hair and finally the Marshall dragging the offender out of the House.[34] There were long accounts of heated exchanges and confrontations that sought to underline the 'womanliness' of the women rulers and the absurdity of their ambition to rule.

---

[30] Ghosh, *Power in Print*, 225.

[31] Ibid., 226, footnote 3.

[32] *Meyeli bhasa* was represented with the predominance of abbreviations, regional dialects (*hala* instead of *shala*, lit. brother-in-law, used abusively—Anon, *Meye Parliament*, 19), the use of expressive words (*shait shait* as a variation of *shaat shaat*, bless you—Ibid., 11; 'mor'—die, used repeatedly—Ibid., 17, 19), abuses (like *porarmukhi*, burnt face; *shotek khoarira*, losers of hundred husbands, etc.—Ibid., 19), and distortion of sanskritic (*tatsama*) words (one early example: *amangule*, harbinger of ill luck, Ibid., 11).

[33] Anon, *Meye Parliament*, 20.

[34] Ibid., 19.

The Women's Question

Tanika Sarkar has argued in *Hindu Wife, Hindu Nation* that the late nineteenth century witnessed a shift in the women's question. As the social reform debate led increasingly to the problematization of the conjugal relationship as unequal and undemocratic, characterized by physical and emotional violence, nationalism sought a more benign template of gender relations in the mother–son relationship. Thus, it was through the image of the woman as mother that nationalism sought to resolve the most troubling of the women's questions.[35] *Meye Parliament*, written in the 1880s, was still concerned with questions of conjugality. It was in fact the central concern. Questions of marriage systems, women's rights and duties within them, and the whole domain of reproduction (for instance, childbearing and housework) were addressed.

The text portrayed a reversal of gender equations in the polity and in the wider social sphere: this was not a land of women, but one ruled by women in which men were suppressed and subordinated. Three major elements of this reversal were treated at some length in the text. The first opening salvo was directed at the most distinctive aspect of the construction of femininity, childbearing. Seen to be embedded in an irreversible natural order, the questioning of women's role in childbirth was an assertion of the illegitimacy and, even more, the impossibility of gender reversal. The issue was first raised in the context of the absence of the President from the House, who was introduced as the epitome of the transgressive woman. Smt. Monomohini Jola was born in a weaver's hut. Her father married her to a man of similar social standing. She grew up to be a beautiful young woman and left her husband for another man. Settling down in Calcutta, she began to attract other men around her (with a hint here that she set herself up as a prostitute) and became notorious in the city's social circles. When the House came to know that Monomohini was pregnant, some members began a debate over women's role in childbirth. Repeated use of the words, 'shame' and 'modesty', sought to highlight the social discomfort with the possibility of women engaged in such discussions. But the force of the argument lay elsewhere. 'Why', asked the Deputy President, 'have women alone had to bear the hateful

---

[35] Tanika Sarkar, *Hindu Wife, Hindu Nation: Community, Religion and Cultural Nationalism* (New Delhi: Permanent Black, 2000).

pains of labour?'[36] Further elaborated in the second session of the Parliament, the point was made that women's 'reproductive power' and the 'processes of childbirth' were determined by the evolutionary strategies of nature—*adi* or lying at the very inception of creation. There was no way to challenge such an order of nature. What then could the sisters do? They petitioned God, that childbearing be reallocated to men, or at least, be distributed between men and women.[37] These sisters, however, did not believe in God (*Ishwar*). God is a man, they said. They wished to rechristen God with a sisterly name. After much floundering, they call him *bhagnipati* (sister's husband) and then struck by the dominance of the word 'pati' (husband or lord) in the name, choose a vulgar appellation of the same relationship and decide to use the term *bonai*. The arguments are contradictory and unconvincing; if the women were set to challenge God as Man, why would they choose the appellation used for the *husband* of a sister? The author steered himself into an impasse; the denouement petered out tamely; and the chapter staggered to a halt. Whether there was any intention of lampooning the Brahmo or other religious reformers is not very clear from these ponderous passages, but the proximity with the question of childbirth suggests the attempt to interlink the 'natural', the 'spiritual', and the 'religious' into a defence of the Hindu gender order.

One of the thrusts in the text was a reversal of work roles. The women ran the country and the men looked after the household. In the fourth session of the parliament, questions of domesticity and conjugality were discussed. There was an informal conversation among the women before the House began. One woman said to another that she was tired of attending the House every evening, to which the addressee responded by asking, 'Why? I hope he does the cooking?' The first speaker replied:

> Dear sister, your question reminds me of something funny. My man is mostly quite settled, but from time to time he goes a bit haywire. He wants to return me to the confines of the home and get me to do the cooking and all the work.

The various members began to compare notes on their husbands. One said that she had just kept a new private secretary and that the earlier

---

[36] Anon, *Meye Parliament*, 11.

[37] Ibid., 35.

one had tried to prevent her doing so. She got her security women to throw him out, since, important members of the House that they were, how could they manage with only one private secretary? A sixth member responded: 'Whether you call him private secretary or head-of-the-house brother, my man is very good.' Clearly, private secretary was a euphemism for husband/sexual partner and a change of private secretaries implied a change in sexual partners. The right to have more than one private secretary was akin to polyandry and a blatant abrogation of the monogamous ideal, increasingly being promoted as the peculiar virtue of Hindu women and the marker of Hindu superiority. Meanwhile, the sixth member described her 'good' man: 'He cooks and cleans happily, does embroidery, is obedient, works silently and with dedicated attention.'[38] The first member spoke up again to spew an 'old-fashioned' superstition: 'Sisters, I do not understand you. After all, these are our husbands. Does it look good that you treat them in this fashion?'[39] The other women laughed and dismissed her with the pious thought that since the men were under their superintendence, they had a duty to ensure their salvation; they deserved and would benefit from the ill-treatment women meted out. Tanika Sarkar emphasizes that towards the late nineteenth century, the focus had shifted from love and equity to pain and discipline in conjugal relations.[40] Was this female justification of punitive treatment, a convoluted defence of wifely subservience even when it involved ill-treatment, pain, and torture?

The argument was then opened out to wider familial questions. One of the major issues of discussion at the time was the ideal of the joint family and conflict among women was being blamed for the increasing nuclearization of families. This was at times expressed in terms of an undesirable focus on the conjugal relationship (the husband-and-wife unit) at the cost of generational obligations, especially filial obligations that were so central to ownership and inheritance of property in Hindu law. Women, theoretically extraneous to but actually participants in distribution of resources, were seen as pivotal to the maintenance of the Hindu family system. This theme was explored in some detail in the text. One member described how she had thrown out her old father-in-law and mother-in-law. Another capped this story by saying that she had thrown

---

[38] Ibid., 31.
[39] Ibid., 32.
[40] Sarkar, *Hindu Wife, Hindu Nation.*

out her husband along with his parents. Another member placed this in the context of 'Population Theory': Those feckless men who were unable to provide for the pleasures of their mistresses were parasites and ought to be eliminated from society. In this heavy satirical vein, the author under-lined the dangers of the New Women's rejection of familial authority. These passages, replete with condemnation of women seeking educa-tion and entry into the new professions, were shot with anxiety about educated-male unemployment and the threat of women emerging as com-petitors. In *Bharata Uddhara*, Bipin, we must not forget, was propelled upon his odyssey by the loss of a job. In 1886, the year this tract was published, Kadambini Basu graduated from Bengal Medical College, and proceeded to practice as a doctor. Women, who were able to access higher education, found, against many odds, jobs as teachers and in other educated/caring professions. Thus, the fear of role reversal had a founda-tion in the anxieties of educated middle-class men, challenged on eco-nomic as well as social and political fronts.[41]

Let us return to the issue of monogamy. Debates over the Hindu mar-riage system began in the 1850s in relation to widow remarriage. The emphatic assertion of the ideal of women's chastity and the sacramental marriage as an irrevocable bond even beyond death brought to the centre stage the discriminatory imposition of monogamy on women in Hindu custom. The reform in marriage law proposed by the Brahmos in 1868 and passed in a much diluted form in 1872 lent an acrimonious edge to these debates, also fuelled by challenges to women's monogamous obli-gations in the case of non-consensual infant marriages. The Rukmabai case, which began in 1884, raised the pitch in the anti-reform lobby. To accept that married women could choose to exit sacramental Hindu marriage seemed to many a step towards the abrogation of marriage and sexual anarchy. The Special Regulation in the Pleasure Equality Laws proposed by the women's parliament was a dystopic vision of such an eventuality.

> The race of brothers is a pleasurable commodity for consumption. From now on women will not be allowed to keep young or old men—as secretary or husband, however they wish to style their men—according to their individual will. The brothers will be classified according to their age and beauty and according to the sections of sisters, they will be distributed in lots. Sisters, according to which section they belong, will receive in respective sequence

---

[41] Ibid., 7–20.

young, middle aged and old men, and thus will have the opportunity of having under their control all types of brothers....This will eliminate the tedium of familiarity and will contribute to variety....[42]

The narrator applauded this system as the fruition not only of modern utility theory but of the ancient republic of Plato. The message rang through every line: To grant women freedom of choice in marriage was to invite the very demise of the marriage system and the family. Female power and liberty would lead inevitably to the rejection of female chastity and an assertion of female promiscuity, destroying the sexual and reproductive economy of Hindu society. The author's position confirms Tanika Sakar's argument that the 'willed subjection' of the woman and her disciplining into its pain and violence was seen as the cornerstone of the Hindu social order.[43]

As a last vignette, the author sketched the terrible consequence of this women-ruled land—a prostitute colony in the outskirts of the city with men as service providers and women as clients. The description covers about seven pages.[44] First, he described the well-addressed and ornamented young men engaged in public in crimping and styling, strikingly similar to descriptions of women soliciting in the 'red light' districts of the city. Second, he emphasized the wealth and ostentation visible in the area coupled with an excess of security measures. It seemed as though 'sisters of the lower order dressed as brothers were standing guard'. Third, he described the hostility and jealousy he encountered when he approached the men for help, having lost his way in the colony. The author's appeal to Hindu *shastric* injunction to give alms was treated with derision and contempt. Finally, he sketched in brief both a set of female reformers who entered the colony to preach temperance and a group of women clients (including the members of parliament): 'well-dressed young sisters flocked to the streets under cover of blankets.... The well-dressed young men grabbed the ends of their garments inviting them to their houses.' He used the word 'fallen' in masculine gender (*patito*) to describe the men, echoing his contemporaries' increasing use of the feminine gender of the noun (*patita*) to describe prostitutes. These descriptions are laden with contempt and condemnation, not

---

[42] Anon, *Meye Parliament*, 55.

[43] Sarkar, *Hindu Wife, Hindu Nation.*

[44] Anon, *Meye Parliament*, 58–65.

so much against prostitution itself (given that the reformers are also cari-
catured harshly), but against the emasculation of those seeking sexual
and financial favours from women.

The Equality Question

Bharata Uddhara was a response to the formation of the Indian Association. *Meye Parliament*, though not so obviously aimed at the Congress
founded a year before its writing, raised a number of similar political
issues. It is now well known that the rebellions of 1857 had not mobil-
ized the urban middle classes of Calcutta. It was only in the 1860s that
a current of protest against colonial policies began. However, while one
group of the *bhadralok* engaged in the new politics of protest, others
continued to count the benefits of colonial rule. Within these contestations, questions of equality, republicanism, and democracy were being
debated. Related to these were issues of 'the market', given the increasing commercialization of agriculture. It is in this context that we may
read the political commentary in *Meye Parliament*.

It is hardly surprising that the Parliament was closely modelled on
the British parliament. Elaborate descriptions of the layout of the House
itself, the posts, and the procedures emphasized the similarity. Given that
the Congress followed in these footsteps, the mimicry may have been
aimed at this organization, which was yet to find any form or identity of
its own. In underlining these similarities, however, the author intended also
to highlight the *dis*similarities. The intention may have been similar to
those in *Bharata Uddhara*, to highlight the inadequacy of the Indian elite
and the inapplicability of British political systems to Indian conditions.

A fracas breaking out in the parliament has been described above:
Starting with a scuffle between the Marshall and Joymani, the session
degenerated into a general melee. The comment is delivered through a
male observer in 'the gallery':

> Brother, perhaps you do not have parliament in your country? Anyway, have
> you heard of debating? This is debating, albeit of a higher variety.... Field
> Marshall *Padir Ma* of the Liberal Party and Joymani of the Conservative
> Party are the best debators in *Bachanabartta*....[45]

---

[45] Ibid., 20.

In long passages of the text, not only were the procedures of democracy ridiculed, but also substantial questions of equality were pilloried. The peg on which much the debates were hung was a petition from Smt. Titumoni Dosad (low caste) against Smt. Harishankari Gangopadhyay (Brahmin), alleging that the latter accumulated fame and wealth as a writer of mysteries. This violated the principle of 'liberty, equality and sorority (sisterhood)',[46] clearly invoking the slogan of the French Revolution, and said to be enshrined in the constitution of the new Republic. This led, eventually, in the sixth session, to a discussion on equality and welfare. These passages could be read as anti-utopian, especially since an explicit contrast was drawn between a putative Hindu ideology and the new tenets of the West. In Hindu practice, welfare involved charity— to provide food for the hungry or to extend aid to those in need. The author invoked this notion of simple and commonsense welfare to contrast with the Utilitarian principles of Mill and Bentham being debated in contemporary educated circles of Calcutta. There is no depth in these discussions, but a quick dismissal of the principles of maximization of benefit and equalizing of individual good. The arithmetic approach to 'happiness' (greatest good of greatest number, good being translated as *sukh*, more akin to happiness) was subjected to derision and mirth by extending it to eliminate all difference, including emotions such as hatred and jealousy. There was a quick elision of inequality and difference in the text. 'As far as I understand the meaning of utility', said one member, 'the purpose is to distribute happiness equally among all members of the society'.[47] This could only be achieved if emotional satisfaction and contentment (as well as material goods) could be distributed equally among all, she argued. Therefore, equality in actual conditions of living, not just of opportunity had to be achieved. This stretching of the equality argument to the demonstrably absurd was a convoluted defence of caste hierarchy.

The inequalities of caste were elaborated in various sections of the text. Sumit Sarkar has pointed out that in the 'Kaliyuga' literature, the social elevation of Shudras and low castes and the correspondent decline of Brahminical power and influence was an important trope. The reversal of the caste order was an emotive symbol of a world turned upside down. In the case of Bengal, he points out, the domination of upper castes within

---

[46] Ibid., 48.
[47] Ibid., 52.

the new urban middle classes meant that caste inequality did not have quite such immediacy.[48] Anindita Ghosh shows that in the publishing industry, however, there was a gradual incursion and at the lower ends of the market, a domination of lower castes. In the *battala* literature at least, caste contestations acquired a special edge.[49]

The issue was first raised in the context of social reform. In response to a long speech by the Prime Minister detailing the reversal of Hindu social customs (focusing on the Special Marriage Act and the reversal of gender roles), one conservative member interjected, 'Why are the rascal (*tikidar*) Brahmins going around delivering speeches?' At the third session of the Parliament, a Conservative member, Rammoni Chang pointed out that the rascal Brahmins had invented God to deceive people and earn a living and that Brahmin domination remained in the Republic of Sisters, since there were many Brahmin ministers. In response, Colonel Chandimani Ganguly (a Brahmin) made a disparaging comment on Rammoni's caste: The Chandal (untouchable caste), she said, was overreaching herself. This altercation led to a heated debate. 'Why not?' Rammoni said, 'I am human, so are you. We are made by the same god....'[50] These debates followed fairly predictable lines and the purpose was to highlight the absurdity of asserting equality across castes. The message is that caste hierarchy is inevitable even 'natural' given the enormous differences in education, social conditioning and natural attributes. These arguments were placed within the context of the women's parliament, but were not specific to women, that is to say, women's specific relationship to caste was not addressed.

In the next passages, however, we see an attempt to think through caste, class, and gender. The author invoked the equation between lower orders and women's culture illustrated in the notion of a *meyeli bhasa* discussed previously. The gender divide was drawn, not only in terms of language but across a wider cultural universe including, for instance, religion. The women challenge the high brahminical precepts of Hinduism, showing no understanding of the weighty issues of spiritual debate. In a long speech, Soudamini Basu attempted to disprove the non-existence of God by quoting not only from Physics, but also History, Algebra, Shakespeare, and Lethbridge. The citation of spurious authorities in English in

---

[48] Sarkar, *Hindu Wife, Hindu Nation*.
[49] Ghosh, *Power in Print*.
[50] Anon, *Meye Parliament*, 24.

parentheses was both a dig at neo-literate women as well as the style of new Western academic scholarship. The women, however, in their own domain—that of reproduction—demonstrated a shared belief in folk deities. Thus, Goddess *Sashthi*, presiding over childbirth and the welfare of children, commanded a discomfort with debate. Women across castes were easily silenced by the invocation of this popular deity, being unable to challenge the powerful force of their own habits of daily worship.[51]

Writing in 1886, the author may not have lived to witness the Salt Satyagraha led by Mahatma Gandhi, but the reader with the benefit of such foresight will appreciate the irony of the fifth session being organized around a new salt tax. The raising of tax on salt led, it was argued in the House, to great misery among common people. The rebuttal was in the usual farcical vein: drawing on a popular and feudal symbolism that associated the partaking of salt with loyalty, Liberals argued that the salt tax had actually helped to stimulate economic development. The issue was, however, stretched to deliver a comment on monetization—'money is a terrible thing' and the 'root of all evil'. And yet, money had to be retained in the hands of the rulers, the women, and was not to be given to men, the subjects. A line was drawn between money, arms, and war. Just as men could not be trusted with money, they could not be trusted with weapons. The rulers, women, who controlled both, were planning to go to war against a neighbouring country, which was not willing to export on the terms the new Republic wanted.[52] The relationship between trade, war, and conquest was an already established understanding of British colonialism, even at the popular level.

Conclusion

The reading of *Meye Parliament* is complicated by the uncertainty of its authorship. However, since it partakes of the elements of many other tracts of same period, we have the option of a historical reading. The text shares, in explicit overtones, the dystopic paradigm of *Kaliyuga* literature. The persistence of this dystopic paradigm is without a synchronous utopian vision unless we posit the notion of a golden age of ancient India, being constructed in this period. One of the chief features of the 'golden

---

[51] Ibid., 25.
[52] Ibid., 39–41.

9

'Empire Builder'

A Utopian Alernative to Citizenship for Early-twentieth-century British 'Ladies'

Martine Spensky

'A utopia is an imaginative account of a perfect society or ideal commonwealth', 'the vision of an alternative society from which present social evils have been eradicated and in which there is complete human fulfilment and well-being through the attainment of perfect justice, freedom, equality and/or other ideals formulated by the Utopia's author'.[1] Sociologist Karl Mannheim, in his book *Ideology and Utopia*, translated into English in 1936, was the first, according to Paul Ricoeur (1986), to analyse ideology and utopia in the same conceptual frame. Paul Ricoeur followed his steps in the *Lectures on Ideology and Utopia* which he gave at the Columbia University, and which were published in 1986. In them, he critically revisits the work of past authors who have dealt with ideology, on the one hand, and utopia, on the other. The link he sees between the two concepts is that they both refer to power and legitimacy: the function of ideology being that of legitimizing power while the function of utopia is that of questioning such legitimacy. The idea that utopia is a 'noplace' is important for Ricoeur because 'extra-territoriality' makes it possible to look at society as it is in a critical way, from the outside. One more link between the two concepts, and this is Ricoeur's hypothesis, it is that both are an example of 'social and

---

[1] Keith Taylor, *Oxford Dictionary of Politics* (Oxford: Oxford University Press, 1996).

cultural imagination'.[2] According to Mannheim, the first to link ideology and utopia, subordinate groups tend to be attracted by utopianism because it emphasizes the possibilities of change, whereas dominant groups want things to stay the way they are and are attracted by ideologies of stability and continuity.

I will look at my main source, the *Imperial Colonist*,[3] from these premises. The *Imperial Colonist* is a women's review—made by women for women—which first appeared on 1 January 1901, with the main object of encouraging the emigration of British women 'of the right sort', that is, 'respectable' women, to the colonies. It is the official organ of the British Women's Emigration Society (BWEA), created in 1884 and of the South African Colonisation Society (SACS or SAX), which sprang from it in 1900 before it split in 1903 to lead its own life. The BWEA is the granddaughter association of the British Ladies Female Emigration Society (BLFES), founded in 1849, and of the Female Middle Class Emigration Society (FMCES), founded in 1862. Both grandmother associations were openly liberal and feminist. The FMCES was housed in the same building as the *English Woman's Journal*, the first feminist British journal founded in 1858 and published by the Langham Place circle of feminists—which included, amongst others, Barbara Leigh Smith (Bodichon), Julia Blake, Emily Faithful (who printed it), Matilda Hays, and Bessie Rayner Parkes, who were its editors. Many articles of the review deal with women's employment. Emigration is seen by them as a source of openings for educated women who had difficulties finding employment in Britain. The journal advertised for the FMCES. It also advertised for the Society for the Employment of Women as well as the National Association for the Promotion of Social Science, which were housed in the same building. These associations were in favour of women's education and of the right, for educated women, to enter the 'professions'.

In 1884, the various existing societies for the emigration of women merged to form the United English Women's Emigration Society and, when in 1888, the Irish and Welsh branches joined the numerous English branches already existing, they changed their name again to United British Women's Emigration Society and then to British Women's Emigration Association. The *Imperial Colonist* published the annual reports of both associations as well as interviews or articles of famous imperialists,

---

[2] Paul Ricoeur, *L'idéologie et l'Utopie*, first published in 1986 (Paris: Seuil, 1997), 17.

[3] *The Imperial Colonist* 1, no. 1 (January 1901 to 1913).

letters and articles from women already living overseas, information about the various self-governing countries of the Empire, about branches of both associations scattered throughout Britain, publicity for imperial training colleges for women, advertisements for jobs abroad, about 'imperial' meetings, book reviews, and so on. Ellen Joyce, an Anglican Minister's widow and a Minister's mother, had been the president of the BWEA since 1884. She is one of the most influential members of the Girl's Friendly Society (GFS) and belongs to other philanthropic societies which catered to women. Lady Knightley of Fawsley was an aristocrat, the widow of a conservative Member of Parliament (MP). She was both the president of SAX and the editor of the *Imperial Colonist*, which bore her mark from its first issue in 1901 to her death in 1913. Lady Knightley of Fawsley is an interesting character. She was born in 1842 and started writing her diary in 1856, which she continued until she died.[4] She was also very active in a number of women's philanthropic organizations, including the GFS, was a member of the Primrose League, and had been a strong supporter of women's suffrage at least since 1867. Eighteen sixty seven is the year in which the Second Parliamentary Reform was voted. It was preceded by a lot of agitation from those groups, excluded from the franchise by the 1832 Parliamentary Reform, who hoped to be included in the body politics; the women's movement was one of them.[5] Lady Knightley signed Millicent Fawcett's petition in favour of women's suffrage which was published in *Nineteenth Century* in June 1889. The statement accompanying Mrs Fawcett's petition was that women needed the vote, not because they were the same as men but because they were different from them, and 'being different, that wherein they differ remains unrepresented',[6] a statement, which, without a doubt, Louisa Knightley of Fawsley, together with Ellen Joyce, would have agreed with, even though the latter was not a suffragist. Louisa Knightley was a member of the NUWSS and became the First President of the Conservative and Unionist Women's Franchise Association (CU-WFA) in December 1908, the same year the suffragettes started their militant strategy, which she strongly opposed. This was also the year

---

[4] Peter Gordon, *Diaries of Lady Knightley of Fawsley*, 1885–1913 (London: Northampton, 1999).

[5] June Purvis and Sandra Stanley Holton, *Votes for Women* (London and New York: Routledge, 2000).

[6] Fawcett, 'Women and Suffrage: A Reply', *Fortnightly Review,* 46, no. 210 (July 1889), 125, cited in Gordon (1999: 16).

in which the *National League Opposing Women's Suffrage* was created, together with its journal *The Anti Suffrage Review*;[7] their views were more in line with the bulk of the Conservatives, even though an important number of the articles they published were written by Liberals. The period during which Louisa Knightley of Fawsley was both the president of the Sax and editor of the *Imperial Colonist* runs parallel to that during which the women's movement was in its most active phase, especially after 1905, when the Liberal government came into power, but which, contrarily to the expectations of the majority of women's organizations, did not grant women the vote.

The 'utopia' of those women who write in the *Imperial Colonist*, and who belonged both to a subordinate group in their own class as women and nonetheless to the dominant group as upper-class and upper-middle-class individuals, is that of an 'ideal England', transplanted somewhere else, a very tight community of blood and culture in which all individuals—of British stock—share a common 'citizenship'. It is a better place, in their mind, than the original one; a good place, not a no-place or a nowhere, but an 'elsewhere'. In this 'elsewhere', men and women are 'more equal' than they are in the mother country. They have different occupations but they work side by side for a common goal: the building of the Empire, and respect each other. Marriage is seen as a partnership of equal individuals working for the common good of the family which coincides with the good of society as a whole and the consolidation of the Empire. Class relations are preserved and the female emigrants travel on board ships providing their customers with different classes—women 'colonists' usually travel second or third class—under the gaze of a different matron. However, in their 'elsewhere' of destination, class relations run more smoothly than they do in Britain; they are much less segregated and social intercourse between the various classes of white Britons are much less formal than they are 'at home'. Race, on the other hand, often endorses the role class still played in England, but for its—not completely mythical—possible upward mobility. Indeed, 'the natives' of their utopia will have the same function as the slaves in Thomas

---

[7] Brian Harrisson, *Separate Spheres: The Opposition to Women's Suffrage in Britain* (Londres: Croom Helm, 1978); Martine Spensky, 'Universalisme des hommes, particularisme des femmes: la légitimation de l'exclusion des sphères du pouvoir', in Martine Spensky, ed. *Universalisme, particularisme et citoyenneté dans les Iles britanniques* (Paris: l'Harmattan, 2000), 127–55. Julia Bush, *Women against the Vote* (New York: Oxford University Press, 2007).

More's *Utopia*, at least as far as the type of work they do. However, his was a slavery based on negative 'merit', a punishment, while the natives have not done anything to deserve their relegation. If they do not deserve a better treatment, it is not because of what they have done but because of what they are; contrarily to the 'British race', they simply are not supposed to belong to a race of freedom-lovers.

What is interesting in the discourse of the *Imperial Colonist* is that both 'utopia' and 'ideology' seem to co-exit: Utopia concerns the transplanted British society of idealized free individuals who are equal 'citizens of the Empire'—despite the existence of different social classes and the absence of enfranchisement for women—while ideology is omnipresent. It serves, at the same time, to cement the 'Imperial citizens' together and to maintain the Aboriginal people outside the realm of the citizenry. It is this intersection of social relations, whereby some will be promoted while others are being downgraded, thanks to the imperial ideology of white supremacy these women endorse, which I intend to look at.

I will argue that both women's emigration societies, whose voice was the *Imperial Colonist*, present prospective emigrants with an alternative to citizenship which is, at the same time, an alternative citizenship. They won't enjoy the vote—unless they emigrate to Australia or New Zealand where women are enfranchised—but they will enjoy some important civil rights which they did not enjoy in Britain. (The main destination of women emigrating through the BWEA was Canada—and to a much lesser extent, Australia and New Zealand—while the SACS only emigrated women to South Africa.) Not only will they find work, which is one of the basic rights of the citizen who owns no property, but by becoming 'Empire builders', that is, social actors in the shaping of the biggest Empire ever, they will impact the destiny of millions of British Subjects. This is not only true of the women 'emigrators' themselves but also, to a lesser extent, of the women who are being emigrated, as the language used by the former to encourage the latter to emigrate constantly puts the 'Empire building' as the primary common goal pursued by all. It is a political goal. If the word 'citizen' appears recurrently in the journal, it bears no legal meaning. (According to Anne Dummett [1994], 'citizenship' had no legal meaning until 1981.[8]) At the time, all British people

---

[8] Anne Dummett, 'The Acquisition of British Citizenship: From Imperial Traditions to National Definitions', in *From Alien to Citizen*, ed. Banböck Rainer (Avebury: European Centre Vienna, 1994).

are subject to the sovereign who symbolizes the state and under whose protection they are. The word 'citizen' often appears in the journal in the phrase 'citizen of the Empire'. It designates white people living under the Union Jack and seems to imply some degree of equality: a member of the same 'imagined community' founded on blood and a shared culture. In the rare instances when the natives are explicitly mentioned with reference to a 'political' status, especially as the First World is approaching, they are referred to as 'our fellow Subject' which is the closest they can ever become, that is, as loyal as 'we' are to the same sovereign. Loyalty does not make them part of the citizenry. 'Citizens of the Empire' are white, British, and 'useful member of their community'. It is their duty to put the good of the Empire above their own or better, to make it coincide with their own. Women and men do not have the same duties towards the Empire as many other authors have shown in the last few years.[9]

Systematic Colonization and Empire-building as Alternative Citizenship

The theory of 'systematic colonization' was elaborated by Edward Gibbon Wakefield,[10] at the beginning of the nineteenth century, even though this idea had existed for some time. It was influential, on and off, throughout the nineteenth century and was still very popular at the turn of the century even if the name of Wakefield is no longer attached to it. According to the latter, 'there are three objects which an old society would have in promoting colonisation, namely, the extension of the market for disposing of surplus produce, relief from excessive numbers, and an enlargement of the field for employing capital'.[11] Another reason for systematic colonization was to find an outlet for the upper fringe of the working class, the educated one, lest they were led to embrace

---

[9] Julia Bush, *Edwardian Ladies and Imperial Power* (Leicester, UK: Leicester University Press, 2000); Anna Davin, 'Imperialism and Motherhood', in *History Workshop Journal*, no. 5 (Spring 1978), 15; Daiva Stasiulis and Nira Yuval Davies, *Unsettling Settler Societies* (London: SAGE Publications, 1995); Catherine Hall, *White, Male and Middle Class*, part III (Cambridge: Polity Press, 1992); Clare Midgley, *Women Against Slavery: The British Campaigns 1780–1870* (London: Routledge, 1992).

[10] E.G. Wakefield, *A View of the Art of Colonization in Present Reference to the British Empire*, 1st edition, 1849 (New York: Augustus M. Kelley, 1969).

[11] Ibid., 94.

Chartism and socialism,[12] a threat to private property. According to Wakefield, 'systematic colonisation' would encourage the best elements of British society to emigrate so as to participate in the building of 'little Englands' around the world. His is also a racial theory. Indeed, these 'little Englands' would be populated with 'Anglo-Saxon' stock, a race supposed to have a great love for liberty, justice and to be law abiding; the colonists would consequently refuse to be governed from London and should be granted autonomy. This would benefit the mother country as the 'daughter colonies' would be loyal to her, her best customer, provider, and faithful protector, in case of conflict. (Wakefield wanted to find a way of preventing 'secession' as had previously happened with the American Revolution which had led to the creation of the United States of America, a rival industrial power. His ideas were very influential in the granting of autonomy to the 'white' colonies: Canada, Australia, and New Zealand. South Africa was also granted autonomy, which benefited the Boers. However, black Africans remained the majority of the population under their tight control.) Women are an important element of his plan as, beyond the biological issue of reproducing the population which is impossible without them, they have a primary role to play in setting the right tone of the colony and building 'English homes' wherever they were, the bridgehead of English culture. The other influential 'theory' of emigration in Britain, according to Carrothers,[13] was that of Malthus, even then a bit outdated. Malthus saw it as a cure, a blood-letting for the mother country that would rid her of her 'surplus' or unwanted elements: the unemployed, the poor, the criminals, and the vicious. It would sanitize both the labour market and society, at home. He was not very interested in what would happen to immigrants once transplanted, but he saw transplantation as a better means of using Poor Law money than investing in more workhouses. Wakefield was in favour of private emigration and loans to buy land rather than land gifts which he thought were a disincentive to work. It is clear that the two emigration societies whose reports are published in the *Imperial Colonist* have been influenced by Wakefield's ideas rather than Malthus', even though none of their names appear in the journal. According to Julia Bush, Ellen Joyce had been in favour of emigrating 'paupers' to the colonies in the earlier days of the BWEA, but had changed her mind later.

---

[12] Ibid., 67.

[13] W.A. Carrothers, *Emigration from the British Iles with Special Reference to the Overseas Dominions* (London: Frank Cass and Co, 1969) (first published in 1929).

The choice of the name of the journal tends to confirm this choice. It emphasizes the membership of those who emigrate, to the Imperial state, transforming their emigration into a political and patriotic act. Indeed if emigration is often a personal response to unbearable conditions at home, colonization, on the other hand, is organized emigration by a dominant group or by the state, to a dominated territory, to the advantage of the former—despite the fact that the British state tended to favour private emigration. Being a 'colonist', or better even, an *imperial* colonist, marked the would-be emigrants as having a special relationship to the British state (often referred to as English), whatever their personal reasons for leaving the UK. The women who ran the journal had no doubt about the public usefulness of what they considered their mission. They were moving out of the private sphere—women's legitimate sphere—but, while remaining under the British flag, they were still 'at home', blurring the frontiers between the public and the private. Moreover, there was no doubt for them that the Empire was as much a women's preserve as a man's, and this was rather subversive of gender relations. Nonetheless, as Lady Knightley of Fawsley wrote in its first issue: 'we hope to appeal to a very large public—no less a public than that which is interested in the great work of building up our Empire'. They were to be 'female' Empire builders, that is, to introduce the 'female side' to Empire building by transforming the Empire into a place where any English 'fellow citizen' would feel at home. 'English women make homes wherever they settle all the world over and are the real builders of Empires.'[14] This is the imperialistic side of 'cosmopolitanism': to feel at home wherever you are because you have transformed the Empire into 'a home from home', without having to transform yourself. This is why their work was supported by the most notorious imperialists of the day, be they conservative or liberal. Indeed, the meetings of both associations, which are reported in the journal, took place at the Imperial Office, the heart of the Empire, which made their work quasi-official. This was reinforced by the aristocratic patronage of emigration societies, especially at the level of their committees.[15]

The would-be colonist was made to feel that she was part of an elite, a messenger of the 'English way of life' and culture which it was her duty to export to less sophisticated shores. This feeling of superiority, the

---

[14] 'Items of Interest', unsigned, *Imperial Colonist*, 1, no. 6 (June 1902), 56.

[15] See Bush, *Edwardian Ladies and Imperial Power*, 18–56.

impression of belonging to an 'elite', was reinforced by the fact that both the BWEA and the SACS carefully selected the women they sent abroad, on the basis of their 'respectability', their physical fitness, and their adaptability. They were supposed to be the 'crème de la crème'. A quote by the Prince of Wales stands at the top of the front page of the first issue of the journal. It runs: 'I would appeal to my fellow-countrymen at home to prove the strength of the attachment of the Motherland to her children by sending them only of their best'[16] The children of the Motherland were her white colonies, that is, settlement colonies. The main destination of those catered for by the BWEA was Canada and, to a lesser extent, Australia and New Zealand. The SACS specialized in emigration to South Africa, which was just recovering from the second Boer war (1899–1902). Because of the context, it seems more inclined than the former association to use a 'patriotic' language in order to appeal to 'women of the right sort'. These were the words of General Baden-Powell, hero of the siege of Mafeking and future founder of the Scouts' Movement (in 1908) who had started six experimental farms in South Africa and wrote a letter to the editor of the journal saying how interested he was by the work of the SACS.[17] (Robert Stephenson Smyth, First Baron of Baden-Powell, had a military career in India, Afghanistan, and South Africa. He founded the Scout movement in 1908. The phrase 'The Right Sort of Women', which is a phrase he used, was taken up by Julia Bush as the title of an article.)

In the journal, the 'colonists' are encouraged to forget about the middle- and upper-class decorum that regulated women's lives 'at home' and put the good of the Empire above their own welfare. In the 1902 obituary on the death of Cecil Rhodes, presented as the greatest visionary imperialist of his times, a light that led the way, Mrs Lyttleton-Gell writes:

... women must bring of their best to the embodiment of his great ideal if his thought is to live. They must lay aside narrow ideas and bring to the work of colonisation an outlook wide as his own 'World's View'. They must slough off the pettiness of the past and rise to the height of Imperial womanhood.[18]

---

[16] George, Prince of Wales, *Imperial Colonist*, 1, no. 1 (1902), 1.
Margaret Amhurst, 'The Women Who Are Wanted in Canada', X, no. 121 (January 1912), 3.
[17] Meeting of the SAX Committee reported by the Lady Knightley of Fawsley, *Imperial Colonist*, 1, no. 6 (June 1902), 50–51.
[18] 'An Augmenter of Empire', obituary of Cecil Rhodes by Mrs Lyttleton Gell, *Imperial Colonist*, 1, no. 5 (May 1902), 1–2.

This model of heroic womanhood is rather alien to that of the soft 'Angel of the House' of the middle-class lady of the turn of the century, back home. The latter, said by 'evolutionist medicine' to need all her vital energy for biological reproduction, was expected to save it, rather than waste it in education, work or politics, let alone interest in imperialistic politics considered as man's preserve! And yet, not only was the Colonial 'lady' expected to work, but she was even expected to work particularly hard in a sometimes difficult environment. As an article written in the June 1912 issue ironically put it '… the woman who is wanted is she who can work, who can, as the saying goes, "put her hands to anything". She can be as ornamental as she likes, but she must, first-of-all, be useful.' A hard life is seen as adding value and strength to those who lived it rather than drawing on their 'vital energy'; 'softies' are not required. 'Citizenship', even alternative, has to be deserved. Post–Boer War South Africa was a good ground for women immigrants to 'serve' the Empire and prove their worth. Indeed, even though the Boer War had ended in 1902, in April 1905, concentration camps for Boer women and children still existed. An inspector of the camp schools in Transvaal is reported to have approached the SACS in despair as he thought he would not find any teacher for, what he called, 'one of the worst camps'. 'He was convinced', said Louisa Knightley,

> … that only the residuum of teachers would be drafted thither. I offered him the first chance of addressing the latest comers and advised him to paint the conditions of life in that camp in the blackest colours. He did so and then asked for volunteers. Four of the best and most refined teachers of this or any other contingent stepped out, and intimated that that was the work for which they had come to South Africa.[19]

This only proved to the editor that the selection had been made properly. Selection is the catch word. Even H.H. Asquith, who would become Chancellor of the Exchequer in the Liberal government in 1906 before he became Prime Minister in 1908 and is reported to have participated in the meeting of SACS for March 1902 (Balfour CPM), had 'strongly emphasised the importance of selection and preparation of the women who go out'.[20]

---

[19] The Lady Knightley of Fawsley, 'Education in South Africa', *Imperial Colonist*, IV, no. 40 (April 1905), 2.

[20] Meeting of the SAX Committee, Report by the Lady Knightley of Fawsley, *Imperial Colonist*, 1, no. 6 (June 1902), 50.

The preparation consisted, whenever possible, in a training course in one of the Colonial Training Homes advertised in the *Imperial Colonist*. There was one in Stoke Prior (Kent), which had been founded in 1890 and gave instruction in 'housework, plain cooking, dairy work and the care of poultry. Laundry work, simple dressmaking, and cutting out'. There was another one in Swanley (also in Kent) which taught the same things, plus 'bee-keeping ... fruit bottling, jam making ... hygiene, etc'.[21] The first training course lasted from three to six months and cost 17 shillings and 6 pence a week, including tuition, board and food. The second one lasted two years and cost 25 shillings a week, which was the equivalent of what an ordinary domestic servant could earn in Canada. The fees excluded the poorest women from colonial training. However, the selection operated by both emigration societies mainly operated on moral grounds; it also operated on 'racial' grounds with 'eugenic' overtones. Indeed, the time was still close when the political elite had realized with horror that the British population was in a very poor state. In 1899, at the outbreak of the Boer War, when the first volunteers had offered themselves for recruitment, 330 out of every 1,000 men had to be rejected because they were unfit for service: 'too small for instance, or too slight, or with heart troubles, weak lungs, rheumatic tendencies, flat feet or bad teeth'.[22] The concern for the quality of its population became an imperial priority. This concern for bio-politics appears clearly in the discourse of the Earl of Onslow who chaired the annual meeting of the SACS in 1905 and who declared that

All new young countries needed a population and it was essential that that population should be of the right kind and quality. The Association only sent out those who were fit for the work they were to undertake in South Africa, and the strongest and healthiest of the British Isles.[23]

At the other end, the white colonies, which were now autonomous dominions, refused to accept those the mother country was only too willing to get rid of. In its April editorial of 1905, the *Imperialist Colonist* reminded its readers,

---

[21] Colonial Training Home (Publicity), *Imperial Colonist*, VI, no. 82 (October 1908), 13.

[22] Anna Davin, 'Imperialism and Motherhood', 15.

[23] Unsigned in Annual meeting of the SACS Report, *Imperial Colonist*, IV, no. 43 (July 1905), 75.

Canada, Australia, New Zealand, Cape Colony and Natal each have statutes to restrict undesirable emigration, which chiefly refers to criminal or diseased, insane or destitute persons; and such are liable to be sent back to the port from which they sailed, the owner of the ship which brought them being liable to a fine of £100.[24]

The 'colonists', therefore, could feel that they were the best: the most respectable, the 'ablest, and the strongest'. The colonies, however, seem to have been much less concerned with the economic situation of female emigrants and those who were destitute would get a grant from the associations which they would reimburse during the first two years of their stay, thanks to their labour. Being destitute, for a woman does not say anything about her social origin, as the class position of women generally depends on that of the man they share their life with. Single women could be poor, whatever their class of origin. Some of the middle-class ones could even suffer from what the Bishop of London elegantly called 'genteel starvation'. As a matter of fact, as long as women were willing to accept a post as a domestic servant, whatever their social origin, they were warmly welcomed everywhere. Canada, however, seems to have absorbed most of the poorest women. A special fund for unemployed factory workers was started by the BWEA in November 1903 to 'help girls in poverty and distress from slackness of work during the winter, to go to Canada ... most girls thus sent out elected to go into domestic service, as the Canadian mistresses are willing to engage and to train inexperienced girls'.[25] Being trained by their mistress who worked along with them saved the working-class woman the cost of a Training College. Most working-class women came from London and manufacturing towns in the North of England. Industrial work was found for a few of them in Canada, but the majority were recruited as domestic servants, despite the 'increasing distaste for domestic service'[26] back home. The 'alternative citizenship', which I referred to before, is much less obvious in the discourse concerning those who go to Canada than it is for those who go to South Africa, Australia, or New Zealand, especially in times

---

[24] Unsigned, 'Rate and State Emigration', *Imperial Colonist*, IV, no. 42 (June 1905), 67.

[25] Unsigned, 'History of the Factory Workers' Fund', *Imperial Colonist*, IV, no. 46 (October 1905), 113.

[26] Lady Knightley of Fawsley, 'The Terms and Conditions of Domestic Service in England and South Africa, Plead read before the Economic Section of the British Association, Cape Town, August 1905', *Imperial Colonist*, IV, no. 48 (December 1905), 137.

of economic slump. Those who go to Canada generally seem to be in a more desperate situation. This appears clearly in the October issue for 1905, which appealed for help in the following words, 'in view of the distress foretold in the coming winter, and indeed already among our poor in the manufacturing centres, we appeal most earnestly for means to transplant many anxious bread-seekers to places where their work will be welcomed and well paid'.[27] This does not mean the association will forgo all selection. As Mrs. Joyce 'cautions' the audience in a paper she gave at the Conference on Unemployment which took place at the Imperial Institute in December 1908: 'it is not every unemployed woman we could accept, the applicants must be respectable, capable and healthy. It is no less than a crime to send women who have had a bad history to a daughter colony ... neither can we send the unemployable'. This discourse bears more resemblance to that of the philanthropist's 'our poor', than the 'heroic' addresses to the Spartan alternative 'citizen'. It is more concerned with rescuing individuals than with building the Empire, even though selecting 'the right sort of woman' has to do with Empire building and eventually with peopling it with 'citizens'. True, the latter did not have the right to vote, but she had the right to work and earn a fair wage, a right she did not enjoy in the mother country. The 'colonist' might even bear weapons, a very unwomanly item. The bearing of arms was indeed one of the symbols of citizenship in Ancient Rome, and the anti-suffragists generally alleged that women could not be granted parliamentary vote because Parliament made decisions about the Empire and the Empire was linked to war: it was acquired and maintained through violence and the citizen might have to defend it, while women were not meant to bear arms. However, one of the first teachers sent out to Rhodesia and who lived in the 'veld', wrote to the *Imperial Colonist* in 1908 that she was a member of the Lady Rifle's Club 'which teaches what is a most useful and fascinating sport, and which might in case of a rebellion be the means of saving many lives'.[28] The existence of a Lady Rifle Association shows that this attraction for weapons did not merely concern one isolated correspondent but a group of white women British colonists. If the female 'colonist' was prepared to save lives, she was

---

[27] Unsigned, 'History of the Factory Workers' Fund', *Imperial Colonist*, IV, no. 46 (October 1905), 113.

[28] 'Life in the Veld in Rhodesia', by 'one of the first teachers sent out to South Africa by the Education Committee SACS' (no name), dated 30 January 1908, *Imperial Colonist*, VI, no. 80 (August 1908), 6.

also prepared to take the lives of those who might jeopardize the project of little Englands which excluded them.

The Ideology of White Supremacy

A possible rebellion on the part of the 'natives' who were not included in the project remained a possibility in the African colonies where the white British remained a tiny minority. This had become very unlikely in Canada, Australia, or even New Zealand where the native population was more numerous. After a violent outburst in 1906, the August editorial remarked that 'the dread spectre of a general native rising still seems to hover around'[29] and that it did not concern South Africa alone. The relationship of the white middle-class women emigrants to the indigenous population, as it can be read in the *Imperialist Colonist*, was that of mistress to servant, 'maternalistic' and benevolent, in time of peace. The women employers seemed to be as amused by their black servants as they would have been with children: they commented on the way they dressed, danced, and played with—and liked—children. 'I find the natives are very kind and fond of children, although they are unreliable' wrote one lady in July 1908. Indeed, the Christian version of 'evolutionism' which runs through the articles and letters of the *Imperialist Colonist* is well summarized by the Bishop of London in his sermon of June 1908:

> God has made of one blood all nations [but] one nation is more forward than another in moral and spiritual education, as the grown son of a family is more forward than the child in the nursery, and can therefore be trusted with greater responsibility.[30]

The responsibility of the white man, or as Kipling would have put it 'the white man's burden' which, in the *Imperial Colonist* had become the 'white woman's burden', is to govern the coloured races for as long as they are in infancy, to lead them towards the light and set for them a good example. According to a piece of advice found in the Notes of the Month rubric,

---

[29] Unsigned, 'Notes of the Month', *Imperial Colonist*, V, no. 56 (August 1906), 30.

[30] From Bishop of London's Sermon in Westminster Abbey, 21 June 1908, *Imperial Colonist*, VI, no. 80 (August 1908), 1 (quoted in rubric 'Notes of the Month', unsigned, front page).

...without attempting equality, which is not yet possible, whatever it may be a few centuries hence, justice, kindness and sympathy should govern all the relations between the white and the coloured races, and above all, the white Christian should set an example to his coloured fellow subjects.[31]

There was a great shortage of white servants in South Africa and the colonists who lived in isolated farms employed African—generally male—servants. Some women colonists learn rudiments of their language so as to be able to give them more efficient orders: 'I speak enough Kaffir to make myself understood, having learnt a good deal from hearing Mr. S give orders to the boys'[32], wrote one lady (July 1908). The use of black servants in English 'homes', however, is recurrently disapproved of in various articles of the *Imperial Colonist* as it was thought to slow down colonization. The 'English home' was considered to be both the proof that England had reached a high degree of civilization and the means of reaching it. The presence of British women was considered of primary importance as it was instrumental in spreading 'little Englands'. Consequently, as Mr L.S. Almery said reproachfully at the meeting of June 1908, 'A country where the domestic duties of the household are performed by natives, where children are largely brought up in contact with the natives, is not a country that can be called a white man's country.' The role of the Association, according to him, should not, therefore merely be 'to strengthen the white element by the addition of some thousand white women, but to help the rest of the white element in South Africa ... to strengthen themselves by making their homes white in the fullest sense of the word'. White servants, attracted by both the good wages and the fact that the heavier work was usually left to the natives, started arriving in greater numbers—but never sufficiently to provide for all the demand—around the years 1904–05. 'Consequently Kaffir help may be—and frequently is—dispensed with in many ways a very desirable change', according to the Notes of the Month Rubric.[33] Not only are native servants not wanted for cultural reasons but also the imperial colonists feel physically ill at ease in their presence. In their published letters, the mistresses seem uneasy about the relationship of the white servants to the black domestics. Of course, the white servants

---

[31] Comment on the Bishop's sermon in rubric 'Notes of the Month', unsigned' *Imperial Colonist*, VI, no. 80 (August 1908) front page.

[32] 'The African Home', by 'one Lady', *Imperial Colonist*, VI, no. 79 (July 1908), 8.

[33] Unsigned, 'Notes of the Month', *Imperial Colonist*, IV, no. 41 (May 1905), 49.

are women while the black servants are men. Some mistresses found their white servants too familiar with the black servants and, at the same time, disapproved of the white servants' feeling superior to them as it made them unmanageable. After all, they were domestic servants. Others reproached them to treat their black servants too harshly or consider them as mere machines, which was a dangerous behaviour as most of them were young men who ought not to be treated with too much familiarity. Lady Knightley of Fawsley, who was thought to be a 'specialist in race relations' (this is how Ellen Joyce described Knightley when she wrote her eulogy after she died, *Imperialist Colonist*, 1913), gave the same kind of advice which she would certainly have given a young aristocratic woman at home as regards her treatment of male servants: 'no familiarity'. The right sort of distance was to be kept.

In the rare instances when native Americans are mentioned, they are also portrayed as children who need to be supervised. A letter by Mrs Bompas, a missionary's wife who lived in the North of Canada (Yukon) expresses mixed feelings about them which are, at the same time, feelings of sympathy and admiration for their great resistance to poverty, 'their fortitude under starvation is quite remarkable'; their solidarity; and their indifference to a very hard climate. She even sympathizes with their sense of independence which was challenged by colonization. 'Maternalism', however, infuses all her discourse, even when she suggests that they should be treated as equals:

> The good Indian woman who comes to do your laundry work will start off because there is no one to direct her, and is probably already half way up the hill picking berries! We need patience in all our dealings with the natives. Indians are a phlegmatic race, and will not consent to be put out or inconvenienced by anyone ... and since the white man has invaded their territory, cut down their fine forests, slaughtered, or driven away their moose and caribou, and is fast possessing himself of their hidden treasure, is it asking too much for his wife or sister to bear patiently with the Indian's idiosyncrasies, to meet them as equals, not inferiors, to deal gently with their failings, and above all, to show towards them under all circumstances 'the summer calm of golden charity.[34]

She exhorts her 'dear sister-settlers among the Indians' to exert their influence upon them. 'It is woman's strongest, most prevailing weapon.' It can be dangerous, she says, but it can be well used 'So will the Indians'

---

[34] 'Our Women in the North', Letter written from Yukon, North Canada, by Mrs Bompas, a missionary's wife, *Imperial Colonist*, VI, no. 83 (November 1908), 4–5.

country grow and prosper, not only from the wealth of its gold mines, but also from the refining, permeating influence of its Christian gentlewomen'.[35]

It seems, however, that the behaviour of some of the immigrants—surely those who hadn't been selected or who had been wrongly selected—do not live up to the project and even endanger the Empire as a purely 'British' empire. In an article entitled 'The Women who are wanted in Canada' signed Margaret Amherst[36], the author cites the case of Chinese cooks who are very much appreciated in Canada because, she said, not only do they cook well for wages as 'large as many a white woman's'—which means much less than a white man's—but, 'in return, they give their untiring work, frequently .... looking after the vegetable garden and poultry and helping in many other ways'. 'Had English women shown the same endurance and taken the same intelligent interest in their work and their masters and mistresses', she goes on, 'this lucrative field would not have been closed to them'. 'What do the Canadians want for their money? To this, there is but one reply WORK. Over and over again I was told 'Don't send us out women who won't work or who are unfitted for work'.[37] It is interesting that the author, for her argument to be brought home more efficiently, compares British women immigrants—negatively—with another dominated group: that of non-white immigrants. The same kind of technique is often used with men who are not deemed to be 'virile' enough, thus shaming them by negatively comparing them with more daring females. In the case quoted above, Chinese men are not promoted to equal 'British citizenship', thanks to their superior efficiency and work ethic—which are 'British' values—but the British women alluded to are meant to feel ashamed by the comparison which is not in their favour. It is not meant to include the Chinese men in the citizenry of the Empire, but rather to exclude particular women from it.

To Conclude

The beginning of the twentieth century is a period of political unrest in the mother country during which the various governments had to cope at

---

[35] Ibid., 9.
[36] *Imperial Colonist*, X (January 1912).
[37] *Imperial Colonist*, X (January 1912).

the same time with Home Rule agitation, socialist agitation, and last but not least, the agitation for women's suffrage. In the eyes of its detractors, the latter resulted from the existence of an 'abnormal' number of those they called 'surplus' women, that is, the number of women which exceeded that of men. It is interesting to note that the men who were called 'surplus men' were the number of men who exceeded the number of jobs available.[38] This demographic imbalance, largely due to the much larger emigration of British men, was said to be a threat to the individual woman's mental health, to the nation and to the race as it upset the ideal gender division of labour based on the male breadwinner–female carer nineteenth-century middle-class model. According to 'evolutionist ideology', which was still very influential at the beginning of the twentieth century, this model was both, the *proof* of a high degree of civilization and the *means* of reaching it. As the famous Swiss naturalist Karl Vogt had put it earlier in his 'Lectures on Man', partly reproduced by the *Family Herald*, 'sexual inequality increased with civilisation. [Also] the lower the state of culture, the more similar the occupations of the sexes'.[39] This still had some scientific value and women's access to the professions and to the vote was generally opposed by the 'intellectually sophisticated' males who opposed women's suffrage on 'evolutionist' grounds: grant it and this is the end of the family, of the nation, of the Empire, and of the white race: a nation that did not progress, regressed irrevocably to a state of barbarism. The Empire was, for them, a male preserve.

Indeed, the most extremist of the anti-suffragists suggested that women activists should be sent to the colonies where—white—women were scarce—so that they would acquire a British husband, calm down, and turn into 'real women': housewives and mothers devoted to their families. Their contribution to the Empire was seen by them as the mere 'close your eyes and think of England' that was necessary to increase its white population. The white supremacist ideology of Empire building was shared by the Imperial Colonist and impregnates the journal. Nonetheless, the women who write in it and select the articles and correspondence for publication do not share this restricted vision of womanhood and women's role. Their utopia is a world of equality and respect—not

---

[38] Sarah Boston, *Women Workers and Trade Unions* (London: Lawrence and Wishart), 1987.

[39] Carl Vogt, 'Family Herald of the 28 àct. 1871', cited by Charles Darwin, *The Descent of Man* (London: John Murray, 1889) (first published in 1871), 564.

similarity—between men and women, a world in which the rigid class hierarchy prevailing in Britain would become softer without disappearing and where respectability and hard work would promote individual women to a much better position than the one they would have been able to reach on the soil of the motherland, while their work would have contributed to building the Empire. This society of 'natural'—if not 'social'—equals the 'citizenry of the empire', whose members would all be geared towards its development and glory would not, however, include all the inhabitants of the 'new' country. The original inhabitants, whatever their country of origin, would remain attached to their low status, that of a dependent children. They would remain so for centuries until, may be one day, they became 'equal' to their British co-subjects, thanks to their Christian teaching and the good example set to them by their 'imperial colonists'.

10

Ladylands and Sacrificial Holes

Utopias and Dystopias in Rokeya Sakhawat Hossain's Writings

Barnita Bagchi

I

'Ladyland' in my title refers to the utopian country of that name described by Rokeya Sakhawat Hossain (1880–1932) in her English-language fictional tour de force, *Sultana's Dream* (1905). In this feminist fable, women's education, in the concrete shape of all-women universities, propels social change and progress. The sacrificial hole, equally, refers to Rokeya's dark, dystopian piece *Baligarta* or 'The Sacrificial Hole' (1927): the allegorically named Baligarta is a sacrificial pit of an Indian village where a boorish, corrupt, oppressive landlord wields his power to keep women and peasant tenants in a state of subjugated misery.

The written oeuvre of the South Asian Bengali Muslim educator–writer Rokeya Sakhawat Hossain is resonant with utopian and dystopian contours. An autodidact, working woman, widow, social worker, school-teacher, headmistress, organizational leader, creative writer, campaigner, and analytical writer, Rokeya packed at least 10 women's lives into her life which spanned 52 years from 1880 to 1932. This woman from co-lonial India had, this chapter argues, both the creative play and sense of the nitty-gritty which contribute to effective utopian and dystopian writing. Of her two principal utopian pieces, *Sultana's Dream* uses the dream vision form. Her novella *Padmarag* or 'The Ruby' is structured as a narrative-romance–cum–novella describing an educative and reformist community founded and administered by women.

Utopias etymologically hinge on the pun in the meaning of the Greek word, at once 'no place', and 'a good place'. Female utopias conjure up an idealized world where the 'wrongs of women' are ameliorated by active, thoughtful women. A combination of yearning and ambition powerfully charges works describing communities of women seeking to dream and ground a good life in a defined place. Across history and across cultures, female utopias dot the literary and social landscape.

Rokeya's utopian/dystopian writings are situated in a highly multivalent context. The creative and ideational experimentation with the good life and feminism that they express inflects her powerful, concrete work and agency in the history of women's education and social reform. Allowing a collocation of the ideal and the real, the practical and the visionary, the utopian dimension in fact becomes a consummate locus to see the connotative, associational richness of Rokeya's agency at the interface between the private, the social, and the political spheres in early-twentieth-century colonial Bengal and India.

Rokeya is recognized today, thanks largely to the work of feminist scholars, as a major figure in the history of women's education in South Asia, and in the history of women as agents of social change.[1] A key debate in the history of such women centres round the place of gender in political and social reform in colonial India. The contentious issue of social versus political reform emerged and crystallized in India by the 1880s. Gender and the 'condition of Indian woman' became the crux of the issue. Partha Chatterjee argued in a provocative and stimulating article[2] that from the late nineteenth century, Indian male nationalists (such as B.G. Tilak) created an ideology in which the category 'woman' was made synonymous with home, spirituality, privacy, and the unsullied purity of the Indian nation. The nationalists demanded that the British should not interfere, through social reform projects, with this private world of women. In the nationalist 'resolution' of the women's question hypothesized by Chatterjee, the 'unpolluted' domain of 'home' and 'woman' was distinguished from the public world of male nationalism,

---

[1] Bharati Ray, *Early Feminists of Colonial India: Sarala Devi Chaudhurani and Rokeya Sakhawat Hossain* (New Delhi: Oxford University Press, 2002); Sonia Nishat Amin, *The World of Muslim Women in Colonial Bengal* (Leiden: E.J. Brill, 1996).

[2] Partha Chatterjee, 'The Nationalist Resolution of the Women's Question', in *Recasting Women: Essays in Colonial History*, eds Kumkum Sangari and Sudesh Vaid (New Delhi: Kali for Women, 1989), 233–53.

which, demanding greater political liberty for Indians, would have its own independent trajectory.

Education for women figures centrally in Chatterjee's thesis. He argues that Indian nationalists created a 'new patriarchy' which approved of women's education, provided it was disciplined, regulatory, and that it furthered the home–world divide perpetuated by nationalist ideology. This kind of education would be designed to inculcate 'orderliness, thrift, cleanliness', 'literacy, accounting, and hygiene, and the ability to run the household according to the new physical and economic conditions set by the outside world'.[3] Women getting this kind of education would even be allowed to set foot outside the home, provided this did not threaten their Indian 'femininity' and culturally visible feminine 'spiritual qualities'. Chatterjee's account would see reformist women active in the field of women's education, such as Rokeya Hossain or Pandita Ramabai, as already inscribed into the 'new patriarchy'. However, the agency, critical questioning, and resourcefulness displayed by a number of colonial Indian women as actors in the public sphere shows that in fact there was no resolution of the woman's question in late-nineteenth-century or early-twentieth-century India, despite attempts on the part of the British colonial state and masculinist nationalism to do so. By 1927, India saw the foundation, through the initiative of the Irishwoman Margaret Cousins and Indian women, of a highly influential all-women platform, the All India Women's Conference (AIWC), which started by working for women's education, but which quickly began campaigning for political issues such as women's suffrage.[4] AIWC was only one, albeit the most influential, of hundreds of such women's organizations in the work of which campaigns for women's education and other sociopolitical issues went hand in hand. These associations, from Pandita Ramabai's Arya Mahila Samaj, founded in 1882, to Rokeya's Bengal branch of the Anjuman-e-Khawateen-e-Islam, founded in 1916, had women bridging the home and the world, banding together in solidarity to campaign on education, and creating training and income-earning schemes for women.

All those working for greater gender equity in colonial India found themselves caught between the devil of the British colonial state and the deep blue sea of revivalist, neo-patriarchal nationalists such as Tilak.

---

[3] Ibid., 247.

[4] Bharati Ray and Aparna Basu, *Women's Struggle: A History of the All India Women's Conference 1927–2002* (New Delhi: Manohar, 2003).

While the former used the 'degraded condition of Indian womanhood' as a stick to beat Indians with when they demanded greater political liberty, the latter felt threatened and deeply hostile to movements for greater female agency and freedom in domains ranging from education and health care to politics. However, articulate, active reformist women active in the field of education challenged private–public boundaries and the Indian patriarchy (both 'old' and 'new'), and through their activities and writing, gave voice to ideologies and views widely at variance with conservative Indian nationalists and hegemonic British colonial officialdom. Work by feminist historians such as Tanika Sarkar, Uma Chakravarti,[5] and Meera Kosambi have been highlighting the complexity, energy, and articulacy of women as agents. While trying to determine the relative importance of structure and agency in the field of gender and reform in Rokeya's time, one can now argue forcefully that colonial Indian women in many cases acted as agents of equity-oriented social change and development, targeting women and other marginal groups, even as they grappled with colonialism, semi-feudal patriarchy, the new patriarchy of revivalist nationalists, and class hierarchies.

Utopian impulses and communities played a powerful role in such women's agency, spanning public and private spheres; education; and social, welfarist, and political work. Pandita Ramabai, the Western–Indian feminist, educator, and activist, created utopia-like female communities, Sharada Sadan, Mukti Sadan, and Kripa Sadan (Halls of Learning, Freedom, and Mercy, respectively) where women and other marginalized groups found refuge and engaged in an astonishing variety of trades, including dairy work and printing. The community was, of course, led by the female reformer, Ramabai herself.[6]

Equally, we have in recent years learnt to recognize the international configurations in the history of female communities and female agency, and the complex role of white women in such activities.[7]

---

[5] Uma Chakravarti, *Rewriting History: The Life and Times of Pandita Ramabai* (New Delhi: Kali for Women, 1998).

[6] Ramabai Saraswati, *Pandita Ramabai through Her Own Words*, edited and part translated by Meera Kosambi (Delhi: Oxford University Press, 2000).

[7] See, for example, Joyce Goodman and Jane Martin, eds., *Gender, Colonialism and Education: The Politics of Experience* (London: Woburn, 2002); Siobhan Lambert-Hurley, 'An Embassy of Equality? Quaker Missionaries in Bhopal State, 1890–1930', in *Rhetoric and Reality: Gender and the Colonial Experience in South Asia*, eds. Avril A. Powell and Siobhan Lambert-Hurley (New Delhi: Oxford University Press, 2006), 247–81.

Such configurations crop up in the work of Rokeya, whose fictional community of Tarini Bhavan in *Padmarag* is inhabited by a white British woman teacher, Helen Horace, whose story reveals the tragic gender inequity of British divorce laws. Figures such as Helen Horace bring to mind the work of the South Asian scholar, Kumari Jayawardena, who has analyzed the trajectories of white women, many of them teachers, reformists, and revolutionaries, who sought to engage with Indian experience at a distance from imperialism.[8]

II

Born into a landholding family in east Bengal, Rokeya never had any formal schooling. Her conservative father discouraged Rokeya's impetus to read and learn, but a supportive elder sister and elder brother helped her pursue her study of English and Bengali, respectively. It was the same elder brother who negotiated Rokeya's marriage at the age of 16 to a much older man who respected Rokeya's powerful mind. After marriage, Rokeya moved to a provincial town, Bhagalpur, in Bihar, where her husband was a government official. Rokeya wrote *Sultana's Dream* while living in Bhagalpur, and the fable was published in a periodical called the *Indian Ladies' Magazine* in 1905. This periodical is itself a major source for understanding the history of Indian women's education. The Indian Tamil Christian writer Kamala Satthianadhan (1879–1950) started it in 1901. Krupabai Satthianadhan (1862–1894), Kamala's husband's first wife, wrote two major novels on Indian women, *Saguna* (1894) and *Kamala* (1895).[9] Kamala herself wrote half the stories in ananthology of short stories co-authored with her husband on Indian Christian life,[10] and the journal she edited published major women writers such as the poet-nationalist Sarojini Naidu, who in turn wrote warmly in 1916 to Rokeya, after reading an annual report of Rokeya's school published in the *Indian Ladies' Magazine*, congratulating her on

---

[8] Kumari Jayawardena, *The White Woman's Other Burden: Western Women and South Asia during British Rule* (New York and London: Routledge, 1995).

[9] Krupabai Satthianadhan, *Kamala: A Story of Hindu Life* (Madras: Srinivasa Varadachari and Co., 1894); Krupabai Satthianadhan, *Saguna: A Story of Native Christian Life* (Madras: Srinivasa Varadachari and Co., 1895).

[10] Kamala Satthianadhan and Samuel Satthianadhan, *Stories of Indian Christian Life* (Madras: Srinivasa Varadachari and Co., 1898).

her educational work.[11] Real-life groupings of women were evolving in early twentieth century India that conversed with and recognized each other's contribution in writing and public action.

By 1904, Rokeya had became a regular writer in Bengali-language periodicals and reviews such as *Nabanoor*, *Mahila*, and *Nabaprabha*, and wrote polemically feminist essays. She collected her early essays into a volume, *Motichur*, volume I, which was published in 1904. Widowed at the age of 29, Rokeya was bequeathed a legacy of ₹10,000 by her husband to start a school for girls. Her first attempt to start this school in her marital hometown, Bhagalpur, proved a failure. Indeed, relations with members of her marital family became unhappy, and she moved alone to Calcutta. In 1911, she started the Sakhawat Hossain Memorial School for Muslim girls in a rented house in Calcutta, with eight students.

In 1916, Rokeya started the Bengal branch of the Anjuman-e-Khawateen-e-Islam, an association for Muslim women, which busied itself in welfarist and developmental work, including sending women into the slums of Calcutta to take literacy and vocational training classes. In 1922, Rokeya became President of two organizations, Narishilpa Vidyalaya (Women's Arts and Industry School) and Narithirtha (Women's Institution), set up by a male social activist and writer, Lutfar Rahman, in Calcutta, to rehabilitate destitute women and prostitutes.

In 1905, when Rokeya's husband read *Sultana's Dream*, he commented, 'A terrible revenge!' *Sultana's Dream* remains fresh and undated even today. It is widely read and appreciated and retains its status as one of the most successful pieces of Indian writing in English. It is evident from the focus of Rokeya's activities that in *Sultana's Dream*, the driving force behind the success of the utopian feminist country of Ladyland is women's education. Rokeya lays particular emphasis on the importance of women familiarizing themselves with the world of science and is unequivocal in her condemnation of male militarism. In the unconventional, inverted world of *Sultana's Dream*, the men, whose advantage is brawn rather than brain, remain confined to the *mardana* and perform the daily mundane chores, while the women, headed by a queen who is ably supported by her deputies—the female principals of the two women's universities—use their superior intellectual abilities to govern

---

[11] Letter from Sarojini Naidu to Rokeya Hossain, 16 September 1916, in Miratun Nahar, ed., *Rokeya Rachanasamgraha* [Collected Works of Rokeya Sakhawat Hossain] (Calcutta: Viswakosh Parishad, 2001), 619.

the country wisely and well. As a fable, *Sultana's Dream* has a compact and clever plot line and a clear moral. The men of a certain nameless country engage in futile and incessant warfare, thereby exhausting themselves and their country's precious resources. The women, on the other hand, are devoted to the more productive goal of cultivating their minds, thanks to their queen who decrees universal female education. In the two universities, built exclusively for women, novel schemes are drawn up and subsequently implemented: one allows water to be drawn directly from the clouds, while the other enables solar heat to be collected, stored, and concentrated.

When the male soldiers of the country prove themselves powerless to thwart the threat of invasion by an enemy nation, the female principals of the universities step into the breach, making the withdrawal of men into the *mardana* a pre-condition for agreeing to defend the country. Using the concentrated solar heat stored by the women's universities as a missile, the enemy is routed. With the men still safely secluded in the *mardana*, the women continue to govern the country, now called Ladyland, creating a utopia where science, technology, and virtue work together in perfect harmony. Air travel is the only mode of transport, land is cultivated by electrically driven motors, and the weather is controlled. Ladyland embodies the triumph of the virtuous, enquiring, scientific, enlightened, and welfare-oriented spirit in women. And its heroines are women educators.

I would like to bring into my analysis two further pieces by Rokeya with significant utopian overtones, namely, her anti-colonial, anti-patriarchal political allegories 'The Fruit of Knowledge' and 'The Fruit of Freedom'. Positing causal links between women's education, women's agency, and political freedom, these allegories argue that British colonialism perpetuated itself by using lies, that it disguised as moral welfarism the fact that imperialism de-industrialized India, and offered very few resources for furthering Indians' welfare in areas such as education and health care. When women take on agency and leadership to both advance their own condition through education and become actors against colonialism, the pieces argue, we walk from dystopia towards utopia.

In 'The Fruit of Knowledge' (1922),[12] Rokeya regards the eating of the Fruit of Knowledge in the garden of Eden, through the agency of

---

[12] Nahar, *Rokeya Rachanasamgraha*, 175–82.

Eve, in a positive light: Rokeya thus reworks, from a colonial Indian perspective, a 'fortunate Fall', a liberal political paradigm.

> Eve requested him to eat the fruit which was in her hands. Adam too awoke to knowledge on eating the rest of the fruit from his wife. Then he began to feel his own deprived condition in every layer of his heart.—Was this paradise? This loveless, workless, lazy life—was this the pleasure of paradise? He also realised that he was a political prisoner; he had no ability to set foot outside the boundary of the garden of Eden!... Now the happy dream of heavenly pleasure, which was in fact ignorance, was shattered—he clearly felt the wakeful condition of knowledge.[13]

In Rokeya's parable, one fruit from the Tree of Knowledge falls onto the earth, and a tree is born from it, though human beings are, by and large, ignorant of the effects of this fruit. Inhabitants of a country called Paristan or Land of Fairies (allegory for Britain) get to drink the juice of some of these fruits and gain knowledge. Becoming imperialist traders, they exploit the great wealth of Kanakadvipa, the Island of Gold (allegory for India and other colonized countries), which overflows with food crops, but whose inhabitants live in a state of innocence. Eventually recognizing that their country is being drained of its wealth through unequal commerce with Paristan, some of the people of Kanakadvipa get to taste the juice of the Fruit of Knowledge. They then go in search of the original tree that bore the Fruit of Knowledge. To do this, they have to withstand opposition from the inhabitants of Paristan, an allegory of the opposition of imperialists to the colonized gaining emancipatory knowledge. After a long search, the search party finds the tree—it is withered and near-dead, and cannot be made to revive, despite much effort. In a dream, a sage appears to the Kanakadvipa explorers, and tells them,

> Even if you sacrifice two hundred thousand humans, the Tree of Knowledge will not be revived. Two hundred years ago, the selfish, shortsighted, foolish wise men of that country forbade the women to eat the fruit of knowledge; in time, that order became a social edict, and the men monopolised that fruit for themselves. Since they were stopped from picking and eating that fruit, the women did not tend or care for that tree. And since the Tree of Knowledge was deprived of the nurture and care of women's tender hands, it died. Go, return to your country; go and sow the seeds of those guavas.... Do not deprive your daughters of guavas! Remember without fail that women have all rights to the fruit which they themselves brought to the earth![14]

---

[13] Hossain, 'The Fruit of Knowledge' (my translation) in *Rokeya Rachanasamgraha*.
[14] Ibid.

In 'The Fruit of Freedom' (1921),[15] Kangalini, the Pauperess, erstwhile queen of the country of Bholapur, and an allegorical representation of the Indian nation, is shown to be dying under colonialism. The ablest of her various sons, Layek ('The Capable One'), dies; the rest are cowards, sycophants of the British, or corrupt (the allegorically named sons include Darpananda, 'One Who Rejoices in His Vanity'; Kritaghna, 'The Traitor'; Ninduk, 'The Villifier'; and Matridrohi, 'Rebel against His Mother'). We are told that the reason for the mother's illness is a curse brought on by an ascetic, due to her treating her daughters as inferior to her sons. The ascetic says to her,

> 'Child, it is very unjust that you love your sons far more, while you don't love or care at all for your daughters.... You will have to suffer the results of being the mother of unworthy sons and of being partial in showing love towards your children.' I ... asked him, touching his feet, 'When will my curse end?' In answer to that, the ascetic said, 'On Mount Kailasha there is a tree bearing the Fruit of Freedom; the day that someone brings you that fruit and feeds it to you, you will recover.'[16]

When Kangalini's cowardly, venal older sons prove incompetent in bringing back the fruit from the closely guarded gardens of Mayapur (Land of Illusion/Fancy, an allegory for the colonizing country), Kanagalini's daughters Srimati and Sumati, along with their younger brothers, decide that they will step outside the home, make the arduous journey to Mayapur, and wrest the Fruit of Freedom. In a politically symbolic gesture, Srimati unbinds her hair, and says that she will keep it loose until she is successful in getting the fruit. This is a reworking of an episode in the epic *Mahabharata* where queen Draupadi decides not to fasten or wash her hair until one of her husbands' can bathe her hair in the blood of the enemy prince Duhshasana, who had disrobed her in public. In Rokeya's story, the defiant woman herself decides to act, instead of depending on males to act on her behalf.

Thus, in both 'The Fruit of Freedom' and 'The Fruit of Knowledge', women's active participation in knowledge-making and action is seen as the sine qua non for overthrowing colonialism. Equally, Rokeya sees knowledge and education in positive terms, even when originating in or mediated by the colonizing countries of the West: she thinks that to reject

---

[15] Nahar, *Rokeya Rachanasamgraha*, 117–35.

[16] Hossain, 'The Fruit of Freedom' (my translation) in *Rokeya Rachanasamgraha*.

knowledge on the grounds that it is 'Western' is to play into the agenda
of colonialism, which seeks to keep Indians enslaved by perpetuating
ignorance.

In 1924 Rokeya published a novella called *Padmarag* or 'The Ruby'.
Describing a female-founded and female-administered welfarist institution called Tarini Bhavan in Calcutta, the work also offers us narrative
after narrative recounting the personal histories of the 'sisters of the
poor' who live and work in this spiritualized but non-religious community. Tarini Bhavan has a school, a workshop or a training institute for
adult women, a shelter for widows, and a home for the ailing and the
needy. Both day scholars and boarders attend the school. The Society
for the Upliftment of Downtrodden Women constitutes the moral, ideological, and institutional core of the project. Nearly each one of the personal life histories of the inhabitants of Tarini Bhavan is a tale of what
Rokeya punningly calls 'biye fail': 'biye' means marriage in Bengali, apart
from the other sense of the educational degree. Among the women is
one we have mentioned earlier, namely, Helen Horace, a white British
woman, who takes her place in the gallery of oppressed wives. She is
described as having married a man who violently made her the butt of
his drunken rages. While the couple is living in Hazaribagh in eastern
India, the man disappears. Years later, following rumours, Helen finds
that Joseph, her husband, has been arrested for murder, been diagnosed
as incurably insane, and shipped off to England. She finds on travelling
to England that though Joseph is now incarcerated in Broadmoor, she is
'tied for life to a lunatic', since her attempt to get divorce from him
fails in the law courts. Rokeya borrows nearly all the details of Helen
Horace's story from the real-life plight of Mrs Norman Cecil Rutherford,
protagonist in the infamous English divorce suit of *Rutherford v.
Rutherford*. Mrs Rutherford was refused divorce from her criminally
lunatic husband. (Colonel Rutherford had been convicted in 1919 of
having murdered a certain Major Seton and was sent to Broadmoor
Asylum.[17]) Rokeya translates into Bengali and quotes[18] excerpts from
the judgment that Lord Birkenhead had offered in this case:

---

[17] 'Lords Deny Divorce from a Lunatic: Birkenhead Declares Mrs Rutherford Unhappy
Victim of British Law', *New York Times*, 4 November 1922, http://query.nytimes.com/
mem/archive-free/pdf?_r=1&res=9504E7DA1F39EF3ABC4C53DFB7678389639EDE&
oref=slogin (accessed 27 September 2010).

[18] Rokeya Sakhawat Hossain, *Sultana's Dream and Padmarag: Two Feminist Utopias*,
introduced and part-translated by Barnita Bagchi (New Delhi: Penguin, 2005), 95–96.

It is an unfortunate circumstance that she should thus be tied for life to a dangerous, violent and homicidal lunatic ... Unless death remove him or release her, she must look forward to a loneliness from which she can escape only by a violation of the moral law. To some, this may appear a harsh, and even an inhuman, result, but such is the Law of England.[19]

The tale of Helen Horace is one of the numerous others in Rokeya's writing which manifest her international and global imagination. Elsewhere in her writing, she translates into Bengali, Marie Corelli's melodrama *The Murder of Delicia* (1896, about the marital oppression and death of a talented woman writer), and translates into Bengali an interview with Begum Tarzi, mother of the deposed Queen Soraya (1892–1960), consort of the reformist King Amanullah of Afghanistan, who abolished slavery, liberalized the family code, limited child marriage, and supported the unveiling of women. Rokeya shows, in numerous such examples in her writing, a lively mind that culls women's lives and women's history from places ranging from England to Turkey to Afghanistan to India. It is as if she is culling out examples of real-life utopia led by women working for the greater good.

Hearing Helen's story, Sakina, a Muslim woman who has also 'failed her marriage', exclaims, 'This England—this noxious, putrid England—claims to be civilized!'[20] Sakina has reasons of her own to be bitter about England: her husband goes off to study for a long period in England, eventually serving his wife with a writ of divorce in a letter. Yet another life story comes from the Hindu community, where Usha's marital family refuses to take her back after she has been abducted by and rescued from robbers. There seems to be a deliberate attempt to show that women from all the major religious communities in Bengal suffered patriarchal oppression in their familial lives. These are the real-life dystopia in which women live in the heart of the sanctified home and family. In a powerful essay entitled 'Griha' (1904), Rokeya argues that women have no home, in the sense of a shelter or refuge: 'No beast in the animal kingdom is as refugeless as us. Everyone has a home—it is we who do not.'[21] Of the two components of home, the family, and a place of refuge, we find that women's oppression within the family makes the possibility of

---

[19] Frederick Edwin Smith Birkenhead, *Last Essays* (first published in 1930) (New York: Books for Libraries Press, 1970), 347.

[20] Hossain, *Sultana's Dream and Padmarag*, 96.

[21] Nahar, *Rokeya Rachanasamgraha*, 59.

home as refuge impossible in practical terms. Women who are victims of the *abarodh* or total seclusion Rokeya indicted in *Abarodhbasini*, ('The Secluded Ones') cannot stir out of their homes into the public sphere; a Muslim married woman cannot keep in touch with her sister because her husband has quarrelled with the sister's husband; a Hindu widow is deprived of maintenance or refuge by her husband's brother. The family emerges as a living dystopia.

In *Baligarta* (The Sacrificial Hole),[22] three women—Jaheda, Kamala, and the narratorial voice—find that the Muslim landowner Khanbahadur Khatkhate, a sycophant and collaborator of the British, invokes a strategically reinvented Islam to condone oppressive practices, yet explicitly refuses to honour the rights and obligations enjoined by Islam which would favour women or peasants: thus, for example, he refuses to allow his 13-year-old widowed sister to remarry, saying that though they are Muslims, in this matter, they should follow the customs of brahminical Hinduism since they live in a Hindu-majority country. He lends money to his tenants, going against Islamic tenets, and yet charges exorbitantly high rates of interest as compensation for violating his religious obligation not to be usurious. His home is filled with female slaves. Explicitly, Rokeya introduces into this dystopia, a woman political activist —Kamala, who is a worker of the Indian National Congress, who campaigns along Gandhian lines, advocating spinning and the wearing of homespun cloth, *khaddar*. Again, Rokeya combines female agency in the private, the social, and the political spheres.

After listening to the dark personal narratives of the women in *Padmarag*, one of the women living and working in Tarini Bhavan asks:

> Is there no treatment for these suppurating sores of society? You either have to remain tied for life to a raving madman or endure being abandoned for no fault of your own.If after being insulted by a drunkard of a husband, you refuse to live with him and his concubine, your own brothers want to truss you up and pack you off to him…is there no redress for these injustices?[23]

And Saudamini, a senior teacher in Tarini Bhavan answers, 'There is! That redress is the Society for the Upliftment of Downtrodden Women at Tarini Bhavan. Come, all you abandoned, destitute, neglected,

---

[22] Ibid., 420–24.
[23] Hossain, *Sultana's Dream and Padmarag*, 104.

helpless, oppressed women—come all. Then we declare war on society! And Tarini Bhavan is our fortress.'[24]

Rokeya has a place in many kinds of history of female communities and female utopias. Most obviously, she is inserted in a Bengali and a South Asian milieu, and the history of female communities in this region. Strikingly, however, because of her status as a Bengali, a Muslim, and an Indian, she now occupies a prominent position in different national histories and in transnational histories: Rokeya's work itself functions as a locus of feminist utopian longings. The fact that she functions simultaneously as a South Asian, a Muslim, a Bengali, a precursor of the Bangladeshi, and as a global/international allows new kinds of associative, regional, transnational, and international histories to be written, woven round her work—while she simultaneously keeps her place as a powerful presence in the national histories of Bangladesh in particular, and secondarily, of India. The place she occupies in Indian and Bangladeshi histories may be different, but there is enough congruence to make dialogue between Bangladeshi and Indian Bengali scholars and readers of Rokeya exciting and fruitful. She also has a distinctive place in a genuinely global mapping of female utopia, in which we can place her in comparison with British, French, Egyptian, and American women.[25] One is excited to think of the resonances of her work, yet to be mapped, with women from other nations and other peoples—West Asia and North Africa spring particularly to mind. In all these senses and more, Rokeya's utopia and dystopia manifest the 'principle of hope', which, as we know, was how Ernst Bloch conceptualized utopia,[26] in all its resonance.

---

[24] Ibid.

[25] Barnita Bagchi, 'Carrying Over: Analysing Female Utopias and Narratives of Female Education Cross-Culturally and Cross-Historically', www.igidr.ac.in/pdf/publication/WP-2003-003.pdf (accessed 22 January 2008).

[26] Ernst Bloch, *The Principle of Hope*, 3 vols., trans. Neville Plaice, Stephen Plaice, and Paul Knight (Cambridge: MIT Press, 1995).

11

Utopia in the Subjunctive Mood

Bessie Head's *When Rain Clouds Gather*

Modhumita Roy

In analysing utopian fiction, Raymond Williams identifies four distinct strains: the paradise that exists elsewhere; the externally altered world—an alteration made possible by some unexpected natural event; the willed transformation—that is, a world changed by human agency and effort; and, lastly, the technological transformation wherein science intervenes to solve all earthly problems.[1] This last category has been the purview of much energetic and imaginative science fiction in the past century while the first has resurfaced with deadly force in the imaginings of religious fanatics in various parts of the world. Though analytically separable, the forms of utopian fiction often overlap to produce visions of a future world where science and human agency are inseparable.

In looking at South African fiction in the 1960s and 1970s, one would be hard-pressed to find experiments with utopian fiction. In fact, apartheid fiction is full of dystopian narratives that capture with force and accuracy the unfolding horrors of a police state. As Lewis Nkosi and others have stressed, the fiction of apartheid felt its first duty to represent the reality of dystopia—leaving implicit/unspoken the desired future. In this chapter, I argue that Bessie Head's *When Rain Clouds Gather* is a lonely and notable exception to the fiction of apartheid. Critics have noted the parallels between Head's own life story and the narrative trajectory of *When Rain Clouds Gather*. The autobiographical echoes are undeniable. As is well known, Head had fled the legalized segregation and repression

---

[1] Raymond Williams, *Problems in Materialism and Culture* (London: Verso, 1980), 196.

of apartheid South Africa in 1964, and so, mimicking Head's own departure from South Africa in search for a place to belong, *When Rain Clouds
Gather* (1968) opens with Makhaya's exit from a nightmarish world of
barbed wire, violence, and destruction into a settlement of people who
have all gathered together to make a 'new' world. The Golema Mmidi of
the novel is based on the Botswana village where Head had settled. Unlike Makhaya, however, who finds a niche in his adopted village, Head's
disenfranchisement continued in Botswana where she remained a stateless refugee for many years. But that was still in the future. Her first
published novel reflects the hope and optimism she had harboured in her
early years. Writing in *A Woman Alone*, Head had already indicated her
own, very personal description of a 'new world' and the centrality of a
tiny Botswana village in the conception of re-making the world:

> I took an obscure and almost unknown village in the Southern African bush
> and made it my own hallowed ground. Here, in the steadiness and peace of
> my own world, I could dream dreams a little ahead of the somewhat vicious ·
> clamor of revolution and the horrible stench of evil social systems. My work
> was always tentative because it was always so completely new; it created new
> worlds out of nothing; it battled with problems of food production in a tough
> semi-desert land; it brought together all kinds of people ... everyone had a
> place in my world.[2]

My chapter analyses the particular version of utopian fiction that
Head is able to create—one which is precariously poised between the
'vicious clamour of revolution' and the 'the horrible stench of evil social
systems'. Among the most notable features of the novel is the making
of a 'feminist' hero—Makhaya—long before the feminist movement had
articulated such a possibility. The novel locates itself in this ambivalent
space, attempting to acknowledge the consequences of human evil as
well as those of compassion and generosity. My point is not to argue
that the novel is a straightforward imagined utopia—a 'primitive' place
'out there' that exists as a counterpoint to the messiness of contemporary life and fulfils the yearnings for a 'simpler' world. The novel is a complicated, somewhat compromised attempt at imagining cooperation as
the lifeblood of utopian living: utopia is place that humans labour to
engender. Head's utopia, thus, deviates from the familiar formulations:
Golema Mmidi is not heaven on earth, nor has it been brought into being

---

[2] Bessie Head, *A Woman Alone: Autobiographical Writings*, ed. Craig Mackenzie
(London: Heinemann, 1990), 28.

through revolutionary change. It is not the futuristic world of science fiction, nor a world from which pain and suffering have been effectively eliminated. It is, as Head herself writes, only 'a little ahead' of its time and 'tentative'. It is, in fact, a novel experiment in creating what might be seen as a contradiction in terms—a realist utopia.

Utopian fiction has had a long and complex history and it would not be possible to do justice to its history in the limited space of this chapter. However, it is important to provide a schematic summary of some of the variations of Utopian fiction in order to situate Head's novel within it. Utopia, first and foremost is a work of *imaginative* fiction in which, unlike other such works, the central subject is 'the good society'. Utopia gestures towards a positive future, it oversteps the immediate reality to depict a condition whose desirability is beyond question. As the meaning of the word itself suggests, it is both nowhere (*outopia*) and somewhere good (*eutopia*). Utopia, therefore, simultaneously indicates its absence (no place) while marking the desire for its existence. Krishan Kumar defines utopia as 'to live in a world that cannot be but where one fervently wishes to be: that is the real essence of Utopia'.[3] Unlike Plato's *Republic,* which left out the mass of citizens who are not 'guardians' (not to mention slaves on whose labour, after all, the 'good life' would be secured), More's *Utopia* published in 1516, generally accepted as the inaugural text of the genre, encompassed all housekeepers and husbandmen. *Utopia* is dedicated to a life of common labour and the homely pleasures and not to, as in Plato's *Republic*, a selective communism of consumption. Here, unlike in the *Republic* which accepts a fundamental inequality of labour, work is not to be left to the private producers while rulers devote themselves to philosophy and politics. Equality is the central value of *Utopia*. There is, of course, a more flamboyant utopian tradition which takes its cue from the idea of Cockaygne—a place of hedonistic extravagance, exuberance, and excess. Cockaygne turns upside down the notions of fastidious simplicity of More's communism. Cockaygne is the poor man's heaven—everything here is free and freely available: youth, abundant food, and promiscuous sex. One of the notable features of this version of utopia is the complete freedom from work. The familiar descendants of More's *Utopia* are to be found, especially in the nineteenth-century Utopian socialists who proclaimed, 'Let cheerfulness abound with industry', in the *Communist Manifesto* and perhaps

---

[3] Krishan Kumar, *Utopianism* (Minneapolis: University of Minnesota Press, 1991).

more generally, in communism's central dictum of 'to each according to his need, from each according to his ability'. One encounters the same desire in the demand for 'bread and roses' which insisted on the inseparability of life free from want and a life filled with beauty. But for all utopian experiments—fictional or otherwise—the question of labour, that is, who will have to work in order for the community to enjoy 'the good life' has been one of the key issues. Though Head distanced herself from explicit political ideologies, *When Rain Clouds Gather* seems to combine the aspirations of socialism without adhering to its politics.

Critics have noted the utopian impulse of the novel though most have found it too romantic. Arthur Ravenscroft, for example, finds the novel 'excessively romantic', its attempted solutions 'rather elusive even mystical'.[4] Similarly, Huma Ibrahim calls the novel 'utopian nostalgia' and reads Head's intention as 'a tendency to create a utopic and euphoric space, namely, a small rural village' which is 'a wondrously idyllic, almost utopian place' exemplifying an exile's nostalgia for 'old Africa'.[5] Head herself describes the village as 'consisting of individuals who had fled there to escape the tragedies of life'.[6] But even a cursory reading of the novel would contradict Ibrahim's conclusions. Golema Mmidi is a much more ambivalent space than 'euphoria' would suggest. The title itself is indicative of this ambivalence: *When* Rain Clouds Gather. The conditional 'when' gestures towards possibilities without specifying what they are and, in the temporal dependence of the clause, 'when' is open-ended, disallowing any easy or straightforward euphoria. We do not know what might happen when (and perhaps 'if') rain clouds gather. The harrowing description of death at the novel's end, though outside the boundaries of the village, nonetheless is within the space of the novel and counters all impulses towards unqualified ('excessive') romanticism. Unlike much utopian fiction, especially in the contemporary moment, which are exercises in fantasy (and would fall within the rubric of 'science fiction'), Head's novel is firmly anchored in the realist mode. It explores the modalities of what *can* be achieved through collective will and co-operative labour, here and now, rather than in some unspecified future time. Makhaya, after all, is not fleeing some hypothetical calamity or

---

[4] Arthur Ravenscroft, 'The Novels of Bessie Head,' in *Aspects of South African Literature*, ed. C. Heywood (London: Heinemann, 1976). 179.

[5] Huma Ibrahim, *Bessie Head: Subversive Identities in Exile* (Charlottesville: University of Virginia Press, 1996), 155.

[6] Bessie Head, *When Rain Clouds Gather* (London: Heinemann, 1969), 6.

dystopia (as the Smales family does in Nadine Gordimer's *July's People*, or as Michael K does in J.M. Coetzee's *Life and Times of Michael K*). Nor does he arrive at a futuristic world, altered beyond recognition. The novel's 'now' is clearly delineated as a historical 'present': Botswana's imminent independence from Britain tells us the year is 1964 which, of course, is also the year of Head's own flight from South Africa. In this delicate play between the actual and the possible, the real and the imagined, Head achieves what H.G. Wells called 'domesticating the impossible hypothesis'.[7]

Kumar usefully reminds us, 'Utopia's value lies not in its relation to present practice but in its relation to a possible future. Its "practical" use is to overstep the immediate reality to depict a condition whose clear desirability draws us on like a magnet'.[8] Fanciful and fabricated though these imagined worlds maybe, it should be remembered that all utopian documents are historically determined; that is, the form of the desired future is deeply influenced, even shaped, by the realities of the society in which they are imagined. It is not difficult to see that Head's ideal village is, indeed, a reaction to lived realities. The shadow of a brutal, racialized state—apartheid South Africa—is clearly the dystopia whose modular opposite is the 'imagined community' of Golema Mmidi. Collectively, the 'wayward lot of misfits'[9] that make up the core of the utopian community allows us to imagine—even see—a possible human alternative to South Africa, 'that cold and loveless country' as Head once described it. By contrast, Golema Mmidi is imagined as the outcome of composite desires, which each individual has contributed to realize; it is the place where racialism, sexism, the effects of poverty and neglect *may* indeed come to an end—though nothing is guaranteed.

The little village stands as an anti-thesis to the logic of a segregationist state. Not only is there friendship and co-operation among races, the marriage of Gilbert and Maria stands as an outright challenge to apartheid's Mixed Marriages Act—the law that, at least in one version of her own life story, had resulted in her mother being committed to an asylum:

> I was born on the 6th of July 1937 in Pietermaritzburg Mental Hospital. The reason for my peculiar birthplace was that my mother was white, and she had

---

[7] Kumar, *Utopianism*, 25.

[8] Ibid., 3.

[9] Head, *When Rain Clouds Gather*, 17.

acquired me from a black man. She was judged insane, and committed to the mental hospital while pregnant.[10]

It is one of Head's achievements that the novel pointedly rejects such an outcome. No such cruel fate can exist in a village where strangers are welcomed and where foreigners are accepted as 'sons'. Gilbert, the white, middle-class British exile accepts the poor 'as though they were his blood brothers'[11] and Dinorego without hesitation accepts both Gilbert and Makhaya: 'Just as I take you [Makhaya] as my own son, so do I take Gilbert as my own son'.[12] The very wording of Dinorego's acceptance of white and black, of foreigner and stranger, 'I take you', is an audacious echo of the marriage vow 'I take thee' and a deliberate challenge to the ideology of racial separation.

The novel opens with the yet-to-be named Makhaya fleeing South Africa to an ambivalent freedom. Makhaya, however, flees across national borders, not across time (as fantasy literature is apt to do). It is not the *imagined* nightmare of a dystopian present that propels him cross the barbed-wire fence. Indeed, the continuity and contiguity of the two worlds—the one he has left behind and the one towards which he is running—is emphasized from the outset. Though this place is distinguished from prison, the inside and outside of barbed-wire fences are not easily separated. He escapes to 'whatever illusion of freedom' lies on the other side of the barbed-wire fence. The 'little Baralong village swept right up to the border fence' we are told and the hut where Makhaya is hiding 'touched the barbed-wire fencing', thus making the escape—and the distinction between the two places—uneasy and ambivalent. Though he has fled from 'a country where black men were called "boy" and "dog" and "kaffir"' to what he escapes remains unclear: 'I *might* like it here'[13] Makhaya thinks before he falls asleep. His decision to follow the road north is similarly qualified: he hoped it would lead him somewhere. Although he feels he has come to the end of his journey, he has arrived, not at a pastoral Eden but in a 'landscape of dryness and bleakness'. It is 'a vast expanse of sand and scrub' that invokes no poetic flight of fancy. The uncertain 'perhaps' repeats itself in each of his reflections:

[10] Susan Gardner, '"Don't Ask for the True Story": A Memoir of Bessie Head', *Hecate* 12 (1986), 114.

[11] Head, *When Rain Clouds Gather*, 18.

[12] Ibid., 21.

[13] Ibid., 16 (emphasis added).

Perhaps he confused it with his own loneliness. *Perhaps* it was those crazy little birds. *Perhaps* it was the way the earth adorned itself ... Or *perhaps* he simply wanted a country to love and chose the first thing at hand. But whatever it was, he simply and silently decided that all this dryness and bleakness amounted to home and somehow he had come to the end of a journey.[14]

This ambivalence and uncertainty will characterize the rest of the narrative.

Fragile and tenuous though the distinction is between what is on either side of the barbed-wire fence, it is one of great moment. The village is immediately contrasted to South Africa, 'that terrible place,' which 'the good God doesn't like'. The village, instead is, 'God's country'. Within the first few pages of the novel, the specialness of the village is remarked upon by a number of people. The village is a 'unique place' and a 'whole new astonishing world'. It is a place where miracles occur. As Makhaya stands with Gilbert, looking at the sparse landscape, Gilbert remarks: 'This is Utopia, Mack'. If, for Gilbert, the uniqueness of Golema Mmidi has something to do with the possibilities it offers ('I have great dreams for it'), then to Makhaya, in the first instance, it allows a step into freedom: 'I just want to step on free ground ... I just want to feel free what it is like to live in a free country'. Makhaya, after all, is not only a 'stateless person' he has daily experienced 'the terror of rape, murder and bloodshed in a city slum' which has 'bred a horror of life' in him. It is not till the novel's end, and not till he has witnessed both the extraordinary deprivations that are part of life in the villages as well as the remarkable resilience of spirit that allowed them to forge ahead, that Makhaya comes to terms with his own yearnings for Utopia. It is only then that he sees Golema Mmidi as an 'enchanting world'.

But it would be shortsighted to argue that Golema Mmidi is the answer *only* to South Africa's nightmarish reality. Head is keenly aware of the consequences of sedimented inequalities based on race, class, and gender. Her indignation and anger at corrupt politicians, avaricious chiefs, and degrading social arrangements also find their way into the novel. The 'deadly chilling society' of 'tribalist' Africa which 'kept out everything new and strange'[15] is part of Head's withering critique. Head's novel makes a serious attempt at imagining human enterprise that is not vitiated by greed or by power. The communal philosophy

---

[14] Ibid., 16–17 (emphasis added).
[15] Ibid., 96.

of the village stands in striking contrast to the boundless consumption of 'hereditary' chiefs, symbolized with telegrammatic precision in the image of Matenge's huge cream Chevrolet. Chief Sekoto who loved 'fast cars, good food and pretty girls', and whose lifestyle is underwritten by slave labour, is immediately contrasted to Golema Mmidi's experimental cattle co-operative which 'belongs to the people and each member is to get a fair price' for their livestock. Though the novel includes the fallibility of humans, it nonetheless holds on to a fundamental assumption that each person, man or woman, black or white, can transcend socially or politically imposed restrictive boundaries to make common cause.

Golema Mmidi is an exercise in imagining 'a deep horizontal comradeship' in Benedict's Anderson's memorable phrase.[16] The village is not the 'natural' outcome of biological descent; rather, it is the result of disparate elements coming together. We are told at the outset that it is 'not a village in the usual meaning of being composed of large tribal or family grouping'. The village community directly challenges the stultifying rigidities of race and class, tradition and tribe, of political affiliation and national belonging. Everyone here is a stranger or a newcomer. The question of the indigene and therefore the question of first or original claim to land and to belonging are overturned; everyone belongs *precisely* because no one can claim belonging. The novel eschews the involuntary community of the 'tribe' where social relations are fixed and reproduced through a grammar of naturalized obligations. Here, too, one can easily see Head's own desire for a belonging that is not determined by birth or by genealogy reflected in the novel. Again and again in the novel, Head enacts what, following Rob Nixon, we can term as the 'compensatory matrix of allegiances' that are based on voluntary acts of acceptance. In place of the filiation of nation, tribe, or family, Head offers the possibility and recompense of affiliation 'as the alternative sources of lineage and belonging'.[17]

A 'village of commoners', Golema Mmidi is the desired alternative to the abysmal darkness of traditional hierarchies. The comradeship forged through meaningful acts of solidarity, exemplified in the Englishman Appleby-Smith's quiet assertion to Makhaya, 'I will still stick my

[16] Benedict Anderson, *Imagined Communities: Reflections on the Origin and Spread of Nationalism* (London: Verso, 1991), 7.

[17] Rob Nixon, *Homelands, Hollywood and Harlem* (London: Routledge, 1994), 102.

neck out for you', is directly contrasted to the flamboyant but empty sloganeering of political parties with their easy mouthing of 'workers of the world unite'. It is not as though the novel (and especially Makhaya) repudiates politics altogether. What he (and the novel) seems to be against is a dogmatic ideology which is bankrupt and misleading, and whose purpose is to exploit. Though the narrative is deeply sceptical about organized political movements and has little faith in revolution as the utopian horizon, on being asked directly whether he will leave politics, Makhaya's answer is an unequivocal 'no'. In direct contrast to the politicking of Joas Tsepe who mouths facile revolutionary slogans, Head offers the sincerity of individual characters. The transformation of the individual is seen as the key to the programmatic tranformation of the collective. Whether it is Gilbert whose oddly conservative gender politics need to be overhauled or the villagers' collective prejudice against millet or maize, it takes *work*, the novel argues, to create an egalitarian communal life.

Set in rural Botswana, with its central preoccupation of land and agriculture, *When Rain Clouds Gather* brings to mind the popular *plaasroman* [the farm novels of South Africa]. The dominant Afrikaans genre in the 1920s and 1930s, these novels, especially in the context of Afrikaner politics, were nostalgic and utopian in their own ways. The *plaasroman*, as critics have noted, reflected Afrikaner settler ideology, functioning to justify the fiction of 'natural' ownership of land, obscuring thereby the contentious history of land appropriation and eviction of peoples. The rural farm, idyllic and pastoral, was of course a fantasy of racial homogeneity and of genealogical continuity. In many a *plaasroman*, 'farms are places of freedom'.[18] I have mentioned earlier the ways in which Head carefully counters the logic of filiation. Golema Mmidi is no pastoral refuge and no appeal is made for a separate/separatist cultural identity. The novel should be seen as a meticulous undoing of the tropes of the *plaasroman*: of birthright and belonging, of inherited claims of ownership of land, and of the racially pure collectivity whose claims are secured by barbed wire and guns. The novel eschews the legitimizing trope of farm/land as place of 'origin'. Though land has to be fenced in Golema Mmidi, the fencing, in fact, turns the usual association of privatization on its head and is reproduced as a necessary component for better collective farming. Unlike, for example, Coetzee's third person

---

[18] J.M. Coetzee, *Boyhood: Scenes from Provincial Life* (New York: Penguin, 1977), 22.

memoir, *Boyhood: Scenes from Provincial Life*, whose narrator claims that 'through the farm he is rooted in the past',[19] what the motley group in Golema Mmidi can claim is a shared 'unbelonging'. Instead of rootedness, what is emphasized is the *uprooting*, though the hope of rooting of both people and plants is everywhere present. Golema Mmidi, after all, is a place of strangers and none can claim a stable and historic connection to the place. Coetzee reminds us that the *plaasroman* held out the 'transcendental justification for the ownership of land' where 'inherited ownership of the farm ... becomes a sacred trust: to alienate the farm means to forsake the bones of ancestors'.[20] In Head's novel, by contrast, it is not the bones of ancestors but those of a child that have to be buried. The bones of Paulina's dead son are not symbolic of a sacred trust but the evidence of incalculable human tragedy. Suffering and death bestow no transcendental spiritual meaning. Instead they are incorporated into the difficult business of living and lend the impetus for overcoming the circumstances that lead to needless death. What is emphasized is not the past but the importance of the present and the desire to create possibilities for the future. The novel, as well, forces us to re-think the generic conventions of the pastoral form, replacing the usual romantic descriptions of nature with harrowing descriptions of drought and famine, dislocation, and death. Head rarely reproduces the sentimental yearning for a vanished idyllic past that is a constitutive feature of pastoral romances. To be sure, there are moments of deep lyricism in the descriptions of the landscape, but these are invariably tempered by the pain and suffering of those who inhabit that space.

If the blood, sweat, and tears that went into making the farm fruitful was the legitimizer of (white) ownership in the *plaasroman*, then black labour had to be erased: 'If the work of hands on a particular patch of earth ... is what inscribes it as the property of its occupiers by right, then the hands of black serfs doing the work had better not be seen'.[21] Head counters the figurative and literal erasure of a black presence by poignantly writing them back into the landscape. Human labour itself is shown to be above and beyond race and gender. The novel pushes the logic of the *plaasroman* to its limit to include labouring hands, black and white, male and female, and young and old.

---

[19] Ibid.

[20] J.M. Coetzee, *White Writing: On the Culture of Letters in South Africa* (New Haven: Yale University Press, 1988), 85, 106.

[21] Ibid., 5.

Head's novel stresses the value of making; that is, the role that active labouring plays in creating the possibility of a utopian space. This small village of foreigners is no cockagyne. Nothing here is free, nothing can be taken for granted. Certainly, there is no abundance, everything has to be worked for, wrested from the sparse landscape. Unlike other villages that are named after 'important chiefs or important events', Golema Mmidi was named 'from the occupation the villagers followed, which was crop growing'.[22] A village of subalterns, the place is named for the work they collectively perform. Head had once remarked of the village in which she had sought refuge that it had 'a sense of wovenness; of wholeness in life'. The metaphor of 'weave' and of fabric that is thus created is a telling one. It centralizes the process of labour in creating ('weaving') wholeness and brings to the mind the warp and weft of the loom. In Golema Mmidi it is the quotidian but necessary work of growing crops, the naming suggests, that weaves the growers together into a cultural fabric. The meaning of life, we are told, is a combination of love and work, and for Gilbert, the very meaning of existence resided in work and the 'lack of work meant death'.[23]

The centrality of work—especially collective work—is nowhere more emphasized than in the chapter which describes in detail the women getting together to build the tobacco sheds. The scene carefully delineates the *making* of a collectivity out of a disparate group. On the morning of the important day, each woman arrives bringing with her provisions tied up in bright, chequered cloths.

> One of the women stood up and collected small helpings of tea leaves and powdered milk from each bundle, and then both the powdered milk and tea leaves were poured at the same time into the boiling water. By the time Paulina emerged ... tea was ready and poured.... Then they all drank the tea with clouds of vapour rising up from the mugs into the cold air. Each woman then carefully rinsed her mug and tied it up once again in the checkered cloth. They arose and walked in a brisk, determined group to the farm.[24]

The description of the women making tea oscillates between the singular and the plural, moving from seriality to collectivity, in a careful choreography till a 'determined group' walks away to start the crucial

---

[22] Head, *When Rain Clouds Gather*, 16.
[23] Ibid., 82.
[24] Ibid., 101.

work of building the shed and, therefore, of building a future. Each of the 10 women contributes towards the effort, bringing with them their individual portion of tea, milk, and sugar. This they gather together to make the communal brew which 'they all drank' together. The almost ceremonial making and drinking of tea inaugurates the moment of coming together for a common purpose. It is a ceremony of co-operation and solidarity. The sentences alternate between the singular and the plural— 'each' giving way to 'they', leading back to the individual 'each'—thus keeping in exquisite balance the individual and the collective. The description ensures that both the individual contribution and the collective outcome are preserved and that one is not subsumed into the other.

Trivial though the purpose may appear (making tea), it stands as a synecdoche for the larger effort of building the first tobacco-curing sheds and, by implication, for the co-operative that the entire village is engaged in creating. Like the Botswana goats 'who just walk about eating at this dry paper and bits of rubble and then turn it into meat and milk', the village of foreigners change the stark desert landscape and, through their collective labour, create a viable co-operative market garden. The novel carefully delineates the interdependence of talents and abilities. Thus, though Makhaya, an urban journalist, knows nothing about village life and even less about agriculture, and though Gilbert knows all about cultivation and has radical new ideas about making it work in Golema Mmidi, he admits that unlike Makhaya, 'I can't teach. I can't put my ideas over somehow, and not only because my Tswana is poor' . But while Makhaya might be able to teach using Gilbert's ideas, it is the women, 'the traditional tillers of the earth, not men', who will have to become partners in this experimental enterprise. To this must be added the interdependence of cattle production and crop cultivation; that is, in an ever-growing circle, the entire community will have to pool their talents, resources, knowledge, and labour to create 'a whole new astonishing world'.

It is no accident that women are the central figures in this description. 'No men,' we are told, 'ever worked harder than Botswana women'. In keeping with the mood of the entire novel which hesitates on the threshold of euphoria, the women's efforts are presented within a larger patriarchal frame. Despite Paulina's bold leadership, only 10 women have joined the tobacco-growing project, while 20 more though willing to join 'had to get the permission of their husbands'. It is hardly surprising that the rapid changes taking place in Golema Mmidi occur in the absence of the patriarch. Matenge, struck down by high blood pressure, spends a month in the hospital and in his absence 'a number of rapid changes took place in Golema Mmidi'. It is for most of the year 'a village of women with all the men away at cattle posts'. But Head's purpose is not to create a separatist feminist utopia. Instead, what she presents is the interdependence of women and men of good will. Thus, Paulina, who is 'daring and different' and an obvious leader, is matched with Makhaya's explicitly egalitarian gender politics. He speaks to the women as equals and each accepts the other as a person, neither male nor female: 'once it struck them that he paid no attention to them as women, they also forgot he was a man and became absorbed in following his explanations'. If Gilbert and Makhaya are seen as the pioneering spirits in the enterprise, the novel is quick to point out that 'perhaps all change in the long run would depend on the women of the country'.[25]

In a remarkable scene where the women begin the hard work of building the tobacco sheds, Makhaya stumbles upon a little girl's efforts at creating a model village, carved out of mud: 'there were mud goats, mud cattle, mud huts and mud people, and grooved little footpaths for them all to walk on'.[26] As the women labour to create the drying sheds, Makhaya sits in a corner carving out the last details for the model village. Head juxtaposes descriptions of work with descriptions of art and in so doing, produces both as instances of labour, and as part of the effort to make a perfectible world. 'The women, with pickaxes and spades, scraped out the foundation' while Makhaya 'had a few short sticks in his hand and took out a pocket knife and began slicing away at the wood. The alternating descriptions of labour and carving suggest both the inseparability and desirability of the two efforts. The child's attempt at carving an entire village out of mud was almost perfect. All it lacked was a palm tree which Makhaya took upon himself to add. He carefully and meticulously carved out trees, 'placed the foot of each tree into the pitch bucket to prevent its future damage by the white ants' and added them to the model village. The child's imagination is supplemented by the adult's vision. Once again, what is emphasized is the collaboration—here one of youthful enthusiasm and mature wisdom. It is this combination that makes the model village perfect. As Makhaya finishes his carving, Gilbert, the original proponent of cooperative farming walks in and 'stood gazing at the complete tobacco sheds with the same delight in his eyes as Makhaya looked on the minute village of mud people and animals'.

[25] Ibid., 38.
[26] Ibid., 103.

The fungibility of the two villages, miniature and real, is further emphasized when Gilbert, taking the finished palm tree from Makhaya, crouches down, and places it in the most suitable spot, saying, 'Each household will have a tap with running water out of it all year round … And not only palm trees, but fruit trees too and flower gardens. It won't take so many years to turn Golema Mmidi into a paradise'.

'I was born in South Africa', Bessie Head was to say, 'and that is syn-onymous with saying that one is born into a very brutal world'[27]. The burden of my argument in this chapter has been to show that *When Rain Clouds Gather* was Bessie Head's attempt at writing herself out of the brutality and into the possibility of a kinder world. Though it is not a utopian in the more familiar idiom of futuristic narratives, it is nonetheless an attempt to counter 'what is' with 'what might be'. Head acknowledged the flaws of her first published novel which she called her 'first amateur effort'.[28] It is a notable effort, nonetheless, a literary antidote to the harshness that had surrounded her life. In *A Woman Alone*, Head poignantly writes, 'I have lived all my life in shattered little bits. Somehow here [in Botswana] the shattered little bits began to come together'.[29] Makhaya too finds his world shattered, but if for Head wholeness remained elusive, she certainly allowed her fictional counterpart to put the pieces back together. It is in the midst of others who have fled their past that Makhaya is able to see the shape of an 'enchanting world'. For Makhaya, too, the world had shattered into fragments but he learns to put his world back together. He realizes that through the act of generosity and human compassion the world is made whole: 'If there was anything he liked on earth, it was human generosity. It made life seem whole and sane to him. It kept the world from shattering into tiny fragments'.[30] Throughout the novel what is seen as redemptive, even in the face of unrelenting nature, death, and destruction, is the human act of compassion and kindness. The co-operation that is central to the success of Golema Mmidi stands in direct contrast to the greed and selfishness of hereditary chiefs and upstart politicians.

But the future is not guaranteed. It appears only as a possibility. Golema Mmidi is not a Christian Paradise of redemption, nor is it a

---

[27] Gardner, 'Don't Ask for the True Story', 114.

[28] Head, *A Woman Alone*, 64.

[29] Ibid., 22.

[30] Head, *When Rain Clouds Gather*, 57.

millenarian fantasy where a saviour inaugurates a new world for the chosen. Head places her trust squarely on human agency in the making of 'no place' into a 'good place': one which, like the child's attempt at creating a perfect village, is incomplete and needs to be improved. Even if never perfect, the attempt at perfectibility is seen as a worthy goal. The entire novel is cast in the subjunctive mood: tentative, hesitant, and conditional. 'Perhaps' and 'maybe' echo through the novel and the possibility of utopia remains tantalizingly available but tenuous: 'Maybe even utopias were just trees. Maybe'.[31] Rain clouds *may* gather and when they do *perhaps* good things will happen. Though we do not know what they are, we imagine what may flow from such a gathering. On closer inspection we realize that within the space of this tentative and tenuous utopia, where rain has not fallen and clouds have not yet gathered, good things *have* already happened. People have gathered and we know that 'all good things and all good people are called rain'. It is as if, here in Golema Mmidi, apartheid's inhuman laws have been overturned and the Freedom Charter's bold declaration, 'The land will belong to all those, black and white, who live on it', has come true.

---

[31] Ibid., 162.

PART III

Coda: Resistance

12

Globalization, Development, and Resistance of Utopian Dreams to the *Praxis* of Dystopian Utopia*

Marie-Claire Caloz-Tschopp

> You take me for the tide and I am the deluge.
>
> Victor Hugo, *The Horrific Year*,
> Epilogue (on the Commune in France)

Introduction

Utopia is an unending dream in human history. Repression rages,[1] hunger torments, inequalities and violence deepen. Yet, man has as much craving for utopia as for bread. Utopia is as stubborn, hidden, and irruptive as dreams, deceits, and madness of human beings in search of an ideal society. Tracing the path of *conquista*, slavery, colonialism, imperialism, world wars, and mass-massacres, the dream gave way to the field of ruin of the totalitarian twentieth century, by contesting the philosophy of history marked by the boundless expansion and the hegemony of the West. Thereafter, what has utopia come to be? For some, it forms

---

* Translation from the French by Trinanjan Chakraborty. Edited by Barnita Bagchi.

[1] On the Commune in France, see Victor Hugo, *L'année terrible* (Paris: Gallimard, 1985); Louise Michel, *Je vous écris de ma nuit: correspondance generale de Louise Michel, 1850–1904* (first published in 1871) (Paris: Les éditions de Paris, 1999). Louise Michel was 41 when she fought on the barricades during 22–28 May 1871, the 'bloody week'; on 24 May, she was jailed and brought before the 4th Council of War, on 2 September, her friend Théophile Ferré, representative of Monmartre was sentenced to death. On 16 December, she was sentenced to life imprisonment.

an integral part of the disaster.[2] It should make room for a sound realism, which would abandon all dreams and idealist notions of progress. For others, its transformation is at work within praxis and thought. It is yet to be discovered.

The photograph of two young Roma girls who died of drowning and were laid out on the beach at Torregaveta, north of Naples, their small feet poking from under the beach towels that cover their corpses, be-tween bathers[3] sitting idly five metres away (26 July 2008), seems to testify that utopia has yielded to cynical indifference. The photograph does not, however, exhaust the real. While the death and detention camps multiply at the frontiers of rich countries,[4] conflicts are experienced and articulated at the frontiers of democracy (war, women's question, migra-tion, development, etc.). It can be postulated that political and philo-sophical praxes are being constructed within these conflicts and one has to attempt to capture their delicate unfolding. It can be postulated that, in these areas, a post-Hegelian philosophy of history is taking shape, a new revolutionary project that could be called, in the absence of any other name, a project of revolutionary resistance[5] of dystopian utopia. In short, the project involves integrating the dialectics between an eman-cipatory desire for utopian justice and an exercise of dystopian memory of capitalist modernity and its utilitarian and annihilative philosophy.

From Prototypical Utopia to Intemperate Dystopia

Inaccessible mountain, unknown island, unearthly city—so much of im-agery abounds on utopia. On the eve of modernity,[6] these represented the search for a perfect place where there would be no private property, no war. Utopia exists nowhere, and yet, it exists (the privative prefix *u*

---

    [2] Bernard Hours, 'L'idéologie sécuritaire: de la gestion des risques à la préparation du désastre', *L'homme et la société*, No.155 (2005): 13–25.

    [3] The two journalists present on the sea beach reported no manifestation of xenophobia in the attitude of tourists.

    [4] Marie-Claire Caloz-Tschopp, *Les réfugiés aux frontières de l'Europe et le spectre des camps* (Paris : La Dispute, 2004).

    [5] For this concept, see Marie-Claire Caloz-Tschopp, *Résister en politique: Résister en philosophie avec Arendt, Castoriadis, Ivekovic* (Paris: La Dispute, 2008).

    [6] See in this context, Bertrand Ogilvie, 'Mondialisation, dé-mondialisation. Qu'est-ce que la modernité ?' in *Lire Hannah Arendt aujourd'hui: pouvoir, guerre, pensee, jugement politique*, ed. Marie-Claire Caloz-Tschopp (Paris: L'Harmattan, 2008), 97–119.

has both the meanings in Greek). Utopia, undoubtedly incorruptible as an idea of a world, surpasses our imagination in search of new topos of the impossible within the possible.

Yet, in the darkness, blood, and fire, dystopia is not far. Along with the limitations, failures, and tragedies, utopia has revealed its flip side, dystopia, described in *Brave New World* by Aldous Huxley (1931) and *1984* by George Orwell (1948). After the historic ruptures of totalitarian capitalist modernity, it is impossible to think of one without the other, whereas praxis and thought are getting transformed. Mountain, island, and city of Thomas More and Plato are found at the frontier amidst the chaos and the politics. Today, the relation between utopia and dystopia has the weight of a long and doubly tragic historicity (individual and mass-mortality, the real possibility of destruction of the human species by humans). We dream of conquering new galaxies, but, as of now, our relation with outer space is one of a finite planet. The question of resistance in extremely unequal power relations rests in still more radicalized forms when we live within an intemperate dystopia.

In the 1960s, the ambiguous[7] utopia explored by Ursula Le Guin[8] in *L'autre côté d'un rêve* (The Lathe of Heaven), was thoroughly optimistic. Yet, in a world criss-crossed by conquests (Kant) and dominated today by a totalizing liberal capitalism, the utopian horizon resembles the big Australian wind-swept desert of solitude, where it rains every 10 years and no one knows when that will be. One would have to understand why this desert escapes even the imaginary of the madness that the Dadaists and the surrealists underwent in their attempt to reshape art, language, and thought in an unusually destructive century. Paul Celan, Primo Levi, David Rousset, Robert Antelme, Catherine Delbo, Anne-Lise Stern,[9] and many others understood this, exploring other barren ways, into other deserts, other much more terrifying abysses. Some others even attempted to describe the 'language of the assassin' (Faye), the Lingua Tertii Imperii (LTI)[10] in order to reshape the possibility of (post)totalitarian narration

---

[7] Maria Mena Yuste, Jordi Bonet Marti, and Alejandra Araiza Díaz, *Distopies feministes: un analisis de genere del libro els Desposseits d'Ursula K. Le Guin*, 2008, http://ca.wikibooks.org/wiki/Distopies_feministes:_un_an%C3%A0lisi_de_g%C3%A8nere_del_llibre_els_Desposseits_d'Ursula_K._Le_Guin (accessed 4 March 2011).

[8] Ursula Le Guin, *L'autre côté du rêve* (Paris: Le livre de poche, 1971).

[9] Anne-Lise Stern, *Le savoir déporté: camps, histoire, psychanalyse* (Paris: Seuil, 2004).

[10] Victor Klemperer, *LTI: La langue du IIIe Reich* (Paris: Pocket, 1975); Jean-Pierre Faye, *Le langage meurtrier* (Paris: Hermann, 1996).

of human history. At the end of the twentieth century, utopia is marked by a deep confusion regarding the philosophy of history. Whether it is cyclical (ancient Greece), or Hegelian, or whether it dreams of imperial hegemony in a 'new world order' (Bush), the philosophy of history is henceforth inhabited by the angel of Walter Benjamin, walking backward on a field of ruins towards the future.

We are confronting a challenge to find an oasis of survival, wrote Hannah Arendt in the 1960s, after having described the totalitarian system as the creation of a desert on earth, borrowing the metaphor from Nietzsche. But within the (post)totalitarian desert, the oases[11] of friendship and love which scraped through after the destruction of politics seem to have disappeared today. They have been swept out by the yellow sand of liquid[12] capitalism. The number of mental breakdowns among students, workers, activists, occupational mental illnesses, more frequent than the physical, in the world (according to World Health Organization, International Labour Organization [ILO])—are all worrisome phenomena. They keep us alerted about what happens to the body, psyche, and thought in professional fields. We are facing the challenge of creating a utopia for the twenty-first century which would combine the experience, victories, failures, and the memory of the defeated.[13] We are in search of a place (topos) where we can refresh our future dreams by embedding ourselves into life and not into survival. We are searching for a place where the relation between man and nature would no more be that of destruction. We are in search of a city of the world where it would be possible for everyone to have an accepted place, to experience a *cosmopolitical* condition of world citizen and, thereby, acquire a secure relation to the world, as in the philosophy of Hannah Arendt.

In the context of globalization where new power networks are webbed within the capitalist hegemony,[14] at the stage of the current crisis of

---

[11] Hannah Arendt, 'Fragment 4', in *Qu'est-ce que la politique?* (Paris: Seuil, 1993), 136–43.

[12] Zygmunt Bauman, *L'amour liquide: de la fragilité des liens entre les hommes* (Paris: Le Rouerge, 2004).

[13] See in this context, *Cahiers d'anthropologie sociale,* No. 4 (2008) Titled 'La Tradition des Vaincus' (which means the tradition of the vanquished), this is devoted to the work of Walter Benjamin.

[14] André Tosel, 'Hégémonie des pouvoirs et hégémonie capitaliste à l'époque de la mondialisation', in Pierre Concialdi, Lucien Guirlinger, Vincent Lépinard, Philippe Raymaud, Myriam Revault d'Allonnes, André Tosel, and Jean-Jacques Wunenburger, *Où est le pouvoir aujourd'hui?* (Paris: éditions Cécildedefaut, 2007), 111–49.

an all-embracing liberal capitalism and development, how do we name/ describe what is happening before our eyes by integrating regimes of historicity[15] relating to various spaces and an unprecedented rupture of civilization, its continued formation (conquest, colonization, imperialism), the tragic possibility of the destruction of the humanity, and the planet which was shaped in the twentieth century by Auschwitz and Hiroshima,[16] Cyclone B of extermination camps, and atom bombs? It has been philosophically characterized by Hannah Arendt as 'Human superfluity'[17] and by Günther Anders as 'the obsolescence of man'.[18] It should be emphasized that these two analyses highlight the national–socialist regime (Nazi) and US imperialism confronting Japan during the world war. These amount to an evaluation of the modernity of Europe and the American empire. The facts they have located are getting more and more pronounced today.

In this perspective, while it is acknowledged that all the possibilities of narrative have not disappeared,[19] how do actions and narrations articulate the crisis of utopia? How is the dialectic between utopia and dystopia being explored? What is recounted to us by these narratives when they overcome desperate muteness or listless silence? After the twentieth century and its continued formation, would dystopian narratives outplay utopian ones in the literature, by negating hope, making us tip over into the camp of anti-enlightenment[20] and withdraw from politics? Discourses on the illusion of progress through economic growth, of *work more earn more*, of self-centred control[21] are permeated with

---

[15] François Hartog, *Régimes d'historicité. Présentisme et expérience du temps* (Paris: Hartog, François, Seuil, 2003).

[16] Enzo Traverso, 'Auschwitz et Hiroshima. Notes pour un portrait intellectuel de Günther Anders', *Lignes*, No. 26: 7–34.

[17] Hannah Arendt, *Les origines du totalitarisme, le système totalitaire* (Paris: Points-Seuil, 1972).

[18] Günther Anders, *L'obsolescence de l'homme. Sur l'âme à l'époque de la deuxième révolution industrielle* (Paris: l'encyclopédie des nuisances, Ivréas, 2001) (1956).

[19] I do not subscribe to Adorno's position (it is impossible to write poetry after Auschwitz), nor to the end of grand narratives in post-modernity as in the philosophy of Lyotard.

[20] Zeev Sternhell, *Les anti-Lumières* (Paris: Fayard, 2006). See also, Enzo Traverso, 'Interpréter le fascisme', *La Revue Internationale des Livres et des Idées*, No. 3 (January–February 2008), http://www.revuedeslivres.net/articles.php?idArt=99 (accessed 14 March 2011).

[21] Writing about what is happening in Kenya, while taking note of the limits of 'right to interfere', a journalist names his article 'Before We Can Count the Number of Deaths' Bernard Getta, *Le Temps,* 2 February 2008.

doubt and scepticism. Moreover, the idea of revolution itself, tinged as it is with historical positivism, and the 'natural' link between war and revolution are being challenged.

Prima facie, facts on the modernity of the twentieth and the beginning of the twenty-first century make us tip over into intemperate and dreadful dystopia. Contemporary novelists articulate better the current impasses than the scientists. Science fiction, comic strips, mangas, sites on the Cyberpunk movement along with their satirical critiques of conditionings and solitude in the engulfing economic existence, disasters of the kind signalled by Huxley's *Brave New World* are replete with dystopian narratives. We are referring to novels such as *Disgrace* by Coetzee, *The Road* by Cormac McCarthy,[22] or George A. Romero's 'trilogy on the dead', fictional horror films.[23] Horribly rickety American tramps, rambling in the streets after a quasi-total end of the world, do not know anymore who they are, where they are. Everything is reduced for them to the poignant infernal present, to the details of their activities, to a few prophetic sentences. In this troubling space, we find maladapted people failing to melt into the streams of the society where they survive. The rest of the humanity still lives in fear, sorrow, compassion, and the curiosity of a child following a completely lost father. Another film, The *Hitchhiker's Guide to the Galaxy* leads to nothingness rather than even to a chaotic cosmos. This precedes *Nothing*,[24] a Canadian film on the power of nothingness staging a comedy of the void. The dialectic between utopia and dystopia seems to be crippled. The intemperate dystopia holds the centre stage.

The theme of the fiction of dystopian utopia through *active desertion* is, however, alive in the three-volume set of novels by Stieg Larsson, *Millennium* and particularly, in *The Girl with the Dragon Tattoo*,[25] where the character of a *hacker*, Lisbeth Salander, a rebellious young woman, disturbed, suffering from social control, prying unusually into family hatreds, financial scandals, and killers. Her only obsession is not to allow anybody to enter her life to control her, usurp her freedom, her body, her life, and thought. Yet, Lisbeth Salander, heroine of *Millennium*, shows us a viable way of active desertion. She thinks a lot, in an acute manner.

---

[22] Cormac McCarthy, *La route* (Paris: De l'Olivier, 2008).

[23] See on this subject, Sylvestre Meininger, 'Le retour des morts-vivants', *Le Monde diplomatique,* March 2008, p. 27.

[24] Natalie de Vincenzo, *Nothing*, DVD (2003).

[25] Stieg Larsson, *Les hommes qui n'aimaient pas les femmes*, Milennium 1 (Paris: Actes Sud), 2006.

She is very sensitive to her autonomy in her dealings and to all forms of submission and acquiescence. When she acts, she uses the latest techno-logical inventions. In the process of construction of her own self within a radical rejection of all bonds with the system, she makes use of de-ceits, she fantasizes, and she acts. She seeks to understand, describe, and denounce finance capitalism; the violence ushered by it; and to pay her enemies back in the same coin. To put it plainly, she resists. We are in front of a narrative indulging in the dystopian utopia. This leads us from the field of destruction to that of new struggles.

As for the nightmares of the humans, the urgent enquiries on secur-ity logics—a temporality reduced to the accelerated immediacy[26] of *channel-hopping*—enquiries on the tangible destruction hide the hori-zon of the future, urging us to break away from the past, historical mem-ories, and generations. And we find ourselves drowned in the dystopian dark night of the end of the world and within a space too cramped on this planet. Yet, exercises and alternatives persevere in dreams, thoughts, and narratives with new orientations. Contributors to this volume have for-mulated new concepts from diverse angles, and dialectically problem-atized utopia and dystopia as forms of resistance. These are the material and symbolic foundation of the most secret dreams and the most hid-den tactics for salvaging the political.

Observations of the conflict zones at the frontiers of democracy (women, foreigners, wars, destruction of the planet, etc.) lead us to pos-tulate that amidst the narratives of totalitarian domination based on ideas of the end of history as given by Francis Fukuyama and democ-racy (Bush), amidst the narratives about the metaphysics of disaster[27] describing the relation between capital and labour, ecological problems of the planet, inceptions of intemperate violence, wars, etc., subsist praxes of resistance, narratives recounting experiences of innovative struggles. What is there inside these praxes and narratives? How do these succeed in blending the most radical interrogations on the contemporary world, for instance, the inevitable questions posed by the social relations of gen-der and human finitude vis-à-vis infinitude of freedom experienced by the human species in regard to the form of chaos and the destruction of politics?

---

[26] Lothar Baier, *Pas le temps! Traité sur l'accélération* (Paris: Actes Sud, 2002).

[27] We cannot but be struck by the impact of an ideology of fatalistic catastrophes stuffed into social and political phenomena, whereas, the energy crisis and ecological problems do not end in political decisions involving immediate actions.

On an experimental plane, these can be described as practices and narratives of *revolutionary resistance of dystopian utopia*. The stake is twofold: gauging the impact on the transformations of practices and thoughts over the ruptures produced in the twentieth century, of new boundaries of mankind and the planet and of new challenges of (in)equality and onslaughts on life; and locating new, alarming signals of submission and de-politicization within the catastrophist and humanitarian discourses and the force of innovative political resistances, perpetually at work, in history.

Cosmos, Chaos and Politics: Abysmal Frontier of Dystopian Utopia

Considering the relation between the twofold concept of cosmos/world and that of politics allows us to bring out at once a primordial ambiguity of the term *mondialisation* which impacts our political and philosophical analyses. The translation of the word *globalization* into *mondialisation* entails an ambiguity on the philosophical plane. This is likely to dissimulate the richness of the Greek word *kosmos*[28] translated as *monde* from the Latin *mundus*. In modern times, the use of the word *monde* constitutes the danger of reducing the *monde* to the current stage of economic globalization. In philosophy, cosmos refers to *monde*, an orderly world in the imaginary of the philosophical thought. What this ambiguity is likely to conceal is the fact that the world does not resemble the idealized cosmos (order). Moreover, in political philosophy, *cosmo-polis* pertains to the articulation between cosmos and polis (city in Greek), one of the foundational political notions of human history. Plato harboured a deep disgust for the word 'democracy' which is to be reconsidered by us within its radicality in the light of recent historical ruptures, since this is one of the possible anchorages of a revolutionary resistance of dystopian utopia.

Let us dwell on traits common to all three terms: cosmos, *monde*, and universe. The reading lays bare a striking tension between the ontological abyss of chaos and the continual concern for establishing an

[28] This term is taken from the Greek *kosmos* and signifies the *world*, 'the world, the same for all, has not been created by either God nor man.' Sylvain Auroux and André Jacob, *Les notions philosophiques*, vol. 1 (Paris: Presses Universitaires de France, 1990), 500.

order by the polity (contract), philosophy (meaning), and science (truth). The cosmos represents a universe considered as a well-organized system. The *monde* represents a whole consisting of everything that exists, which is shaped by the earth and the visible celestial bodies conceived as an organized whole. Against this order of the cosmos, the totally disordered multiplicity is named 'chaos'. 'According to ancient philosophy, the world is an organized and meaningful whole within which every being finds its natural place. All the philosophers, from Heraclitus to the Stoics are in search of this single law.'[29] The world is also the dwelling place for man, the place as well as the symbol of human life. From the seventeenth century onwards, the universe (*universus*) comes to represent everything that exists, considered, according to the philosophies, as the totality of things created (creation), of beings, of perceptible objects including, or not including, human consciousness.

The word cosmos, *kosmos* comes from Greek; the word *monde*, *mundus* comes from Medieval Latin. We are treading the footprints of the tradition of Greco-Roman philosophy. These words send us back also to the words *Loka*, *Svarga* (Indian philosophy) and *Ten*, *Ukiyo* (Japanese philosophy). Seen from the other side, that of political and philosophical privation of cosmos and *monde*, cosmos becomes *acosmia*, the world—*monde*—becomes *immonde* (wretched). To put it plainly, they have an evidently positive and negative philosophical and political significance. From an atheistic approach towards the *monde* (world), Hegel forged the word *acosmia*, which signifies for him the negation of the reality of the world. He used it in his critique of Spinoza's pantheism.[30] Hannah Arendt, in her turn, overwhelmed by the totalitarian life situation, described the link between the privation of rights pertaining to the political and the *acosmia* situation, that is, privation of the possibility of relating to the world[31] following the privation of the political. She will therefore

---

[29] Jean François Robinet, 'Monde', in *Les notions philosophiques,* vol. 2 (Paris: Presses Universitaires de France, 1990), 1671.

[30] Pierre Macherey, *Hegel ou Spinoza* (Paris: Maspero, 1979); Yimiyahu Yovel, 'Le dialogue Hegel-Spinoza. Sa structure logique et sa voix humaine', *Cahiers de Fontenay* no. 36–38 (1985): 103–13.

[31] The tragedy (turbulence) is the fact that this catastrophe is not born out of a lack of civilization, a backward state, or merely, tyranny, rather, on the contrary, it is inescapable, because, there was not a single non-civilized place on the earth—because , willy-nilly, we really started to live in One World. Only a fully organized humanity could act in a way that the loss of home and political status would amount to being expelled from the entire humanity.

Arendt, *L'impérialisme*, vol. II, *Origines du totalitarisme* (Paris: Point-essai, 1972, 282).

ask, how is it possible to become contemporary to this world, possible to envision it, think it, dream it within the life span and the space for living that has been offered to us without any legitimate room for politics? As for the term, *immonde* (wretched), it comes to us from 1220, from the word *mundus*, understood as 'clean', 'pure'. In Christian theology, it used to signify impure, in the sense of wretched animals, wretched spirit, the devil, temptations of the flesh, desires, foul (*immonde*) thoughts, as in the philosophy of Ste Beuve. The classification refers here to the pure Being (God) and whatever moves away from Him and does not form part of Him. In the eighteenth century, it referred to dirtiness, or ugliness arousing disgust and horror. Transferred into the ethical field, it signified an extreme vice, something obscene and abject. The word *immondice*, which conjures up garbage, directs us towards the word-collection of clean or pure, which would inspire a lot of the anthropologists of dirt, like Mary Douglas and the sociologists and political scientists who are inspired by what transgresses the boundary, by the modes of radical political exclusions (xenophobia,[32] racism), which, following different paths of tradition, refer to *acosmia* in the sense Arendt used the term.

Science (cosmology, theoretical physics) and philosophy have both enquired about order, dynamics, totality, and infinitude, about man's place on Earth and also the possibility for man to know about the world (Kant) by displacing the relation of man to time and space. However, 'space and time have ceased to be, for relativity physics, part of the bare bones of the world, and are now admitted to be constructions'.[33] The debate on determinism and freedom and choice of 'being in the world', 'inhabiting the world' has been displaced from metaphysics to its critique. And reason associated with consciousness has gained in importance. From Plato,[34] Socrates, Heraclitus to Leibniz, Pascal, Guillaume d'Occam,[35] Hegel, Marx, Kant, Einstein, Negri, to Foucault, these themes

---

[32] Oliver Le Cour Grandmaison, 'Xénophobie d'Etat et politique de la peur', *Lignes*, No. 26, (2008): 23–38; 'Colonisés immigrés et "périls migratoires"': origines et permanence du racisme et d'une xénophobie d'Etat (1924–2007)', *Cultures et Conflits*, No. 69, (2008): 18–32.

[33] Bertrand Russell, *Our Knowledge of the External World as a Field for Scientific Method in Philosophy* (first published in 1914) (London: George Allen and Unwin, 1952), 109.

[34] J.-C. Fraisse, 'L'unicité du *monde* dans le Timée de Platon', *Revue philosophique de la France et de l'étranger*, No. 2 (1982), 249–54.

[35] J. Biard, 'L'unité du *monde* selon Guillaume d'Occam (ou la logique de la cosmologie okhamiste', *Vivarium*, 22, No. 1, (1984): 63–83.

are explored and interrogated. In the beginning of the twentieth century, advances in astronomical observations and physical theories led to an increasing systematization of the objects of the universe and to a debate centring on its boundary and finitude. Cosmology propped by relativity physics gives forth new knowledge about the structure and spatial expanse of the universe (finitude, infinitude, expansion or re-contraction of the universe); its evolution, beginning, and eventual end; origin of matter and explanation about a structuration on a big scale (galaxies, etc.); the place and solitude of the human kind, its fate, and destiny. On the other hand, new researches on the colonization of the moon (cost: a million dollars per minute of stay) bring to focus the curiosity over the commercialization of Helium 3, which could replace fossil fuels. The transformation of moon dusts into potable water along with the possibility of producing breathable oxygen would allow man to establish a self-sufficient lunar colony that would help escape the terrestrial sphere (without any possibility of return: this would be colonization as far off as possible, leading to a radical transformation in the imaginary regarding the cosmos and geopolitical displacements of power of a different order, international relations evolving into interplanetary relations).

After our visions of the universe, references of pre-totalitarian tradition are blurred in society. However, after the totalitarian rupture of the twentieth century taken together with the long continuance of slavery, colonialism, and imperialism, it is important to take note of two problems which mark the entire theoretical domain and emphasize the link between politics and history. Like Galileo and Machiavelli in their time, and Arendt and the Frankfurt school in the twentieth century, we are also in a very uncomfortable position. Galileo is a notable example of the political resistance to the new scientific discovery.

> We had always said that planets were fixed on the limpid sky so that they do not fall. Now we have plucked up courage and we allow them to remain suspended without support in space, with great ease. And the Earth rotates merrily around the Sun, and fishmongers, merchants, princes, cardinals and even the Pope rotate with it.[36]

Machiavelli, in his days, as explained by Althusser,[37] sought to decipher an emerging event, a beginning, a new form of organization and

---

[36] Bertolt Brecht, *La vie de Galilée* (Paris: L'Arche, 1990), cover blurb.
[37] Louis Althusser, *Politique et Histoire. De Machiavel à Marx. Cours à l'Ecole normale supérieure 1955–1972* (Paris: Seuil, 2006).

political existence, an irreversible fact of modern history that was taking shape within the tensions between absolute monarchy and the constitution of the United States. He attempted to think the New Prince, the New Kingdom without knowing properly the way this newness would come to be, writes Althusser. Arendt explains, on several occasions in her work, how difficult it is for a researcher to think and assess newness, given the 'unique novelty' of the regime, the totalitarian system, and the temptation to retreat when it comes to the question of investing concepts, arguments and old categories that are inadequate to capture the newness and to conceive by analogy (reducing the totalitarian system to a tyranny or a dictatorship) and we end up blindly robbing the political and philosophical novelty of the twentieth century of its originality.

Taking note of the euphoria about the chaos at the root of liberty and also the possible wreaking by politics, (which is a fact of human life)— of not only individual death but mass-killing—not by a vengeful God or natural disaster, but destruction of humans by the humans is a major challenge posed to science, philosophy, and politics. The existential anxiety over individual death articulated in Greek philosophy has been displaced (this can be noticed, for instance, in the employment situation, or policies concerning health, ecology) towards an enquiry on the possible annihilation of mankind and the planet. In such a context, what would become of the anxiety and desire for survival and life within a project of dystopian utopia? A political anthropology, an epistemology going along with the construction of a dystopian utopia, involves integrating the ontological chaos, the gaping abyss of political destruction and the mechanism—so admirably described by Freud—of resistance to see, understand, and know things lying before our eyes, which we reject and struggle to imagine, think, and judge.

At the current stage of globalization, let us dwell a moment on the theories and practices of development, war, and on the current features, particularly, of the policies of migration. Since the 1960s to 1970s, a critical debate within discourses on development has unfolded along three axes: progress adapted to the growth of capitalism (critique of liberalism, enlightenment/anti-enlightenment debate around the notion of progress), (in)equality (ILO, unions, migrants' country of origin), and the environment (environmentalist movement).[38] During the same period, the debate within political philosophy over justice has been polarized by the works

---

[38] The gender perspective is rather much less elaborated within these debates.

of John Rawls, which bear on interests of North American Empire. An Indian development economist, Amiya Kumar Bagchi, has shown the inadequacies of such theorization of justice relating to development[39] and migration.[40]

The concept of development has undergone consecutive formulations, one of which is the notion of sustainable development of the 1980s. It was formalized and propagated by the report *Our Common Future* (called *Brundtland Report* of the World Commission on Environment and Development, under the auspices of the UN General Assembly in 1987).[41] Since 1986, this concept has been contested by new social movements (underdevelopment/maldevelopment,[42] inequality, de-growth); yet, at the same time this is affirmed as 'right'.[43] Since then, the concept has assimilated an extension of the temporal (or generational, following the thinking of the philosopher Hans Jonas[44]) approach and the spatial global approach. It has articulated the economic, the social, the environmental, and the ideals of being bearable, viable, sustainable, equitable, without,

---

[39] Amiya Kumar Bagchi, 'Migration and Morality: Sovereign Finance and Dehumanized Immigrants ', in *Mondialisation, migration et droits de l'homme: un nouveau paradigme pour la recherche et la citoyenneté* vol. 1, eds. Marie-Claire Caloz-Tschopp and Pierre Dasen (Brussels: Bruylant, 2007), 647–81.

[40] Amiya Kumar Bagchi, 'Immigrants, Morality and Neoliberalism', *Development and Change* 39, No. 2 (March 2008): 197–218.

[41] We have to underscore that the argument of financial analysts that the sustainability had a positive impact on the profit of enterprises explains that more than 50 per cent of 2,500 bigger companies rated in stock markets are enlisted in a sustainable fund and that it has prompted the concept of sustainable development in the financial market to be reduced to stock profits (see on this subject the site of the Fondation Ethos).

[42] Jean Batou, *Cent ans de résistance au sous-développement* (Geneva: Droz, 1990).

[43] Led by the non-alignment movement, the UN declaration on the right to development of 4 December 1986, approved by 146 countries (more than 90 per cent of the world population, vetoed by USA, and with 10 abstentions (twentieth anniversary) proposes the following definition of development:

> A global economic, social, cultural and political process which aims at a perpetual betterment of the well being of the entire population and of all individuals on the basis of their active, free and significant participation to the development and equitable distribution of benefits resulting from this.

This founding text was accompanied by other texts: the Charter of economic rights and duties of the states (1974) along with its famous article 20 (Chapter III) expressing the need for the application of norms of protection, conservation, and development of the environment.

[44] Hans Jonas, *Le principe responsabilité. Une éthique pour la civilisation technologique* (Paris: Cerf, 1990).

however, integrating the gender perspective and a heterogeneity of history and territories.

In order to capture the concept of sustainable development within its radicality, it is necessary to go a little further. With the stage of imperialism—the current stage of financial capitalism—we find, contrary to what Cecil Rhodes longed for ('If I could, I would have annexed all the planets'), that it is not yet possible for capitalism to expand markets out of the Earth into the infinitude of the universe. There is a *fundamental contradiction between* the logic of infinite expansion of the exploitation of resources from a utilitarian angle and the logic of the workforce and the mortality-situation of the human race. Trapped in a pincer movement within this contradiction, labour, action, human life, and politics—all become bereft of their significance. This contradiction cannot be superseded within the periphery of the current capitalist system.

Some researchers address these issues from the perspective of *the need for de-growth* by locating the current data in the history of the long period. Jacques Grinevald describes our time as 'anthropocene',[45] that is, a geological age dominated by human beings since the coming of the Industrial Revolution. The anthropocene follows the Holocene which had lasted 10,000 years. It is a tiny and fragile moment in the history of the planet. What becomes then of labour in a perspective of de-growth? In this perspective, the paradigm of exploitation and over-exploitation of nature and the workforce has to be radically called into question.

The category of anthropocene is necessary for locating man's place in the world and for confronting new facts within the long history of our planet: the quantity of matter used by the human species has surpassed the stocks and the flows of nature. Our economic development has become the most powerful force of transformation, of not only social relations but also the planet (stronger than volcanoes). Our growth is on a collision course with biochemical cycles that regulate the stability of the Earth.[46] To come out of it, it is essential to acknowledge realities of the biosphere; further,

---

[45] Jacques Grinevald, *La Biosphère de l'Anthropocène. Climat et pétrole, la double menace: Repères transdisciplinaires 1824–2007* (Éditions Médecine and Hygiène: Geneva, 2007).

[46] The current proportion of carbon dioxide is the highest since 800,000 years, a fact identified by the research project, European Project for Ice Coring in Antarctica, *Nature*, 15 May 2008. Hence, it is no more possible to attribute the present global warming to the events which took place during the shifts from glacial to interglacial periods.

… everyone should admit the fact that we are an animal species unable to live without nature, which is an extension of the species itself. We have to slow down the pace of our life if we are to negotiate the bend coming closer to us at a great speed. The rich people and the West will have to set the example, because it is especially the West which led the world to this mad race. Or we will run into the wall headfirst.[47]

Since the inception of utopias calling development into question—not within the context of the growth/de-growth tension, but within the philosophy of the capitalist and totalitarian experience, an unusual space/ displacement of utopia most often hidden at the root of development theories—has come to the surface, the *Terra nullius*.[48] The concept of *Terra nullius* put forward by international law is described as land belonging to no one. In fact, this fiction allowed European predation against lands to be conquered by them by driving away and subjugating other peoples. The utopia of *Terra nullius* served to legitimize conquests, invasions, extermination of indigenous peoples, and slavery. It was radicalized in the twentieth century by Carl Schmitt.[49] Moreover, the utopia of *Terra nullius* is not only a utopia over a utilitarian conquest leading to plundering of territories and wealth. It also evokes an imaginary of destruction (*Terra nullius, land where nobody lives, therefore, if anyone lives out there, he/she will be exterminated for the benefit of the settlers.*[50]) One can say that it indicated a strange amalgam of utilitarian expansionist thought of the conqueror and the totalitarian nihilist thought of destruction and extermination.

In short, since the 1960s, ambiguous theories of development rubbed out from collective memory the imperial philosophical heritage of the conqueror—*Terra nullius*. Within the dominant policies of development, utopia merged into economic progress, although conquest, colonization, and plunders were never called into question. Interpretations of internal class relations within the states, and imperialist and developmentalist theories on the 'north–south' relations had a common point. These have

---

[47] Jacques Grinewald, 'On ne vit pas en mangeant des dollars', *Campus*, no. 90 (2008), 2.

[48] Sven Lindqvist, *Terra Nullius* (Paris: Les arènes, 2007).

[49] François Rigaux, 'L'histoire du droit international revue par Carl Schmitt', *Journal of the History of International Law*, no. 9 (2007), 233–62.

[50] Among several examples of history of *conquista* and colonization, we can cite Argentina. Before the conquest, Argentina was inhabited by numerous Indian races. Today it is the country in Latin America with the smallest number of Indians (around 3 per cent).

combined within the utopia of worldwide economic development, the eclipse of the ideology of *Terra nullius*, and the argument of catching up, in order to create a world market and simultaneously pursue a 'separate development policy' (apartheid) on the planetary level, replacing the class struggles of industrial capitalism.

Within the globalization of the labour market, we can notice such a philosophy at work, close at hand, between a cynical utilitarian economy and a nihilist approach of the destruction of the workforce. The terrain of the world market of labour at two levels of selective immigration (*care* and *brain drain*) is the right place to observe oblivion and contradictions with respect to the concept of development[51] from a perspective of social relations relating to gender, and at the same time, to (post)totalitarian justice.

The modes of governance of the new migratory order urged by *Lex Migratoria*[52] point to present transformations of the world labour market. In short, the new governance of migrations turns human workers into temporary and insecure beneficiaries of services, whatever their character may be—clandestine women migrant workers in custody or casual, knowledge workers in brain drain. The human workforce is being continually transformed by the logic of capitalism in terms of value, as proposed by Marx, and as a commodity. From a condition of human beings enjoying political rights, migrant workers become exploitable and exchangeable goods—non-entities evicted from politics. The present stage of labour market globalization exacerbates exploitation, essentialization, and naturalization of workforce. Hence, we badly need a critical review of the place of the human species within the concept of sustainable development by assimilating in this concept the *human factor, the meaning of work, the international democratization of the labour market* for all the men and women living as migrant workers. It is essential to link the concern for protecting nature as expressed in 'sustainable development' with the protection of human workers at a time when the survival of both nature and the human species is threatened. The ongoing

[51] Marie-Claire Caloz-Tschopp, 'Scientific Diasporas, Migration and Development: A Perspective from Philosophy and Political Theory', in *Scientific Diasporas as Development Partners: Skilled Migrants from Colombia, India and South Africa in Switzerland: Empirical Evidence and Policy Responses*, eds. Gabriela Tejada and Jean-Claude Bolay (Bern: Peter Lang, 2010), 21–136.

[52] Hélène Pellerin, 'Governing Labor Migration in the era of Gats. The Growing Influence of Lex Mercatoria', in *Governing International Labour, Migration. Current issues, challenges and Dilemmas*, eds. Christina Gabriel, Hélène Pellerin (London: Routledge, 2008).

DEVELOPMENT AND RESISTANCE OF UTOPIAN DREAMS 213

process of destructive cannibalism requires development to be focused on *human labour* without opposing it to the protection of nature. The issue is to expose the particular and typical inclinations for the destruction of nature and man and to rediscover labour within *care*, and also within cognitive capitalism—two ends of the labour market chain, which are not to be separated so that we can observe the market also within a species perspective. This involves a new ontology and a new political anthropology which would combine nature with man as a unique species-being.

On a different terrain, that of war, utopian discourses on progress through war appertain to a utilitarian and destructive thought whose determinism is not faultless. Discourses on the legitimation of war travel across history, gaining strength since the seventeenth century. They resurfaced after 11 September 2001 in a situation in which war as a concept was diluted and captured between imperialist wars and social wars[53]—redefining relations between violence from the top and power from below. In modern times, the term 'military revolution' has been utilized to interpret the predominance of the West since the sixteenth century, and the emergence of 'absolute' war, as given by Clausewitz, along with co-operation among the European states, came gradually to take the centre stage in debates[54] since the eighteenth century. Whereas the republican Kant—an apprehensive admirer of the French revolution—contemplates perpetual peace (built on rights of the people and not only of the state, hospitality, abolition of slavery, opposing private property in a finite world),[55] the state of war serves as the inevitable reference point in international and internal (civil war) relations. Before him, for Hobbes, 'the nature of war consisteth not in actual fighting, but in the known disposition thereto, during all the time there is no assurance to the contrary'.[56]

---

[53] See Jacques Bidet, ed., *Guerre impériale, guerre sociale* (Paris: Actuel Marx, 2005).

[54] A veteran colonel of the 1870 Franco-Prussian war, engaged in the defence of Captain Dreyfus, predicted that the cannon would outshine the bayonet and the war of the future would be a chronic war bringing face to face two human walls that would be forcibly razed to the ground. Vincent Duclert, *Le colonel Mayer. De l'affire Dreyfus à de Gaulle* (Paris: Armand Colin, 2007).

[55] Immanuel Kant, *Projet de paix perpétuelle, OEuvres III, les derniers écrits* (Paris: Gallimard, 1986) (first published in 1795) 350–53; M. David-Ménard, *Les constructions de l'universel* (Paris: PUF, 1997).

[56] Thomas Hobbes, Part I, Chapter XIII, in trans. F. Tricaud, *Léviathan* (Paris: Sirey, 1971).

The French Revolution and Napoleon dominate the imaginary of the eighteenth and nineteenth centuries, whereas the Russian communist revolution and 'total war' dominate the twentieth century. Two references of the philosophy dominating the nineteenth century, Hegel and Clausewitz, are rooted in the experience of Napoleonic wars, leading to an excessive onslaught and total mobilization. They enquired about how to curb the disarray of war[57] and achieve rapid and permanent victory. Both of them laid down a 'natural' relation between war and politics. The 'world spirit' was for Hegel the face of Napoleon, an outcome of the French Revolution, reaching the city of Lena on horseback.[58] The modern (Napoleonic) war, for Clausewitz, has given rise to one of his leading slogans regarding the meaning (and not the definition) of war: 'war [is] an extension of State politics through different means or a combination of different means',[59] and to his distinction between 'absolute war' (abstraction leading to the rise to the extremes)[60] and 'real war'

---

[57] The idea that it would be possible to control the limitless violence by means of force is at the core of the reflection of Clausewitz after his experience in the Prussian army in 1806 in the battle of Jena. The army of Frederick II was positioned in the time of 'limited warfares' and was facing Napoleon whose logic was to go to extremes. Clausewitz concluded: 'The one who does not retreat before a bloodbath will take advantage of the other who does not act similarly.' His principle of non-limitation of violence will be confirmed with the modern 'total' war, millions of people killed in the twentieth century, emergence of nuclear arm. We encounter such a logic in numerous conflicts, from Algeria to Columbia, and also in tortures and forms of imprisonment as those of Guantanamo which, while coming within the scope of the same logic, strengthen the same. Whoever does not submit to this logic, due to his respect towards life and humanist values, runs the risk of becoming more vulnerable.

[58] In the twentieth century, Theodor Adorno sees the spirit of the world reaching on the wings of Hitlerian V-2 missiles, those robot bombs with technical perfection and the most total blindness.

[59] Karl von Clauswitz, *De la Guerre*, Denise Naville, trans (Paris: De Minuit, 1955), 703, 728.

[60] René Girard, *Achever Clausewitz* (Paris: Carnets Nord, 2007). René Girard, in his theory of mimetism, his theory of sacrifice and murder in archaic religions (scapegoat) in order to 'complete Clausewitz' who theorized the Napoleonian model and who, for Girard, has become the absolute model. In these religions the goal was production of the sacred, but today, 'the violence which used to produce the sacred, now produces nothing else than itself' (Ibid., 11). The model of Clausewitz 'has been taken up afresh by Lenin, Mao, Al-qaeda' (Ibid., 363). Girard reads Clausewitz in dialogue with the texts on Apocalypse and a re-interpretation of the religious novelty of Christ. Clausewitz, whom he puts in opposition to Hegel had a 'dazzling intuition', in his admiration of Napoleon regarding the link/relation between war and mimetism. He identified the apocalyptic nature of the modern warfare captured within a momentum of history, the 'rise to the extremes', this political

(historical circumstances). Lenin, inspired by Clausewitz will write later that war prepares the conditions for revolution. We encounter another discourse on war relating to humanitarian acts (not to revolution) in the work of Henri Dunand, founder of the International Red Cross, after his visit to Solferino,[61] which is striking for its acceptance of the inevitability of war.

Raymond Aron asks, 'Why do wars take sometimes subtle forms of fencing, then erupt with violence of tempests and cruelty of instincts?'[62] But he does not de-link war and politics. He explains that two principles (*Grundsätze*) derived from a conceptual analysis help us deliberate upon the Clausewitzian theory: the principle of destruction and annihilation and the perpetuation of politics through other forms. The gaze on the work of Clausewitz changes according to the principle we adhere to. In a 1975 article written for the *Revue militaire Suisse*, on *La société des Etats et la guerre* (The Society of the States and War), Aron explains that these two principles are neither contradictory nor incompatible 'in the strict sense of the term'. They are adjusted according to the place assigned to 'political supremacy' with respect to the war.[63] To put it simply, politics must look after the links between the utilitarian and the destructive aspects of war. It is true that Aron addresses the issue during his reflections over the supreme legislator—the State—and peace being sought

---

inability to contain the inexorable violence of mimetism out of reciprocity which became imperative like the only law of history. It is necessary to finish his book by analysing the flip side of the reciprocity. Girard attempts, religiously, at a rehabilitation of Christianity in the face of Islam and the 'clash of civilizations' as put forth by Samuel Huntington. 'The possibility of the end of Europe, the western world, and the world as a whole. This possible has become real today' (Ibid., 9). 'Christianity can rekindle the love which turned cold. Given that the passion of Christ has unveiled once and for all the sacrificial origin of the humanity…. The Passion has unleashed the violence ad at the same time liberated the holiness' (Ibid., 12). Christ was opposed to reprisals, the rise to the extremes, and introduced reconciliation and love. He laid down the reciprocity within a non-warrior and relational framework. I cannot discuss his theses here, his method, the absence of all relation to history and even to the facts, neither some ambiguities of the argumentation, but I claim to indicate them to the extent that some of his arguments cater to other readers of Clausewitz.

[61] Henri Dunant, *Un souvenir de Solferino* (Paris: Croix Rouge Française, 2009).

[62] Aron Raymond, *Sur Clausewitz* (Brussels: Complexe, 1987), 45.

[63] The natural intention of knife is to slice: this doesn't lead to the fact that the user of the knife should always look forward to slice. There are various ways, for the butcher, of using his knife, albeit, the proposition expressing the natural intention of knife does not cease to be true.

Ibid., 103.

out through the balance between the States in a context preceding the wars of extermination and the nuclear weapons of the twentieth century. He opts for an 'optimistic' position,[64] yet, he observes that the criteria of balance and intensity are profoundly modified with the emergence of two world wars and the nuclear weapons,[65] without denying, for all that, the link between war and politics.

This opens up a new field of reflection on the links between war and politics. In the twentieth century, with the totalitarian domination, emerges the concept of 'absolute' war, as in the philosophy of Carl Schmitt, which, with the pair *friend–foe*, and the state of exception, dictatorship demanding final solutions, shapes a new theoretical debate. Without wrangling over interpretations of the Clausewitzian position, or dwelling on Carl Schmitt, let us remember that war is deliberated upon through articulations of life/death and war/politics.[66] This position will be taken up once more on a different plane (so-called bio-power) by Foucault.[67] With the experience of extremes of the 'short-lived 20th century',[68] Arendt breaks the obvious link between violence and revolution (1950–60).[69] For Arendt, the rupture starts from a critical reflection on another dominantly perceived link, the one between war and revolution. This leads her to enquire about the meaning of politics and separate war from politics. In short, with the totalitarian construction, the field of politics became the field of mass extinction and destruction, the metamorphosis of the world into the desert. It is *the horizon, the logic, the grammar* of all politics and no more an *alternative path* to preserve politics. Arendt reinterprets the famous notion of Clausewitz and denounces a utilitarian conception of politics associated with the philosophy of the war of destruction and capture—an unprecedented transformation which marks a fundamental

---

[64] Emmanuel Terray, *Clausewitz* (Paris: Fayard, 1999): 72–85.

[65] 'Since then, at higher bars of the ladder of violence, emerge nuclear arms. And they force to choose decisively between two Clausewitzian principles: the destruction, annihilation and decision, on the one hand and, on the other, the supremacy of the politics.' Aron, *Sur Clausewitz*, 106.

[66] Zygmunt Bauman, 'Living and Dying in the Planetary Frontier-land', *Society under Siege* (Cambridge: Polty, 2002), 87–117.

[67] See Michel Foucault, *Il faut défendre la société*, (Paris: Gallimard/Seuils, 1997), 16—his concept of silent war by turning upside down the famous thesis of Clausewitz.

[68] Eric Hobsbawm, *L'âge des extrêmes. Histoire du court XXe siècle* (Paris: Complexe/Le Monde diplomatique, 1994).

[69] Hannah Arendt, *La politique a-t-elle encore un sens?* (Paris: L'Herne, 2006), 85, and 101–02.

change of the conception of politics and its practice. It is from this vantage point that she enquires about what connects and, at the same time, separates war and politics, and about what radically transforms the idea of revolution from the twentieth century.[70] Following suit, first Derrida, and then Balibar, in the beginning of the twenty-first century, starting from the ambiguity of the term *Gewalt* (voilence and power), shift their conceptual theorization of violence and war.

Emergence of a New Dystopian Utopia

The frontier is not an essence within the conflicts at the frontiers of democracy. It is a field of relations which is at the same time over-determined, polysemic, heterogeneous[71] belonging to *an ontological, anthropological*, and *political* order. In other words, the frontier is a lieu/non-lieu, within which political relations, the dialectics between chaos and nothingness, between the social-historical being and non-being, and the possibility of building *a political relation of cosmo-political citizen-ship* come into play.

In the preface to the sociologist Abdelmalik Sayad's book on migration, Pierre Bourdieu asks, 'What is an immigrant?' He writes:

... like Socrates, the migrant is *atopos*, without clinging to any place, displaced, defies all classification. Neither citizen nor foreigner, neither really belonging to the Same nor totally to the Other, the migrant is placed in that twilight zone mentioned by Plato, the frontier of social entity and non-entity.[72]

He is the inhabitant par excellence of lieu/non-lieu of utopia. The *atopos* migrant of today does not belong any more to the working class within the internationalized nation state system, but to a globalized

---

[70] Marie-Claire Caloz-Tschopp and Hannah Arendt, 'Le fil rompu entre violence et révolution' (unpublished, seminar Violence and Revolution in the Twentieth Century, December 2007).

[71] Etienne Balibar, 'Qu'est-ce qu'une frontière?', in *Asile, violence, exclusion en Europe. Histoire, analyse, prospective, Cahiers des Sciences de l'Education*, eds. Marie-Claire Caloz-Tschopp, Axel Clévenot, and Maria-Pia Tschopp (Geneva: University of Geneva and Groupe de Genève 'Violence et droit d'asile en Europe', 1994), 335–43.

[72] Sayad Abdelmalek, *L'immigration ou les paradoxes de l'altérité* (Brussels: de Boeck, 1991), 9.

working class. This class has changed its face and has taken on new functions, producing care workers and knowledge workers.

The life conditions of the *atopos* migrant, of the illegal immigrants are maligned and negativized 'to the extent of war',[73] writes Antonio Negri. We may recall here the camps at the frontiers of Europe. We may also recall the European directive on preventive detention for administrative reasons[74] and the European pact recommended by the Sarkozy government to formulate selective immigration policy. We may also recall the famous model of circles[75] (for which Switzerland has been condemned before the UN for State racism) or 'no entry on asylum' (NEM) in Switzerland.[76] We may recall the current debate on 'pure' cultural identity, and protecting Christian Europe from Islamist contamination. From the standpoint that Europe would not owe its wisdom to Islam, a researcher would attempt to reinstate the Greek roots of the Christian empire in France and Aristotle in Mont Saint-Michel.[77] Other researches make an opposite trajectory by recognizing an Arabic domination within European thought.[78] These facts underline the power relation in the context of domination.

In the struggles of the migrants at the frontiers of democracy, following the course of emergence of new configurations, concepts, words, examples to depict the existential condition of resistance, we discover new, valuable narratives combining a utopian and dystopian approach. The conflicts at the frontiers of democracy let us observe the

---

[73] Antonio Negri, 'Nomadisme et métissage: Entretien Fait par Sonia Dayan-Herzbrun', *Tumultes,* no. 24 (2005), 179–89.

[74] One of the last European measures in the making is the subject of a vast debate in Brussels. It is about a project of directives on the clandestine setting of common norms applicable to the expulsion of clandestine immigrants (18 months of administrative retention as per plan).

[75] Marie-Claire Caloz-Tschopp, 'Les trois cercles de la démocratie sécuritaire', in *Transeuropéennes,* no. 9 (1997), 31–41.

[76] Federal department of Justice and Police refused to enlist those without any identity papers, having applied for asylum and classified them in an administrative category (non entrée en matière/without introduction) for denying them all rights and benefits and forcing them to leave, thereby, the Swiss territory. This measure has been regarded as anti-constitutional.

[77] Sylvain Gougenheim, *Aristote au Mont-Saint-Michel: Les racines grecques de l'Europe chrétienne* (Paris: Seuil, 2007).

[78] Ernst Bloch, *Avicenne et la gauche aristotélicienne* (Paris: Premières pierres, 2008); Kurt Flasch and Jacob Schmutz, *D'Averroès à Maître Eckhart, Les sources arabes de la mystique allemande* (Paris: Vrin, 2008).

coexistence of two antagonistic logics which confront one another, namely, security versus support for essential necessaries and rights, as explained by Carretero.[79] Let us also locate in these conflicts the emergence of a utopian revolutionary resistance of dystopian politics from which emerges an alternative project of cosmopolitan citizenship in this era of globalization.

From the perspective of utopia, giving passports to 'illegal workers' and shifting the notion of people towards that of the multitude (following Negri) represent the transformations of the notion of political class, articulating them in what Spinoza called the force of *conatus*, of becoming the Being.[80] 'No one can desire to be blessed, to act rightly, and to live rightly, without at the same time wishing to be, to act and to live, in other words, to actually exist.'[81] At the same time it makes it understandable what 'illegal' meant when they might ascribe illegality to the call for the recognition of the 'right to transit' for illegal workers in Europe.[82]

The majority of the migrants are in fact women, and it is mostly their material and political fate which is labelled, laid out, narrated, and proclaimed. Rada Ivekovic provides a critical analysis of the logic and the categories of the partitioning of thought and the politics relating to fundamentalist war in Europe.[83] Besides the concept of apartheid—put forward to define the current societies of immigration/emigration—her project is enriched by the introduction of the perspective of social relations of gender, by the notion of an 'apartheid regime of gender'[84] for describing the situation of female migrants.

These political and theoretical experiences are all rooted in the material conditions of concrete existence of male and female migrants.

---

[79] Antonio Ajo Carretero, 'Citoyenneté et mouvements migratoires', in Caloz-Tschopp and Dasen, *Mondialisation, migration, droits de*, 441–51.

[80] Laurent Bove, *La stratégie du conatus* (Paris: Vrin, 1996).

[81] Bairuch Spinoza, 'L'Ethique: de la servitude humaine', in *Oeuvres* (Paris: Gallimard, coll. La Pléiade, 1957), 507.

[82] Jean-Michel Dolivo, Tafelmacher Christophe, 'Sans-papiers et demandeurs d'asile: faire reconnaître le droit d'être là', in Caloz-Tschopp and Dasen, *Mondialisation, migration, droits de*, 459–519; Mezzadra Sandro, *Diritto de fuga: Migrazioni, cittadinanza, globalizzazione* (Verona: ombre corte, 2001).

[83] Rada Ivekovic, 'Une guerre de fondation en Europe?', in *Asile, violence, exclusion en Europe: histoire, analyse, prospective*, eds. Caloz-Tschopp, Clévenot, and Tschopp (Geneva: co-éd. FPSE, University of Geneva, Groupe de Genève 'Violence et droit d'asile en Europe', University of Geneva, 1994), 5–10.

[84] Marie-Claire Caloz-Tschopp, 'Clandestinity of Female Migrants. Regime of Gender Apartheid. Violence, Globalization', Proceedings of the Seminar in Free University of Brussels, 18–19 November 2005, 'Living in Clandestinity'.

The words used (to describe them) underscore their political exclusion (illegal, clandestine). These experiences call in question the link between economic globalization and security mechanisms (of the State making way for the privatization) within migration policies, which has been labelled as the complex of *Liberty–Security–Justice* in Europe[85] (Tampere) and as *Perimeter Security*, a term borrowed from the world of computer science.

A *utopian* vision would locate a project of globalized society outside the apartheid of the nation state system and utilitarian globalization propped by security mechanisms. These experiences radically question an imaginary—apartheid practices with respect to gender and class entrenched in the categories of the national and the race, sometimes involving ethnic cleansing.

These experiences of treatment of migrants become a part of a dystopian utopia. They challenge the dominant imaginary and epistemology, where the political and philosophical categories blend with utilitarianism and a political culture of destruction that sanctions forced repatriations.[86] The accounts of these experiences of struggles at the frontiers are not told like the dream of an unlimited freedom of movement which would *naturalize* the migratory movement, and would amount to an abolition of frontiers. It melds with competitive economic utilitarianism comprising free circulation of capital, and goods, and drastically limits the intervention of State control, social movement, unions, parties, along with the weakening of solidarity.

On the contrary, these experiences relate to a citizenship rooted in the material conditions of existence of the male and female workers who are compelled to move for survival and not impelled by dreams of ceaseless travel. The innovative political and philosophical significance of a revolutionary resistance of these experiences can be interpreted in terms of a dual debate around the right to have rights and radical democracy.

The theoretical works by Arendt and Castoriadis were inspired by two major experiences of the twentieth century, namely, Nazi destruction, and failure of communism, respectively. On the one hand, within

---

[85] Council of the European Union: The Hague Programme to strengthen liberty, security and justice in EU as approved by the European Council during its meeting on 5 November 2004, Brussels, 13 December 2004 (no. 6054/04).

[86] Marie-Claire Caloz-Tschopp, *Les réfugiés aux frontières de l'Europe et le spectre des camps* (Paris: La Dispute, 2004); 'Ce Qui Fait ... Ceux Qui Font le Lit du Totalitarisme Neoliberal a Venir?' *Revue québéquoise de droit international, Montréal* 13, No. 2, (2000): 71–97.

the nihilist convulsions of the history of the twentieth century, an exiled woman, Hannah Arendt attempted to understand the totalitarian system and construct a political foundation of 'the right to have rights' by making room for thought and judgment as activities of freedom and plurality. On the other hand, a concept of radical democracy, allowing space for human creativity, was developed by the group *Socialisme ou Barbarie*, led by Castoriadis, an exiled Greek communist.

The Right to Have Rights (Arendt)

Everyone Had a Place in My World is the utopia of Bessie Head, as has been well analysed by Modhumita Roy in the present volume. An identical concern is found in the work of Arendt, who inspired by Spinoza and Marx, posited that every human being has a place in politics and, hence, in the world. Arendt built up her reflections from the vantage point of non-statist conceptions in Europe and in the colonies in diverse forms. We may pick out two things from her work.

Starting from a critical analysis of the rights of man and non-statist conceptions,[87] Arendt laid a foundation for politics, citizenship, and rights of man without giving in to relativism, even in the name of a constructivism that differentiates between 'universalizing and universalizable',[88] and wears down all the legitimacy of the rights of man, struggles for the rights of man, and the need for sanctions related to these rights, as reminded by Monique Chemillier-Gendreau.[89] That constructivism would also disallow rights based on diverse fields of practice; for instance, the right to employment.[90] Arendt spoke about 'the right to have rights' as:

---

[87] Marie-Claire Caloz-Tschopp, *Les sans-Etat dans la philosophie de Hannah Arendt. Les humains superflus, le droit d'avoir des droits et la citoyenneté* (Lausanne: Payot, 2000).

[88] Julien François, *De l'universel, de l'uniforme, du commun et du dialogue entre les cultures* (Paris: Fayard, 2008). See also, Universels les droits de l'homme? *Le Monde diplomatique* (February 2008): 24–25.

[89] Monique Chemillier-Gendreau, *Humanité et souveraineté. Essai sur la fonction du droit international* (Paris: La Découverte, 1995); *Droit international et démocratie mondiale. Les raisons d'un échec* (Paris: Textuel, 2002); Monique Chemillier-Gendreau and Moulier-Boutang Yann, eds, *Le droit dans la mondialisation* (Paris: Presses Universitaires de France, 2001).

[90] With respect to the right to employment, see Alain Supiot, 'Lier l'humanité: du bon usage des droits de l'homme', *Esprit* (February 2005): 134–63.

[W]e become aware of the existence of a right to have rights (and that means to live in a framework where one is judged by one's actions and opinions) and a right to belong to some kind of organized community, only when millions of people emerge who had lost and could not regain these rights because of the new global political situation.[91]

In a (post)totalitarian perspective, through her *right to have rights*, Arendt reverses the destruction of politics and humans rendered super-fluous by a narrow view of rights. To eschew all ambiguities, let us clar-ify that she does not go for the same logic as does Burke in penning a severe critique of the rights of man. Arendt is interested in the loss that we are unaware of, resulting from the destruction of politics.

Her statement of the right to have rights is neither a right figuring in a list of demands, nor for an institution like the others. This is a foun-dation, a framework, an arch which precedes every political institution. This appears in an extreme political situation of non-adherence, and genocide, which can be brought back to positivity through actions by the individuals building up a collective consciousness about the situation. This is a kind of theorem for political thought which underscores the im-portance of action in the process of re-instituting politics. No authority, no sovereign grants the right to have rights. The only immanent certitude is that the individuals grant each other the right to have rights and remain committed to the same.

The loss of political position and citizenship or the annihilation of a person's humanity leads to the situation that a person loses the quality that allows others to consider him (her) as their fellow being. Those who have lost every political adherence 'appear as the first signs of a pos-sible regression in civilization'.[92] For these people, what remains only is an existence reduced to the qualities of a private reality (sympathy, friendship, intelligence, gift of love) which cannot replace the loss of the politics that relates her to the world.

Arendt makes her demonstration by a method which I called the dynamics of 'lack and desire'[93] with respect to politics where adherence

---

[91] Hannah Arendt, *Les origines du totalitarisme*, vol. 2 (Paris: Point-essais, 1972), 281–82.

[92] Hannah Arendt, *L'impérialisme*, vol. 2, *Les origines du totalitarisme* (Paris: Points-seuil), 289.

[93] Marie-Claire Caloz-Tschopp, *Les sans-Etat dans la philosophie de Hannah Arendt. Les humains superflus, le droit d'avoir des droits et la citoyenneté* (Lausanne: Payot, 2000).

to politics and political consciousness (aftermath) about the situation and the political condition are built up at the same time. This explains the relation between the 'right to have rights' and the reflective and critical practice in her work.

According to Arendt, the paradoxical character of the role of reason is a result of the crisis which does not allow an escape route of open dialectics. Do we opt for game theory to overcome the deficiencies of theories of intentionality? When the theories of revolutionary choice[94] are subjected to it, game theory says that something goes beyond its purview, that revolutions remain unforeseeable and unknowable (which is perhaps the most important discovery).[95] The dominant mainstream philosophy of history would have us believe that with the end of history and democracy, there is no more place and space to fall on, to think, and to act. Dialectical reason gets into a tangle within the paradigm of progress and it refuses to explore its own limit and determinism. Can poetic reason—only beauty matters—replace it? It is the dressing of the soul, but it doesn't replace the urgency of the polis, and politics.

How can we imagine and think in such a scenario? By retrieving and formulating thought as shared public practice along with action and public judgment, 'reflecting on what we are doing', that is, what Arendt, once again, convincingly argued in *Life of the Mind* and other texts. I extracted a praxis from it, a practical exercise of thought activity within quotidian action, open to the world as a whole. I called this 'the exploratory postulate of the total liberal capitalism'[96] which has to be supplemented by public judgement. Playing tricks with fear, working on the anxiety, establishing a possible link with the world (cosmos), to be

---

[94] Tarik Tazdaït, Rabia Nessah, *Les théories du choix révolutionnaires* (Paris: La Découverte, 2007).

[95] The revolutionary, socialist, communist utopia is constituted by the infinitude of liberty, plurality, and equality which are the essence of man (Arendt) and is not reducible to destructive passion (thesis of Furet), neither to any particular type of political regime. Utopia cannot be defined by the boundary of history and of the unforeseeable of which totalitarianism has been the political regime par excellence. As for communism, its history presupposes the consideration of the leftist opposition to the dictatorship of the proletariat of Lenin and to the totalitarian system of Stalin. The analysis of Soviet totalitarianism cannot be confined to the condemnation of the evil spells of a doctrine, Marxism, socialism, egalitarianism. Without being totalitarian, egalitarianism belongs to the democratic conceptualization, which is constituted at its frontiers by those having no part. (Socialisme ou Barbarie, Castoriadis, Rancière).

[96] On this subject, see Marie-Claire Caloz-Tschopp, *Résister en politique. Résister en philosophie avec Hannah Arendt, Castoriadis, Ivekovic* (Paris: La Dispute, 2008).

contemporary to the world, where we live, we have to turn the surge of reflection into shared creative activity.

Imaginary Project of a 'Radical' Democracy (Castoriadis)

At a time which was not yet doubly tragic as ours (individual death and the possibility of destruction of humanity and even the planet), the democrats of ancient Greece were confronted with other challenges—war, mortality, chaos, social relations of gender, for example, the absence of a father with his authoritarian substitutes in politics, personified by the tyrant and tackled through the creation of the genres of tragedy, philosophy, and democracy. They passed on to us questions about power, the State, submission and freedom, a father-free society, and a society of brothers. These questions were taken up again by Freud, Federn,[97] and much later by the feminists (What are the functions of mothers and sisters in politics and war?).

The crisis of reason and philosophy demands a deep transformation of rationality and philosophy, enabling us to rethink philosophy and thereby a project of dystopian utopia—but in what direction? Deliberating upon the imaginary institution of society, Castoriadis writes that from Plato to Marx, political thought has been introduced as an application of a theory of essence of society and history. An ontology of identity for which being has always signified being determined, has concealed the being of the social-historical as imaginary radical. This ontology has thereby suppressed various germs contained in the contemplative exercise by the thinkers such as Plato, Marx, and Freud. Castoriadis advances the thesis that a new institution of society, a new relation to history involves a supersession of established reason. This is about seeing history as creation, the instituting society, or the social imaginary at work within the instituted society, the social-historical Being as unknown mode of being of inherited thought. Human beings have conceived both Auschwitz and democracy. The determinism of destruction, although it is clearly present and difficult to conceive, is not inescapable. The social-historical being perpetually contains determinism and freedom, chaos and order, the instituted and the created, and war and revolution. For Castoriadis,

---

[97] Paul Federn, 'Contribution à la psychologie de la révolution: la société sans pères', *Incidences*, no. 3 (2007): 221–37.

resurrection of an open dialectical thought is possible, thanks to the power of imagination of individuals and societies.

In his open method of political and logical ontology which enlivens dialectics, the method of Castoriadis is put to the test of integrating the fact that, under the influence of wars and struggles,[98] foundations are shaken, the constants may vary to such an extent that the framework that holds the political life completely disappears.[99] To put it simply, the dynamics of the becoming of the social-historical being transforms theory, logic, and philosophy.

History, transformation of power relations, and reorientations of temporality and territorializaton within global geopolitics urge foundational philosophy and political theory to shift towards a political ontology of becoming, and the power of connecting multiplicities and networks,[100] towards an open and creative logic, and a theory of relations between the States on their frontiers and outside their territories. It is encouraging that Arendt, Castoriadis along with other scholars have engaged in a new political anthropology for the twenty-first century. It is precisely here that one of the basic issues of contemplation about the dystopian utopia of the twenty-first century has to be located.

For Castoriadis, the rediscovery of the power of radical imagination is linked to a resurrection of logic, and political ontology of individual autonomy. That resurrection would transform the praxis and the relation between politics and philosophy. Along with the group *Socialisme ou Barbarie*, in a debate over the substance of socialism, Castoriadis put forward the issue of democracy in the workplace, in the parties and the unions by recalling the experiences of the revolutionary committees at the time of the Soviet revolution. He emphasizes the tension between the conceptualization of law and autonomy, and between society and subjectivation. Then in dialogues with Pierre Vidal-Naquet, Jean-Pierre Vernant, Nicole Loraux (who emphasized conflicts over the place of woman in society), he goes deeper into his conceptualization of democracy

---

[98] Michael Hardt and Antonio Negri, *Multitude. Guerre et démocratie à l'âge de l'empire* (Paris: La Découverte, 2004).

[99] It suffices to keep in mind the situation of ex-Yugoslavia, Columbia and some African countries.

[100] See particularly, Gilles Deleuze and Felix Guattari, *Mille Plateaux* (Paris: Minuit, 1980); Toni Negri, *Les nouveaux espaces de liberté* (Paris: Dominique Bedou, 1985); Gilles Deleuze, *Pourparlers* (Paris: Minuit, 1990), *L'île déserte et autres textes (1953–1974)* (Paris: Minuit, 2002).

as a 'germ'[101] and the theorization of the same. He engages in polemics with Plato (like Arendt) by reviewing the dialogues of Plato—and by demonstrating that Plato is the major enemy of democracy.

For Castoriadis, democracy is neither a model nor a regime in the classical sense of these terms in political science. *This is a mode of creation of collective power which is continually open and uncertain*—'democratic creation is the creation of an unlimited enquiry in all domains: truth and falsehood, the just and the unjust, good and evil, the beautiful and the ugly'.[102] He locates in democracy the notion of radical workers' control which he already developed in his 'On the Content of Socialism', on the basis of experiences of workers' management in the working-class movement. He goes back to Ancient Greece between eighth and fifth century BC, the fifth century being the golden century, by putting aside the fourth century and Plato[103] (but by assigning a privileged position to the authors of tragedy, to Protagoras and to doxa—speech, debate, judgment—and not to episteme nor to techne[104]). This implies profound political and philosophical ruptures for retrieving the power of creation inherent in human finitude. Jacques Rancière adds another stone to the edifice by taking up afresh the issues of (in)equality, *Disagreement*[105] and the excluded. This helps establish links with the non-statist conceptions of Arendt and with issues of *post-colonial studies* by integrating the gender perspective.[106]

The instituting power of demos, by constituting itself politically and constructing its autonomy, sets limits, particularly to secure human rights.

---

[101] I am not taking up again the critiques of the Athenian democratic experiment (place of women, imperialism, war, slavery).

[102] Cornélius Castoriadis, 'La culture dans une société démocratique', *La montée de l'insignifiance* (Paris: Seuil), 200.

[103] Castoriadis decried, apart from the relation to the history as *Geschick* (destiny), three blindnesses in the Heideggerian interpretation of Greece, 'We are now in front of a bizarre spectacle of a philosopher who incessantly talks about the greeks and in the thought of whom we find holes in the place of *polis*, *eros* and *psyche*.' Cornélius Castoriadis, 'La fin de la philosophie?' *Le monde morcelé* (Paris: Seuil), 228.

[104] '...our genesis cannot be the philosophers of 4th Century and in any case certainly not Plato, filled with an ineradicable hatred for the democracy and the demos.' Castoriadis, *La montée de l'insignifiance*, 163.

[105]Jacques Rancière, *La Mésentente. Politique et philosophie* (Paris: Galilée, 1995).

[106] Danielle Haase-Dubosc and Maneesha Lal, 'De la postcolonie et des femmes: apports théoriques du postcolonialisme anglophone aux études féministes', *Nouvelles Questions Féministes*, 25, no. 3 (2006), 32–55.

The meaning of tragedy for humans is all about the unruly hubris (castigated by the Decalogue, gospels, Koran, etc.). The need for autonomy or self-limitation is always there and never resolved. That is why this is a political and not a technical or normative question. The law is not reducible to the imposed norm. Castoriadis explains that *The Trojan Women* stages the Greeks after the destruction of Troy—the Auschwitz or the Katyn of that period. 'Democracy is a power which institutes itself in a permanent way.' Moreover, democracy articulates autonomy and equality, which is not a social but political equality. 'Strictly speaking, equality means: equal chance for all to participate in power.'[107]

The practice of autonomy and democratic self-limitation currently faces the challenge of combining the dual experiences of Auschwitz and Hiroshima and their long genesis (*conquista*, slavery, colonization, imperialism) by reconsidering *de-growth* and radically reshaping nuclear politics into *de-nuclearization*.

An Action Plan for Dystopian Utopia (Chemillier-Gendreau)

Embedded within the perspective of struggles, coupled with theoretical breakthroughs, an action plan by a judicial expert—a woman teaching international human rights in Paris—calls for an International Court for Human Rights.[108] The proposal was expounded in the following terms: '7. *consolidating* theoretical tools and practices for denouncing violations of Human Rights by the Nation-States or any other inter-governmental or para-governmental players before the Council of Human Rights, Zonal Courts (Europe, Asia, America).' We should institute 'an extensive legal body of controls and sanctions for application of Human Rights in migration policies and right to seek political asylum on a global scale.'[109]

How does such a proposal, shaped by the struggles at the frontiers and the works of Arendt and Castoriadis, come within the scope of a praxis of

---

[107] Cornelius Castoriadis, 'Quelle démocratie?' in *Figures du pensable* (Paris: Seuil, 1999), 145–79.

[108] For the elaborations on the conditions, see Caloz-Tschopp and Dasen, *Mondialisation, migration et droits de l'homme*, 41 (clause 7, note 18).

[109] Marie-Claire Caloz-Tschopp and Pierre Dasen, *Mondialisation, migration et droits de l'homme: un nouveau paradigme pour la recherche et la citoyenneté* (Paris: Bruylant, 2007) 40–41.

dystopian utopia? First of all, it *differentiates between conflict and war* in constructing politics in between polis and cosmos. Machiavelli, the thinker of disorder may help us to re-assess conflict by distinguishing it from war. The one who wrote about 'the art of war' in the *The Prince* had not experienced Napoleonian wars like Clausewitz, the theorist of modern warfare. Other thinkers on democracy would take up afresh the issue of conflict to contemplate the disagreement of the excluded (Rancière), or the constituent dynamics of conflict in politics and democracy (Loraux, Mouffe). In this perspective, as explained by Marx, and later by Castoriadis, autonomy, or political democracy, is nothing without the democratization of labour relations and the relations of social life as a whole and, hence, also of international relations. Next, the Geneva proposal ought to be located within the struggles for the democratization of societies and of the UN. In the context of post-colonial struggles, this may bring forth the emergence of political spaces of subjectivation and collective practices.[110]

The promotion of regional International Courts of Justice for adjudicating economic crimes and crimes against humanity has a symbolic *and* a practical significance. The Geneva proposal is aimed at constructing a framework for *pluricentric* political dynamics. The goal of the experiment is a wide participation in constructing democratic foundations of a new society on a global scale with a special emphasis on *autonomy* and *self-limitation*. This ought to be simultaneously a laboratory and an observatory (learning a democratic practice of self-limitation and law, control, and sanctions) where governments, social movements, non-government organizations would play their part within the international institutions. To avoid being instrumentalized by dominant powers, it has to be supported by forums and opinion tribunals for reflecting on a justice which would work out the question of law along with autonomy and democratic self-limitation.

Between law, autonomy, and self-limitation is present a dialectics which is not to be reduced to the imposition of norms emanating from hegemonic relations of domination. How will law originate then, if it does not descend from the top and is not assured by some absolute reference? The answer is that law belongs to everyone irrespective of gender.

---

[110] Ranabir Samaddar, 'The Politics of Autonomy. An introduction', *The Politics of Autonomy. Indian experiences* (New Delhi: Sage, 2005), 9–31; Paula Banerjee, 'Women's Autonomy: Beyond Rights and Representations', Ranabir Samaddar, *The Politics of Autonomy. Indian experiences* (New Delhi: Sage, 2005), 49–70.

The Geneva proposal rejects any confinement of the question of norms to the State and to the field of specialists or any hegemonic force which would instrumentalize it.

In the current political crisis, the aberrations of justice turning into rituals of absolution institutionalizing amnesty, necessitate a philosophical, political, and epistemological shift of the referents, deliberations, and practices of norms that are, thereby, *de-democratized.* Law is matter and the responsibility for everyone. Laws cannot be confused with morals. The politics lying within the scope of law cannot be confused with humanitarian action. Its re-appropriation is the sign of a resurrection of the debate on projects, regimes, and the imaginary). Moreover, the framing of law through autonomy and self-limitation entails exit from a sort of irresolute consensus in face of new forms of populism that appeared as new forms of 'civility' which trivialize transgressions of norms by legitimizing war (the Iraq war, for example) and violence (for example, attacks on immigrants).

Such a perspective is much larger than the articulation between politics and right, between right and norm, and it cannot stay content with the illusion that laws would cool down political passions. This perspective involves the awakening of a self-instituting and self-limiting democratic aspiration entailing a new philosophy and a new political anthropology. Therefore, the process of elaboration does not only aim at strengthening the internal coherence of the mechanism of United Nations and forging a new instrument of dialogue between the States or strengthening the power of the judges regardless of any other powers (executive, parliamentary, counter-powers). The Geneva proposal is not about getting embroiled in tactical debates over the avatars of the defunct Commission and the limits of the mandate of Human Rights Council, of the UN, of existing Conventions and the consolidation of specialists. Mere technicalities or the failure of the UN reform should not invalidate the Geneva. project.

In the globalized world, the democratization of societies or of the UN does not depend on jurists harbouring the illusion of taking the heat off political debate by their expertise. The issue is to re-evaluate the *conatus* (Spinoza)—the instituting power—constituting itself as a globalized framework combining autonomy and self-limitation in the formulation of laws. The principal political engagement in the Geneva proposal is involving the multitude of players in the constituent process of the world public space, revitalizing, thereby, the autonomous and self-limiting democratic activity.

It is not by accident that the proposal has been formulated at one of the frontiers of democracy—with research on the conditions of male and female migrant workers put to the test of the human rights. It can be, therefore, at one and the same time, a place for dystopian utopia, a public space, and a positive frontier against despotism and destruction. It deserves to be part of the global public debate.

Instead of a Conclusion

Utopia has been the mother of exact sciences, and like many fecund mothers, it has often produced sterile or excessively weak germs, prematurely born or born under bad conditions.[111]

Within the dialectics between utopia and dystopia in the beginning of the twenty-first century, various praxes, narratives, fragments of a many-shaped, heterogeneous project of revolutionary resistance of utopian dystopia emerge. These raise numbers of questions and critiques. The emergent project carries forward struggles and various, disparate, even contradictory, collective consciousnesses. But it is worth keeping alive as history exists after destructions of the modernity which culminated in the twentieth century and is not sparing the twenty-first. It is fragile, open, vague, caught in between chaos and destructive nothingness of a worldwide total liberal capitalism.

Re-engaging with utopia and dystopia from the viewpoint of praxis of dystopian utopia implies that they combine the Greek rupture, the rupture of the capitalist modernity (utilitarianism, limitless exploitation), and the totalitarian rupture (annihilation)—all captured within the course of a long history (*conquista*, slavery, colonization, imperialism). These tragic ruptures have shown that the world is not created; rather, it can be auto-created or also destroyed by the humans.

These ruptures hold the means to surpass a deterministic position, a sense of infirmity and to make a bet on the 'rights to have rights', autonomy, and self-limitation, through the re-discovery of democracy in its radicality; the means to re-situate the debate between submissive creationism and active democratic auto-creation; the means to rethink the debates over cynical economic utilitarianism (migrations, use of raw materials,

---

[111] *Témoignage d'un prolétaire* (1890) in Jacques Rancière, *La nuit des prolétaires* (Paris: Fayard, 1981) 437.

finances, etc.) and the illusions over the balance of war terror (theories of dissuasion) without forgetting the dangerous acts of denial; the means to rely on emergent discoveries leading to the restructuring of action plans by radically shifting the way of conceiving and implementing them.

Today, therefore, it becomes possible to consider dystopian utopia as a project of revolutionary resistance. Such a fragile project emerges through experiments, in a quandary, while, at the same time, it carries forward resistance to think over what is destroyed and also what is being created. It is one of the places where emerges a new philosophy of history of the infinitude and finitude of freedom.

About the Editor and Contributors

The Editor

Barnita Bagchi is faculty in Literary Studies at Utrecht University, the Netherlands. She was previously a faculty member at Institute of Development Studies Kolkata (IDSK), India. She is an Executive Committee Member of the International Standing Conference for the History of Education (ISCHE).

Her published books include *Pliable Pupils and Sufficient Self-Directors: Narratives of Female Education by Five British Women Writers, 1778–1814* (2004); *Webs of History: Information, Communication, and Technology from Early to Post-Colonial India* (co-edited with A.K. Bagchi and D. Sinha, 2005); and a critical edition and part-translation, *Sultana's Dream and Padmarag: Two Feminist Utopias.*

The Contributors

Miguel Abensour is Emeritus Professor of Political Philosophy, University of Paris VII Diderot, Paris, France.

Marie-Claire Caloz-Tschopp is Director of Programmes, Collège Internationale de Philosophie, Paris, France.

Subhoranjan Dasgupta is Professor of Human Sciences, Institute of Development Studies Kolkata, India.

Sonia Dayan-Herzbrun is Emeritus Professor of Sociology, University of Paris VII Denis Diderot, Paris, France.

Rachel Foxley is Lecturer of in History, University of Reading, Berkshire, UK.

Peter Kulchyski is Professor of Native Studies, University of Manitoba, Winnipeg, Canada.

Theresa Moriarty is an independent scholar and historian based in Ireland.

Modhumita Roy is Associate Professor in English Literature, Tufts University, Boston, USA.

Samita Sen is Professor of Women's Studies and Director of the School of Women's Studies at Jadavpur University, Kolkata, India.

Martine Spensky is Emeritus Professor of British Studies, Blaise Pascal University, Clermont-Ferrand, France.

Index